JOSEPH SMITH
FOR PRESIDENT

JOSEPH SMITH FOR PRESIDENT

. . . .

The Prophet, the Assassins,
and the Fight for American
Religious Freedom

SPENCER W. MCBRIDE

OXFORD
UNIVERSITY PRESS

OXFORD
UNIVERSITY PRESS

Oxford University Press is a department of the University of Oxford. It furthers
the University's objective of excellence in research, scholarship, and education
by publishing worldwide. Oxford is a registered trade mark of Oxford University
Press in the UK and certain other countries.

Published in the United States of America by Oxford University Press
198 Madison Avenue, New York, NY 10016, United States of America.

Library of Congress Cataloging-in-Publication Data
Names: McBride, Spencer W., author.
Title: Joseph Smith for President : the prophet, the assassins, and the
fight for American religious freedom / Spencer W. McBride.
Description: New York, NY, United States of America : Oxford University Press, [2021] |
Includes bibliographical references and index.
Identifiers: LCCN 2020051798 (print) | LCCN 2020051799 (ebook) |
ISBN 9780190909413 (hb) | ISBN 9780190909437 (epub)
Subjects: LCSH: Smith, Joseph, Jr., 1805–1844—Political activity. |
Church of Jesus Christ of Latter-day Saints—Political activity. |
Presidents—United States—Election—1844. |
Presidential candidates—United States—Biography. |
Political campaigns—United States—History—19th century.
Classification: LCC BX8695.S6 M287 2021 (print) | LCC BX8695.S6 (ebook) |
DDC 289.3092 [B]—dc23
LC record available at https://lccn.loc.gov/2020051798
LC ebook record available at https://lccn.loc.gov/2020051799

DOI: 10.1093/oso/9780190909413.001.0001

3 5 7 9 8 6 4 2

Printed by Sheridan Books, Inc., United States of America

To my parents, Monroe and Laurie McBride

CONTENTS

· · · ·

CONTENTS

ACKNOWLEDGMENTS

. . . .

IN RESEARCHING AND WRITING THIS BOOK, I BENEFITED from the support of many others. Ultimately, I alone am responsible for the book's content, but I am delighted to acknowledge the assistance I received.

Several friends and colleagues read drafts of the manuscript in part or in full and offered constructive feedback. These individuals include Mason Allred, Bryon Andreasen, Mark Cheathem, Steve Evans, Brian Franklin, Matthew Godfrey, Amy Greenberg, Adam Jortner, Jody Lane, Brent Rogers, and Alex Smith. I refined my arguments with frequent conversations, both in person and via text message, with friend and fellow historian Benjamin Park. Through much of this time, Ben was researching his own book project about Nauvoo, Illinois, and it was helpful to compare notes and ideas with him.

I have spent years immersed in Joseph Smith's surviving documents as a historian at the Joseph Smith Papers Project. My colleagues on that project—individually and collectively—contain a wealth of knowledge about Smith and early Latter-day Saint history from which I gratefully benefited. For this I especially thank Mark Ashurst-McGee, Brett Dowdle, David Grua, Christian Heimburger, Sharalyn Howcroft, Robin Jensen, J. Chase Kirkham, Elizabeth Kuehn, Jeffrey Mahas, Jessica Nelson, Sharon Nielsen, and Adam Petty. The leadership of the Church History Department, the institutional home of the Joseph Smith Papers, has been supportive of my research endeavors, particularly Legrand Curtis

Jr., Matthew Grow, Matthew McBride, Kyle McKay, Reid Neilson, and Steven Snow. That department also has a group of scholars who meet to critique works in progress, and this book benefited from the feedback that members of that group provided. Those members included Anne Berryhill, Christopher Blythe, Joseph Darowski, Kay Darowski, Alan Morrell, Jacob Olmstead, Steve Olsen, Ben Pykles, Mark Staker, Emily Utt, and Jordan Watkins. With an office in the heart of a research library, I never ceased to marvel that I could work with many of the relevant primary source documents at my own desk. I thank the many staff members of the Church History Library in Salt Lake City for their assistance in accessing these records.

I am fortunate that several of my professors from my days as a graduate student have become close friends. In particular I thank Andrew Burstein and Nancy Isenberg, who were instrumental in helping me publish my first book and assisting me in refining the ideas and arguments of this project.

This book was further refined through feedback that I obtained when presenting on related material to several scholarly organizations, including the Center for Presidential History at Southern Methodist University, the Society for Historians of the Early American Republic (SHEAR), the American Historical Association, the American Society of Church History, the Mormon History Association, and a special symposium on Mormons in American political culture. SHEAR's inaugural Second Book Workshop in 2017 was a tremendous help for navigating the world of publishing.

I thank my literary agent Rebecca Friedman, who believed in this project from the start and worked hard to make it a reality. Similarly, it was a pleasure to work with the wonderful team at Oxford University Press, especially my editor, Theo Calderara.

In acknowledgment sections of books, family members are often listed last. This may be merely convention for some, but for me, I save my family members for the end because their contributions are the most difficult to adequately enumerate and my gratitude for them the most difficult to sufficiently articulate. May their placement in these pages be read as a sign of my deepest appreciation. Kris and Gail Budinger, my father-in-law and mother-in-law, have long been strong supporters of my research and writing and I thank them for this. Monroe and Laurie McBride, my parents and the people to whom this book is dedicated, were my first teachers. At an early age they placed me on a path of historical inquiry that has led to a life of rewarding discovery. Most of all, I thank my wife, Lindsay, and our four children, Erik, Laney, Joshua, and Thomas, for their unconditional love and unwavering support.

NOTES ON STYLE

. . . .

THIS BOOK RELIES HEAVILY ON NINETEENTH-CENTURY DOCUMENTS in which the spelling and grammar is often erratic. In quotations from these documents I have preserved the original spelling and grammar.

The church founded by Joseph Smith in 1830 was called the Church of Christ. In 1834 the name changed to the Church of the Latter Day Saints. Then, in 1838, the church adopted the name the Church of Jesus Christ of Latter-day Saints. While this has remained the church's official name since, throughout its history the church has been alternately referred to as the Mormon Church or the LDS Church. The term "Mormon" has also been used to refer to other individuals, institutions, and practices that trace their origins to Joseph Smith. When referring to members of the Church of Jesus Christ of Latter-day Saints in this book, I have used "Mormons," "Latter-day Saints," and "Saints" interchangeably, just as church members of the 1830s and 1840s did.

INTRODUCTION

Religious Intolerance in the "Land of the Free"

AFTER NIGHTFALL ON MAY 17, 1844, THOUSANDS of men assembled on the streets of Nauvoo, Illinois. They brought with them a barrel of tar. Some were residents of the city; others had traveled from elsewhere in the state. But they all shared a common grievance. And so they marched through the streets to the home of the city's controversial mayor, Joseph Smith. When they got there, they set the barrel of tar ablaze.

But this wasn't an act of violence; it was a celebration. They had even brought a band with them. Smith had previously been the target of violent mobs, but he had nothing to fear from these men. After a day of political speeches, those assembled had nominated Smith as their candidate for president of the United States. They had resolved that he was the ideal man to "carry out the principles of liberty and equal rights" from the country's highest elected office.[1]

In the glow of the burning tar and with musical accompaniment, the crowd hoisted Smith and his running mate, Sidney Rigdon, upon their shoulders and marched them around the fire twice before returning the men to the front of Smith's home.[2] It was a fitting end to a jubilant evening, and a triumphant moment for Smith.

Yet, it was a moment that he would find difficult to savor. In the coming days he would become mired in civic and legal crises. Just six weeks later a crowd of men would again surround Smith. This time they were not intent on making him president but were determined to take his life.

WHO WAS THIS MAYOR, THIS UNLIKELY PRESIDENTIAL candidate, this target of mob violence? Despite his common name, the thirty-eight-year-old Smith was far from ordinary. His primary claim to fame was as a religious leader—indeed, a prophet. Smith had declared that in 1820—when he was only fourteen—God and Jesus Christ had appeared to him in the woods near his family's home in western New York and instructed him not to join any church at that time but to wait for the fullness of the gospel of Jesus Christ to be revealed to him at a later date. In 1830, at the age of twenty-four, he published the Book of Mormon, which he said was a translation of an ancient scriptural record preserved on gold plates. That same year he formally established the Church of Christ (later renamed the Church of Jesus Christ of Latter-day Saints); in addition to "Saints" and "Latter-day Saints," Smith and his followers were often called "Mormons." Eventually they set out for what was then considered the American West, where he took on the roles of urban planner, newspaper editor, mayor, and lieutenant general of his community's militia. Yet, his candidacy for president was not the next step in a traditional political career. It was an act of desperation.

For years, Smith had been lobbying the federal government to protect the civil rights of his followers. The Mormons had fled persecution during the 1830s in New York and then Ohio, but those experiences paled in comparison to what awaited them when they moved on to Missouri—a war waged against them by vigilante mobs and militiamen. After the Mormons took up arms to defend themselves and their homes, and after they made preemptive strikes against neighbors whom they believed sympathized with their persecutors, Missouri's governor, Lilburn W. Boggs, ordered that "The Mormons must be treated as enemies, and must be exterminated or driven from the state if necessary for the public peace."[3] It was an extreme act for sure, one that Missourians would largely forget but that would be seared into Mormon memory as the infamous "extermination order."

Starting in the frigid winter of 1838 and continuing into the following spring, the Mormons lived as refugees on the banks of the Mississippi River in western Illinois. Exiled from their homes, they began to pick up the pieces of their lives while Smith and other church leaders petitioned Congress for redress and reparations for their lost property in Missouri. However, by the end of 1843 all such petitions had failed. In a desperate final plea for federal support—and with new persecution rearing its head in Illinois—Smith wrote a letter to each of the five men expected to run for president. He asked each one what he would do as president to aid the Mormons in their petitioning efforts. Only three of the men responded, and none of them pledged to help.[4] Believing that the only way to obtain federal support for their rights as Americans was to effect a major philosophical change within the national government, in January 1844 Smith announced his candidacy for president.[5]

SMITH WAS A PRESIDENTIAL CANDIDATE UNLIKE ANY other the United States had seen. In a country that earnestly sought the separation of powers in its burgeoning democratic system, many Americans saw in Smith a dangerous combination of religious, civic, and military authority. Some 25,000 Mormons throughout the United States followed his revelations because they viewed him as a prophet delivering the word and will of God; approximately 12,000 citizens of Nauvoo, Illinois, followed his civic orders as their mayor; and the nearly 2,500 men enlisted in that city's militia followed his calls to battle as their commanding officer.[6] While some Americans openly laughed at the prospect that Smith might win the White House, behind much of the mockery was a profound fear of what a Smith presidency would mean for the nation's still-fragile democracy.

It wasn't just Smith's background that made him an unusual candidate; so did his campaign platform. In a widely distributed pamphlet, Smith weighed in on several of the most controversial issues of his day. Combining innovative pragmatism with naïve idealism, he called for extreme action to halt what he described as the country's decline. He called for the total abolition of slavery through the purchase and subsequent manumission of slaves by the federal government. He advocated for the complete closure of the country's penitentiaries. He called for the re-establishment of the national bank to stabilize an economy susceptible to extreme booms and busts. Furthermore, he made an appeal for the expansion of the country's borders until it filled all of North America, but only after the Native Americans in those territories consented to the expansion.[7]

But his most prominent campaign position was a call to empower the federal government to protect the religious freedom of all Americans. By 1844 the history of the United States was already littered with cases of religious persecution. Jews throughout the country had experienced frequent discrimination and occasional violence since the colonial era.[8] Many mainline Protestant Christians worked to keep the country's rapidly growing Catholic population relegated to a second-class citizenship and, in some of the most violent expressions of their religious intolerance, destroyed private property and took the lives of their Catholic countrymen.[9] In addition, smaller religious groups such as the Shakers faced systemic religious discrimination through state laws and abuse at the hands of angry mobs.[10] The Mormons were definitely a persecuted religious minority, but they were hardly the only one.

Yet, for as common and consistent as religious discrimination and persecution have been throughout the history of the United States, such historical episodes are not widely known by twenty-first-century Americans. Then, as now, many Americans have chosen to focus on a dramatic narrative of the country's past in which the blood of American patriots stained the soil of their homeland to preserve a set of freedoms that included the right for all men and women to worship as they please. These simplistic, celebratory accounts of the country's founding cement the misguided notion that the disestablishment of state churches during the years that followed the Revolution and the protection of religious expression in the Bill of Rights brought about universal religious freedom. The reality is that these actions merely established an American ideal; the lived experiences of religious minorities throughout the history of the United States clearly demonstrate the persistence of intense, and at times violent, religious inequality in the country that lauds itself "the land of the free."[11]

To celebrate the sincere efforts of several early American leaders to bring about universal religious liberty without considering the many moments in which their countrymen fell short of such a noble ideal is to perpetuate what one historian has termed "fables we forget by."[12] In forgetting—or worse, never learning—the troubling plights of religious minorities in the history of a country that aspires to loftier heights, Americans comfortably situated in the cultural mainstream celebrate their exceptional level of freedom while many of their fellow citizens suffer the effects of systemic discrimination and fear-driven persecution. The perpetuation of such myths, cherished though they may be by some, nearly ensures that the country will fail to make good on its promise of "liberty and justice for all."

If we want to understand the persistence of religious inequality in American society, Smith's presidential campaign offers an indispensable lens.

1
····

A LESSON IN POLITICAL
NEGOTIATIONS

JOSEPH SMITH WAS IMPRESSED BY THE WHITE HOUSE; by its occupant, less
so. At least that is what he reported to his brother, Hyrum, in a December
1839 letter. "We found a very large and splendid palace, surrounded with
a splendid enclosure decorated with all the fineries and elegancies of this
world," Smith wrote. But as for Martin Van Buren, "He is a small man,"
Smith stated, with a "sandy complexion, and ordinary features; with
frowning brow and considerable body but not well proportioned, as his
arms and legs—and to use his own words is quite fat."[1]

Smith's unflattering description of the president's physique squares
with contemporary descriptions of Van Buren, but it was also fueled by
a recently acquired animus toward the eighth president. When Smith
journeyed to Washington, D.C., from Nauvoo, Illinois, in the fall of
1839, it was not to see the nation's capital as a tourist or to hobnob with
that city's influential men. Instead, the leader of the fledgling Church
of Jesus Christ of Latter-day Saints sought redress and reparations from
the federal government for the persecution he and some 10,000 of his
followers had experienced at the hands of vigilantes and the Missouri
state militia. These persecutions included the destruction of their homes,

the confiscation of their property, the murder and rape of some of their family members and friends, and, ultimately, their expulsion from the state under the threat of extermination ordered by Missouri's Governor, Lilburn W. Boggs.[2] By 1839, all attempts Smith and his fellow church leaders had made to have their property and citizenship rights restored by Missouri courts had failed, as had their many appeals to the state's elected officials.[3] Smith claimed that by endorsing and perpetuating the mob violence that led to the loss of life, liberty, and property of its Mormon citizens, Missouri had failed to protect the inalienable rights set forth in the country's founding documents. Frustrated and desperate, he turned to the federal government as one of his last hopes.

On November 29, 1839, Illinois Congressman John Reynolds accompanied Smith and another church leader, Elias Higbee, to the White House door. Things were different back then. Appointments were neither necessary nor common for men who sought an audience with the president; Reynolds, Smith, and Higbee simply knocked on the door. A porter welcomed the men into the magnificent residence and escorted them to the ornate second-floor parlor, a room where Van Buren received visitors almost daily.

Smith was a nearly destitute refugee rebuilding a life on the country's rural western frontier, and he looked with awe upon the building and its contents. But its rich oil paintings, fine furniture, and intricate decorations did not intimidate him. If anything, they swelled his confidence, as he reported to his friends in Illinois that "he felt at home in the White House . . . that he had a perfect right [to be] there, as much right as Van Buren, because it belonged to the people, and he was one of the people."[4] This was a fiercely democratic view, one that provides a glimpse into Smith's mindset at that moment. He did not intend to meekly request a favor from a ruler; he would insist on redress from a man elected to serve the people. However, Smith soon learned that while gaining access to the president's home was relatively easy, securing the attention—or, for that matter, the political support—of the president himself was a much more difficult task. Smith's personal charm and charisma could not compensate for what he lacked in political savvy.

The men jockeyed for face time with the president in the crowded parlor and eventually snatched his attention. Just before Reynolds formally introduced the men to Van Buren, Smith quietly instructed the congressman to present him simply "as a 'Latter Day Saint.'" Reynolds was shocked at the request. He wondered why Smith would "urge such non-sense on this occasion to the president."[5] But Smith insisted and Reynolds obliged. It was a strange introduction, and a grin began to appear between the auburn mutton chops that framed the president's round face.[6]

This odd and seemingly plain introduction might baffle modern readers, just as it did Reynolds, or it might amuse them, just as it did Van Buren. But to Smith, "Latter-day Saint" was more than a descriptor for members of the religious community he led. The term carried nearly two decades of history, history that included stories of divine visions, spiritual enthusiasm, religious innovation, and social transformation—all of which had been met with staunch opposition and violent persecution. That history had driven Smith to the president's parlor. And it is the key to understanding his engagement with the American political system that eventually resulted in his candidacy for president.

"I HAD SEEN A VISION"

Smith's personal history was marked with trials. The fifth child of Lucy Mack and Joseph Smith Sr., Joseph was born on December 5, 1805, in the rural community of Sharon, Vermont. For New England, it was a period of population growth and social and cultural transformation. For the Smiths, it was a time of economic hardship. A few years earlier, Joseph Smith Sr. had made an investment in the China ginseng trade. By 1803, the investment had gone bad and brought financial ruin down upon the growing family. Almost overnight the Smiths tumbled down the economic ladder, from property owners with a bright commercial future to tenant farmers working for meager profits on land that belonged to someone else. Between 1803 and 1817, the family moved eleven times. Consequently, Joseph Smith grew up as a poor farm boy with limited education. As he wrote in his personal history several years later, he "was mearly instructtid in reading writing and the ground rules of Arithmatic."[7]

When Smith was ten, his family—having grown weary of the endless cycle of tenant farming—joined thousands of others in bursting free from the economic constraints of New England by moving to western New York, a place where land was cheaper and more plentiful. They purchased a farm just south of Palmyra, a little village that exuded the energy of a much larger town. The construction of the Erie Canal along

9

the northern edge of the village enlivened the hopes of residents for the growth and prosperity that the artificial waterway promised to bring.

Yet, the prospect of an economic boom was not the only reason for excitement in the area. Fiery itinerant preachers traversed the region intent on rousing the area's settlers with the fervor of Christian conversion. A series of religious revivals—a part of a national spiritual "awakening"— brought a number of these preachers into Smith's neighborhood. Revivals held in churches and in front of makeshift outdoor stages captured the attention of local residents. However, as church attendance and membership rose rapidly in these rural communities, so, too, did the tide of religious debate.[8]

Starting in late 1817, the Smiths found themselves in the midst of what Smith later described as "an unusual excitement on the subject of religion." Although he was only twelve years old, Smith's mind became "seriously impressed with regard to the all-important concerns for the welfare" of his "immortal Soul." In such a religious environment, he had "intimate acquaintance with those of different denominations," including members of the clergy who sought to recruit him to their particular forms of Christian worship. Yet, Smith rebuffed their invitations, explaining that these clergymen caused him "to marvel exceedingly, for I discovered that they did not adorn their profession by a holy walk and Godly conversation."[9]

The seeming hypocrisy of the local clergy was not all that troubled the teenaged Smith. He expressed confusion about which of all the denominations seeking converts in the area practiced the religion of Jesus Christ as set forth in the Bible. "In the midst of this war of words and tumults of opinions," Smith recalled, "I often said to myself: What is to be done? Who of all these parties are right; or, are they all wrong together?"[10] After nearly two years of spiritual exploration and contemplation, the fourteen-year-old Smith determined that he would find a private place to pray to God in the hopes of obtaining clarity.

Sometime in the spring of 1820, Smith ventured into the woods near his family's small log cabin. The woods were part of a dense deciduous forest. The trunks of beech, maple, and poplar trees reached upward as their branches stretched outward, seemingly intertwining with each other in a chaotic effort to provide shelter for the forest floor. Adorning each branch were countless tiny buds waiting impatiently for warmer weather to arrive. Smith found solitude in this space and began to pray.

Several times over the years that followed, Smith told the story of what happened in the woods that day. Reactions from audiences ranged from sincere belief to utter disdain, with sizable amounts of easy dismissal and lighthearted mockery scattered in between. According to Smith, on that fateful day a pillar of light illuminated the forest around him, and in that pillar two divine persons appeared. One introduced the other as his "Only Begotten Son" and told Smith to "hear him." Smith reported that they instructed him to not join any of the churches then vying for his loyalty. The true Christian church—the church of Jesus's time—would be revealed to him at a later date.[11]

Over the next several years, as Smith recounted, he experienced a series of angelic visits directing him to a nearby hill, where he unearthed a set of thin gold plates. Written on these plates, in a language Smith had never seen, was the religious and secular history of some of the ancient inhabitants of the American continents. Claiming that he translated the record by the "gift and power of God," Smith published them as the Book of Mormon in 1830, when he was just twenty-four.[12] The book's text claimed that its publication was a sign that mankind was in the prophesied "last days" before the Second Coming of Jesus. That same year Smith founded a church, the members of which viewed him as more than a minister. They followed him as a prophet akin to those whose lives were captured in the pages of the Old Testament.

The farm-boy-turned-prophet had come a long way from his obscure childhood. In every town and city he entered from that point on, Smith attracted attention: sometimes praise, but often severe criticism. The same can be said of the religious community he led. Wherever the Mormons went, converts followed, as did controversy and violent opposition. Through it all Smith remained adamant that his spiritual encounters were real. "I had actually seen a vision," he averred in his personal history, adding somewhat poetically, "I knew it, and I knew that God knew it, and I could not deny it, neither dare I do it."[13]

"THE CITY OF ZION"

Smith dreamed big. He was not content to lead just another church in an expanding American religious landscape. He believed he was called by God to do something more. Indeed, it was Smith's grand visions—and the charisma with which he articulated them—that helped attract thousands of converts in a relatively short period of time. Still, the attraction to Smith and Mormonism went deeper. To a growing number of Americans dissatisfied with their options in the religious marketplace, Smith and his claims of divine encounters seemed to promise a more direct connection to the sacred. In ways that were increasingly popular among new Christian denominations in the early 1800s, Smith urged men and women to read ancient scriptures with fresh eyes and to discover religious truth without the interference of established clergymen. But he took these popular religious developments a step further, encouraging his followers to see their day and age as a continuation—a restoration—of biblical times, in which prophets acted as spokesmen for an unseen God.[14]

Smith's eagerness to cast his new Christian denomination as the restoration of an ancient one is apparent in the term he and his followers soon used to describe themselves: "Latter-day Saints." According to the New Testament, members of the primitive church were called saints—it was only centuries later that the Catholic Church started applying the term to deceased men and women whom it wished to honor for living virtuous lives. By calling themselves "Latter-day Saints," they were declaring that their church was the primitive church restored to modern society and linking themselves to the men and women who communed with Jesus during his lifetime and his apostles after his crucifixion. Although Smith eventually used the term from time to time to refer to himself, his followers, and their religious movement, "Mormon" was initially a derogatory term used by critics.[15]

Smith maintained that in order to restore the original church, believers needed to build their own communities. Accordingly, Mormon converts would often relocate as soon as their circumstances allowed so that they could live in close proximity to their fellow believers. It was a lot to ask, but many Mormons gladly shouldered the load, believing that their lives had taken on a deeper significance.[16]

While the settlement patterns, economic development, and religious revivals of western New York combined to create an environment conducive to the rise of this new, homegrown religious movement, the region could not contain Smith for long. He and many of his earliest followers were simultaneously pushed and pulled from the state. The push came from the severe and sometimes violent opposition they faced, often centered on a bevy of unorthodox doctrines, including the beliefs that God had recommenced directing mankind through a mortal prophet, that the Book of Mormon was as much a scripture as the Old and New Testaments, and that the scriptural canon was open—which was to say that more scripture was coming. The pull was the reprieve from persecution they hoped would come from joining a large number of enthusiastic new converts who had already settled in Ohio. In 1831, Smith moved the headquarters of the church to the burgeoning town of Kirtland, just 20 miles east of present-day Cleveland.[17]

Shortly thereafter, in July 1831, Smith became focused on land even farther west. He prophesied that he and his followers would build the New Jerusalem spoken of in the biblical Book of Revelation in western Missouri. According to the Bible, the New Jerusalem—or Zion—was the city to which Jesus Christ would return to usher in a thousand-year period of peace on earth that modern Christians have termed "the Millennium."[18] A revelation published by the church declared that Jackson County, Missouri, was "the land of promise & the place for the City of Zion" and urged church members to purchase land around the small settlement of Independence "that they may obtain it for an ever-lasting inheritance." Tapping into the language of millennialism and an early form of American exceptionalism, Smith pointed the gaze of his followers to the end of world foretold by biblical prophets, assuring them that the church they had joined would do far more than direct their worship and religious education on Sundays. It would usher in the Second Coming.[19]

Smith's enthusiasm was contagious and filled his followers with a sense of mission and importance. After all, Christians had waited nearly 1,800 years for Jesus to return, and the Mormons believed that, through a prophet, they had been selected by God to make the final preparations. In essence, though they were a relatively small and inconsequential part of America's religious landscape at the time, Smith's prophesy encouraged his followers to see themselves at the center of God's plan for the moral redemption of mankind.

And so, even as Smith and the Mormons began to thrive in Kirtland, they were aware that it was not to be their permanent home. Over the next two years some 1,200 Mormons rushed to the western edge of the Missouri and gathered on thousands of acres of land they purchased just miles to the east of modern-day Kansas City. Their belief in Smith's prophecy made the land sacred in their eyes, and they arrived brimming with optimism that they would transform the open prairie into a magnificent city to which the world's inhabitants would flock during the earth's final days.

Smith remained headquartered in Ohio and directed the establishment of Zion through several trusted church leaders who had made the move to the south and west. The Latter-day Saints in Missouri faced several obstacles in building their utopian society, including a degree of tension between the leaders of the church in the two states, but ultimately much of their correspondence relayed positive news. By 1833, the results of the Mormons' religious zeal and communal industry were clear. Having acquired more than 2,000 acres in the county, they had commenced their communal farming endeavors and built up towns to support them. Wood-framed homes and finely constructed brick buildings seemed to sprout from the ground, promising a prosperous future. They even established a printing office that published, among other things, a Mormon newspaper. All things pointed to the realization of Smith's vision for an American Zion.[20]

But that summer brought troubling accounts of a rapidly escalating conflict. As the prosperity of the Mormon's Missouri settlement increased, so, too, did the uneasiness of the area's non-Mormon residents. The uneasiness sprang from several different sources. Some were racial. The first Mormons who arrived in the area came to preach to Native Americans, whom the country's political leaders had forcibly removed behind an imaginary line they intended as a boundary between the "civilized" and the "savage." The Mormons preached that the Native Americans were the descendants of Book of Mormon peoples and, with white Christians, heirs to God's covenant and its promised land. To some of the area's white settlers, the Mormons threatened to turn a fragile society on its head by disrupting the racial hierarchy upon which it was built.[21]

Other sources of unease were political and economic. For instance, slavery was legal in Missouri, and the predominately Yankee background of the Mormons fueled suspicion among many of the settlers who had moved there from Southern states that the Mormons intended to undermine the socioeconomic system of race-based slavery that they were trying to install. In addition, non-Mormons feared the potential of the tight-knit and rapidly growing Mormon community to eventually decide local elections and to control the area's economy. These fears were compounded by religious prejudice and bigotry. In their beliefs and practices, the Mormons appeared fanatical—too far outside the norms of mainstream Protestant Christianity to ever fully acclimate into secular society. Stacked upon each other, these concerns were like kindling awaiting a match.[22]

The igniting spark came in July 1833 when the editor of the Mormon newspaper, William W. Phelps, published an editorial in which he insinuated that free people of color were welcome to settle with the Mormons in Missouri. "Slaves are real estate in this and other states," Phelps wrote, but "So long as we have no special rule in the church, as to people of color, let prudence guide."[23] The editorial read as a gesture of goodwill and acceptance to people of all races where the religious practices of Mormonism were concerned, but it essentially confirmed the suspicions of some wary non-Mormons who feared that they were plotting to undermine slavery in the county. Sensing that blowback would only escalate, Phelps quickly tried to placate his critics by publishing a clarification of his intent—that he was merely warning future Mormon settlers of the state's laws regarding slaves and free people of color. But the damage was already done. A few days after the editorial appeared, more than 300 citizens of Jackson County, Missouri, convened a series of public meetings to devise a strategy for dealing with their "Mormon problem."[24]

Those present at these meetings eventually adopted an extreme solution: half of the Mormons must leave the county by January 1, 1834, with the rest to follow by that April. The organizers of the meeting even drafted a statement that sought to justify this course of action, a statement that was signed by many of those in attendance. In the statement, they tried to preempt any claims that they were persecuting the Mormons because of their faith by calling them "a pretended religious sect." They were "fanatics" and "knaves" who pretended "to hold personal communication and converse, face to face with the most high God," and "to perform all the wonderworking miracles wrought by the inspired apostles & prophets of old." They expressed fear that the Mormons were "daily increasing in numbers" and "declare openly that their God has given them this County of land, and that sooner or later they must and will have the possession of our lands for an inheritance." In addition to casting "contempt" on God's "holy religion by pretending to receive revelations direct from Heaven," the Mormons were accused of "tampering with our slaves and endeavoring to sow dissensions and raise seditions among them" by "inviting free Negroes & Mullattoes from other States to become Mormons and remove and settle among them." For these reasons, the signers of this statement declared that the Mormons had five months to leave the county peacefully, or else they would "use such means as may be sufficient to remove them." Invoking the Declaration of Independence, they pledged their "lives, fortunes, and sacred honor" to the expulsion of this menace.[25]

This was an extreme and intolerant statement, but it was no empty threat. These angry citizens let the Mormons know that they were serious in the way that they chose to deliver their edict. On July 20, 1833, they surrounded a Mormon town and declared their intention to expel all of its residents. When the Mormons did not immediately agree to the terms of the statement, the surrounding mob descended upon the town. They rushed upon the printing office—the spot from which the offending newspaper had originated—where they destroyed the printing press and other furniture before razing the building itself. They then dragged the town's presiding ecclesiastical authority, Bishop Edward Partridge, to the public square, where they tarred and feathered him "from head to foot." A week later, the Mormons had still not agreed to the outrageous terms of the proposed eviction, and the vigilantes continued their violent coercion until—out of total desperation—the Mormons agreed to leave the county by the start of the new year.[26]

Joseph Smith was appalled when he read of the mob rule that precipitated such violence upon his followers. He fired off several letters in response, ultimately directing church members to disregard their agreement to leave the county and instead to insist upon their rights as property owners and citizens of the United States. "As you know we are all friends to the Constitution yea true friends to that Country for which our fathers bled," Smith admonished, before declaring that it was the will of God that "not one foot of land perchased should be given to the enimies of God or sold to them."[27] Apparently bolstered by Smith's bold decree and his appeal to American constitutional rights, church members in Missouri prepared legal action against their oppressors, signaling their insistence on remaining on their land despite the terms they had agreed to under duress.[28]

The response was an eruption of violence. Over the course of several weeks, vigilantes in Missouri descended on Mormon settlements, where they captured and whipped several men and shot at many others. Bursting into Mormon homes, they raped young women and forced some of the women's mothers to watch. Outnumbered nearly two to one, the

Mormons ultimately surrendered. Emboldened, the vigilantes went house to house, threatening each Mormon family with death if they did not immediately flee. By the end of November, the Latter-day Saints had fully vacated the county.[29] Their Zion was lost.

"THE MORMONS MUST BE EXTERMINATED"

The Mormons found temporary refuge in a neighboring county until the State of Missouri devised a plan for the Mormons' resettlement. State officials formed a new county that they designated as a place where the Latter-day Saints could live and practice their religion in peace. In essence, Caldwell County, Missouri, was created as Mormon country. These geographic restrictions to settlement appear at once as both a method of maintaining peace and an indication that state leaders viewed the Latter-day Saints as undeserving of their full citizenship rights as Americans. But with no other options, the Mormons moved.[30]

Their sagging morale was lifted when they were joined by their prophet and an influx of other church members who relocated to northern Missouri after the situation in Kirtland, Ohio, became untenable. A number of factors contributed to the backlash Smith experienced there, but chief among them was the 1837 failure of a financial institution called the Kirtland Safety Society. A national economic crisis that year resulted in failed banks throughout the United States, often followed by claims of mismanagement and wrongdoing by the men who directed them. When Smith's bank failed, his ecclesiastical position and claim to a prophetic mantle resulted in a unique form of unrest among church members who lost much of their savings. Some wondered how a prophet could not foresee such an economic downturn. Others who had once gleefully invested their money in an institution operated by several of their church leaders started to second-guess the propriety of mixing the economic with the religious. While thousands of Ohio Mormons stood stalwartly behind Smith, others abandoned him and the church. Yet, disassociation from the church was not enough for some of these dissenters, and they looked for ways to exact revenge on Smith and other church leaders, including prosecution. Starting in 1838 and amid this turmoil, Smith and thousands of other church members left Ohio to join their coreligionists in Missouri.[31]

With such a rapid surge in their numbers, the Mormons started to purchase land outside the confines of Caldwell County, and very soon the unmitigated fear and anger that had so inflamed the residents of Jackson County earlier that decade had returned. But this time the violence would be far bloodier.

The 1838 Mormon War commenced with an Election Day brawl. As Mormons arrived at a polling place in Gallatin, Missouri, a group of antagonistic citizens tried to prevent them from voting. Demonstrating the low station they perceived the Mormons to occupy in Missouri society, their leader declared that "A Mormon had no more right to vote than a Negro."[32] Determined to cast ballots for their preferred candidates, the Mormons were undeterred. The altercation escalated to an all-out brawl. Election Day brawls were common in the 1830s, but this one was different. Although the Mormons won the fight, it set in motion an armed conflict they had virtually no chance of winning on their own.[33]

Many of the non-Mormons in the area armed and organized themselves, seeking to rid their state of its Mormon residents once and for all. The Mormons responded by forming themselves into militia units, determined to defend their property and their rights to remain on it. With the makings of a civil war on their hands, state leaders ordered the Missouri militia to stand between the two sides, but an overwhelming number of its members shared the anti-Mormon prejudices of the vigilantes, and so the violence continued.[34] In this heated moment, some of the more militant Mormons made controversial preemptive strikes, raiding and burning the homes of several of the vigilantes who had gathered against them, actions that further enraged their enemies.[35]

Smith and other church leaders pleaded with Governor Lilburn W. Boggs to take whatever actions were necessary to protect the lives and citizenship rights of his people. But the governor responded with neither sympathetic gestures nor supportive action. In language that stands out within the deeply tragic history of religious persecution in the United States, Boggs issued an executive order to his militia officers on October 27, 1838, stating that "The Mormons must be treated as enemies, and must be exterminated or driven from the state if necessary for the public peace—their outrages are beyond all description."[36] Four days later, militia officers arrested and jailed Smith and several other Mormon leaders on charges that included treason.[37]

Smith's incarceration and the executive order rallied the Mormons' enemies. The vigilantes—aided at times by members of the state militia—proceeded to overwhelm the Mormon forces. But they did not stop there. They took the fight to the Mormon communities, destroying many of their buildings, raping several women, and killing several men. In one harrowing instance, two small children were shot in the presence of their parents. In another, a woman was tied to a bench and gang raped by members of the attacking mob.[38]

True to the governor's order, the Mormons were driven from Missouri. Many of them fled across the Mississippi River to Illinois, where they spent a long and dreary winter as destitute refugees. In the spring of 1839, Smith and company were allowed to escape from jail and soon thereafter arrived in Illinois. Setting out to once again rebuild their society, they acquired several adjoining tracts of swampy, undesirable land surrounding the quiet river town of Commerce. Smith once again donned the role of urban planner as he laid out a vision that would transform the dismal swamplands into the city of Nauvoo, a municipality that at its height would eventually become the largest in the state.[39]

Yet, even as the Mormons sought a fresh start in a new place, they carried with them the physical, mental, and financial wounds they had sustained in Missouri. Smith consulted with other church leaders on the best way to proceed. The courts and elected officials in Missouri had refused to protect their rights to life, liberty, and property. They had refused to prosecute those who persecuted them for their religious beliefs and practices. The Latter-day Saints were convinced that the last earthly option for redress and reparations—the most dependable course of action for the redemption of their Zion—was an appeal to the United States Congress, ideally with the president on their side.[40] Accordingly, on October 27, 1839, Smith left Nauvoo for Washington, D.C., intent on obtaining justice for his people. The frailty of his family and religious community in the wake of their troubles in Missouri made it an inopportune moment in which to make the lengthy journey to the nation's capital. "Nothing but a sense of humanity could have urged me on to so great a sacrifice," he wrote to his wife, Emma, while on the road. "Shall I see so many perish and not seek redress?"[41]

"I CAN DO NOTHING FOR YOU"

So it was that, on November 29, 1839, Smith found himself face to face with the President of the United States. Smith was confident that when he informed the president of the harrowing experiences of the Latter-day Saints in Missouri, he would elicit some degree of the same moral outrage that had brought Smith to the capital in the first place. Smith apparently hoped that Van Buren would speak in support of their appeal for redress in his annual address to Congress—a constitutionally mandated ritual that has come to be called the State of the Union Address. With the Democratic president's endorsement of their petition for reparations, Smith believed the Democratically controlled Congress would follow in lockstep.[42]

Once Smith captured the president's attention, however, all such hope evaporated. Van Buren quickly demonstrated just how ill-prepared Smith was to navigate the partisan environment of the nation's capital. In the arena of the White House parlor, Smith's constitutional idealism was no match for Van Buren's political pragmatism.

After the initial introductions, Smith handed Van Buren several letters from prominent officials in Illinois vouching for his character and sympathizing with the plight of the Latter-day Saints. "As soon as he read one of them," Smith reported, "he looked upon us with a kind of half frown and said, what can I do? I can do nothing for you—if I do anything, I shall come in contact with the whole state of Missouri."[43] Van Buren was stating, in effect, that supporting the Mormons would automatically lose him support in Missouri, one of the few states that he could depend on in his re-election bid later that year. Electoral politics, not constitutional principles, led Van Buren to do nothing, and by doing nothing to condone the Missouri's governor's extermination order and the violent actions of some of Missouri's citizens.[44]

This meeting with Van Buren revealed Smith's political naïveté. Opponents of the Mormons charged that they represented a powerful voting bloc that could be directed by church leaders. And, in fact, this was true. Yet, Smith frequently denied such accusations. If ever there was a time to own up to this charge, this was it. Smith could have countered with a declaration that refusing to support the Mormons would cost the president Illinois—which was, coincidentally, a swing state in the election of 1840. But he did not. Instead, Smith wrote privately to his brother after his meeting with Van Buren that he did not "say that the

Saints shall not vote for him, but we do say boldly, (though it need not be published in the streets of Nauvoo, neither among the daughters of the Gentiles,) that we do not intend he shall have our votes."[45] Indeed, the state's thousands of Mormon voters did vote overwhelmingly for William Henry Harrison that fall, but Van Buren still eked out victory in Illinois by fewer than 2,000 votes.[46]

Of course, openly threatening to withhold a community's vote from the president while in the White House parlor is something few would have dared to do. Still, Smith's reluctance to boast about the power of the Mormon vote is indicative of the way he viewed American politics. Smith thought the government operated on the ideals enshrined in the country's founding documents, that his case would be judged on its merits alone. For all his concerns of anti-Mormon prejudice influencing elected officials, he seems to have given little thought to the partisan workings of the federal government.[47] Smith refused to play political hardball when political hardball was precisely what the men empowered to grant his petition were accustomed to playing.

Van Buren's unwillingness to support Smith's appeal did not end the Mormon petitioning efforts—an appeal to Congress remained their primary point of emphasis. But this interview in the White House ended any good feelings Smith may have held for Van Buren. He openly campaigned against the president in the ensuing months, declaring publicly that Van Buren "was not as fit . . . as my dog, for the chair of state; for my dog will make an effort to protect his abused and insulted master, while the present chief magistrate will not so much as lift his finger to relieve an oppressed and persecuted community of free-men, whose glory it has been that they were citizens of the United States."[48]

In another sermon delivered shortly after returning to Illinois, Smith recounted that when meeting with Van Buren in the parlor of the White House, "a member of Congress waited upon him, and in conversation, among other things, told the President that he was getting fat . . . The President replied that he was aware of the fact; that he had to go every few days to the tailor's to get his clothes let out, or purchase a new coat." Smith then added at the top of his voice that he hoped Van Buren "would continue to grow fat, and swell, and before the next election, burst!"[49] For nineteenth-century Mormons, the eighth president came to stand as a symbol of political corruption that fostered an environment of religious intolerance and inequality.

2

. . . .

SHATTERED AMERICAN
IDEALISM

AFTER LEAVING THE WHITE HOUSE, BUT BEFORE returning to Illinois to publicly unleash his vitriol upon Martin Van Buren, Joseph Smith aimed his energy at Congress. After all, it had been the Mormons' intent to obtain reparations from the national legislature ever since they devised their plan to petition the federal government for redress. Van Buren's endorsement certainly would have helped win over congressional Democrats. Yet, even without the president on his side, Smith remained hopeful. Letters home made it clear that while the president had cracked Smith's robust sense of American idealism, it had not crumbled. Could it survive the painfully slow bureaucracy of a bitterly partisan Congress?

"A DISPLAY OF FOLLY AND SHOW"

For several days Smith and Elias Higbee became fixtures in the halls of the Capitol and on the surrounding streets. "We have spent the remainder of our time hunting up Representatives," they reported to church leaders back in Illinois, adding that they had "already commenced forming some very honorable acquaintances."[1] Among these new acquaintances were perennial presidential candidate Henry Clay, who represented Kentucky in the Senate, and John C. Calhoun, a senator from South Carolina and one of the staunchest defenders of states' rights. The reactions of these two power brokers to the Mormon petitioning efforts could not have been any more different. Whereas Clay signaled a willingness to aid the Mormon refugees by supporting their petition on the floor of the Senate, Calhoun was hostile to the notion that the federal government might intervene in the affair.[2]

Of course, the most immediately important of Smith and Higbee's new acquaintances were the men elected to represent the Mormons' new home state of Illinois. It was an overwhelmingly Democratic delegation, a fact that boded well for the Mormons, since the Democrats held a slight majority in both chambers. Both Illinois senators, Richard M. Young and John M. Robinson, were Democrats, as were two of its three representatives, Zadok Casey and John Reynolds. John Todd Stuart was the delegation's lone Whig.[3]

News of the Mormons' political mission had reached the Illinois congressmen ahead of Smith's arrival in Washington. While en route to the capital, Smith and his traveling party had stopped in Springfield, Illinois, where they lobbied members of the state legislature for support.[4] "I had received letters," Reynolds recalled, "as well as the other Democratic members of Congress, that Smith was a very important character in Illinois, and to give him the civilities and attention that was due to him. He stood at the time fair and honorable, as far as we knew at the City of Washington, except his fanaticism on religion. The sympathies of the people were in his favor."[5]

Indeed, the rapid influx of Mormon refugees into Illinois over the previous year represented a monumental opportunity for the state's political leadership. For years the state had elected Democrats to office at all levels of government, but the partisan tides were beginning to shift. The Whigs' popularity and influence were rising and eroding the Democrats' control. If the Democrats could win over the Mormons—who tended to vote as a bloc—they could shore up their electoral control in a rapidly growing state.[6] Political opportunism was certainly an important motivator for members of Illinois's congressional delegation to go out of their way to assist Smith with his petitioning efforts. Still, it is nearly impossible to distinguish political motives from humanitarian ones. Both were at play.

Senator Young stands out among the delegation for going particularly beyond the call of duty. When Young discovered the poverty in which Smith and his traveling party had undertaken their journey to the capital, he offered to finance their trip and to help fund the publication of a book describing the Mormons' plight to the American public.[7]

Prior to embarking on their trip to the nation's capital, Smith and others had started work on a petition to Congress that told the story of the conflict over the Mormons' presence in Missouri during the 1830s. It commenced with the first Mormon settlements in Jackson County in 1831 and concluded with their expulsion from the state during the frigid winter of 1838–1839. In anticipation of submitting the petition to Congress, members of the Illinois delegation helped Smith and Higbee put the finishing touches on the document they hoped would be their ticket to federal redress.[8]

Handwritten on twenty-eight pages of white paper, the Mormons' petition employed the language of American patriotism. It emphatically declared that the Mormons' religious beliefs and desire to gather in communities to observe their religion did not—and should not—disqualify them from enjoying their full rights as citizens of the United States. The Mormons had moved to Missouri "in the hope of improving their condition," the petition maintained, that they "might worship their creator, according to the dictates of their own consciences." Even though "they had wandered far from the homes of their childhood, still they had been taught to believe, that a citizen born in any one State in this great Republic, might remove to another and enjoy all the rights and immunities guaranteed to the citizens of the State of his adoption; that wherever waved the American flag, beneath its Stars and Stripes, an American citizen might look for protection and justice—liberty in person, and in conscience."[9]

Of course, the Mormon experience did not match this lofty ideal. Smith and company recounted the violent opposition his followers faced in Missouri at nearly every turn. After establishing the grand narrative of their abuse and ultimate expulsion, the petition focused on two particularly harrowing occurrences. The first was the gang rape of a Mormon woman by sixteen vigilantes who had tied their victim to a wooden bench. The second was the slaughter of a little boy at the settlement of Hawn's Mill as he was crying at the side of his murdered father. "Fifteen thousand souls . . . abandoned their homes, and property, and fled in terror from the

Country," Smith and his fellow petitioners declared in summation of the horrific events. "What can be said in extenuation when humanity would shudder and hide herself in shame, if one half only of the house burnings, destruction of property, robbery, rapes, and murder should be told?"[10]

While the Mormon petitioners did not explicitly request reparations in their memorial to Congress, it was implied. They estimated the loss of Mormon property at $2,000,000 and insisted that Congress was the last remaining avenue for redress. "It is the theory of our Constitution and laws, that, for the violation of every legal right, there is provided a legal remedy," the petition averred. "What then we would respectfully ask, is the remedy for these violations of right in the persons and property of the Mormons?" Their various applications to the Missouri legislature for relief had been "treated with silence and contempt." The federal courts in Missouri were not a viable venue because, based on Governor Boggs's executive order, the Mormons were "not permitted to go there; and their juries would be made up of citizens of that state with all their prejudices against them." In the end, the Mormons declared, "we seek no redress, unless it be awarded by the Congress of the United States." And so it was to that legislative body that they made their "solemn, last appeal, as American citizens—as Christians—and as men."[11]

Such a conclusion to the petition encapsulated the sentiment at the heart of the Mormons' lobbying efforts. In declaring their victim status, Smith and company seem to have recognized that their critics might claim that the Mormons had brought such persecution upon themselves by willingly departing from the consensus of mainstream American society. Underlying such arguments was a belief that Americans who did not fully integrate into the country's dominant societal norms deserved whatever poor treatment followed. By emphasizing their American citizenship, the Christian beliefs at the heart of their unconventional religion, and their basic humanity, the petitioners implied that the Mormons were just as entitled to the protections guaranteed in the Constitution as were mainline Protestant Christians.

With the petition ready for congressional consideration, Smith and Higbee strategized with the Illinois delegation on the ideal way to get their document on the floor of Congress. Ultimately, they determined that the House of Representatives—considered the "people's chamber" within the legislative branch—was the ideal setting in which to introduce their appeal. Reynolds, the same Democratic representative who had introduced Smith to President Van Buren, agreed to bring the petition to the House floor.[12]

However, the plan quickly went awry. Contested elections in New Jersey delayed the organization of the House of Representatives and, by extension, the start of the 26th Congress. It was a particularly messy scenario. Eleven men arrived in Washington to assume New Jersey's six seats in the House. The state had not yet sorted out whether the Democratic candidates or their Whig opponents were the actual winners, and evidence had emerged that several county clerks had strategically suppressed voting returns in an effort to swing the election in the favor of the Whig candidates. Control of the House hung in the balance. House Democrats called for the federal government to intervene in order to resolve the matter while their Whig counterparts insisted that such elections fell under the purview of the states.[13] "There is a great deal of wind blown off on the occasion each day," Smith reported to his friends at home, lamenting the gridlock that the affair was causing. Congress "can do nothing of consequence until the House is organized."[14]

It probably should have concerned Smith to see the states' rights doctrine wielded and dismissed as a strategy rather than upheld as an unwavering principle of governance. The Democrats had long trumpeted states' rights, but when it appeared that they might lose their majority in the House, they were more than willing to throw the doctrine overboard. Similarly, many in the Whig Party had called for a stronger federal government, but when that government sought to intervene in state elections that had supposedly turned out in their favor, they fought the prospect tooth and nail. With states' rights subject to political expediency, was there any way to predict how the principle—if, in light of these political machinations, it could still be called a principle—would be applied to the Mormons' case against Missouri? Smith made no mention of these seemingly arbitrary invocations of states' rights and federal authority in his letters home, but the delay in the House meant that Smith and company would need to divert the petition to the Senate.

From his front row seat to the unfolding drama in Congress, Smith provided plenty of commentary. "For a general thing," Smith wrote to his brother, "there is but little solidity and honorable deportment among those who are sent here to represent the people, but a great deal of pomposity and show." He elaborated: "There is such an itching disposition to display oratory on the most trivial occasions, and so much etiquette, bowing and scraping, twisting and turning to, make a display of their witticism that it seems to us rather a display of folly and show more than substance & gravity, such as becomes a great nation like ours."[15] While the Mormon leaders were impressed by the grandeur of the Capitol, they were dismayed to find the men who conducted business in that building be more concerned with pomp and posturing than with efficiency and lawmaking.

The failure of Congress to meet Smith's expectations demonstrates a disconnect between what many Americans living far from the capital thought happened in the houses of the federal government and what actually occurred. The posturing and speechifying that Smith witnessed in Washington, D.C., and the seemingly endless committee process through which bills were shaped, were not new to that city. But they were new—and troubling—to him.

Smith was hardly the only American dismayed by this disconnect. Famed journalist and political commentator Anne Royall had made similar observations in 1830. She asked rhetorically, "What can the people mean by sending such boobies to Congress only to be laughed and pointed at. It would seem they looked for the worst, instead of the best men."[16] Up close and with the reverent facade of prestige pulled back, Americans such as Smith and Royal caught a true glimpse of the American Congress, warts and all.

Seeing the way Congress functioned tested Smith's democratic idealism. He thought highly of the Illinois delegation. "They are worthy men, who have treated us with the greatest kindness, and are ready to do all in their power," he informed his friends at home. But Smith tempered this optimism with caution. "They with us have all the prejudices, superstition and bigotry of an ignorant generation to contend with."[17] The reality of what they were up against had started to sink in.

"AN APPEAL TO THE AMERICAN PEOPLE"

While the rancorous debate in Congress over the contested elections spilled into 1840, there was little that Smith and his fellow church leaders could do to aid their case within the federal government. So they turned their attention to winning over the American people. Until Congress could hear their case, they would try it in the court of public opinion.

This public relations campaign was not limited to Washington, D.C. The delay in Congress afforded Smith and company time to travel to Philadelphia and New Jersey. While visiting Latter-day Saint congregations in those states, Smith tried to assuage public fears that Mormon political practices represented a danger to American democracy. Smith even wrote a letter to the editor of a newspaper in Brandywine, Pennsylvania, in which he countered "many false rumors" about him and the church and tried to put to rest claims that he and his religious movement were a threat to "Earthly governments and laws in general."[18]

Smith's efforts to gain public support for their case against Missouri were aided by the publication of two books by church leaders. Parley Pratt, a member of the church's high-ranking Quorum of the Twelve Apostles, published an 84-page book titled *History of the Late Persecution Inflicted by the State of Missouri upon the Mormons*, which, according to Pratt, laid "open to the broad light of the day, the horrid scenes of murder, treason, robbery and plunder which have been acted in our renowned Republic, and scenes which would put tyranny itself to the blush, and almost bring tears of blood from the heathen of the darkest age."[19] In addition, Sidney Rigdon, one of Smith's most trusted advisors and a counselor in the church's highest governing body, the First Presidency, published the aptly titled *An Appeal to the American People*, in which he described the Missouri conflict in great detail in an effort to "disabuse the public mind, and give it a fair understanding" of the Mormon experience in Missouri.[20] In an age in which the reach of American print media was skyrocketing, the Mormons used the technology to their benefit.

Yet, Smith was at his best when he could employ his dynamic extemporaneous speaking style to convince non-Mormons to sympathize with the plight of his followers. In Washington, hundreds of men and women flocked to hear him speak, if for no other reason than out of curiosity— to see for themselves the man who claimed to interact with the divine and who was called a prophet by his followers. According to the account of one of his traveling companions, Robert D. Foster, in January 1840 Smith addressed a large audience that included "a great many members of Congress and heads of departments," including Henry Clay and John Quincy Adams, as well as President Van Buren.[21] Apparently, even in a city where politicians were constantly making speeches, Smith's public addresses were events.

Smith did not deny the controversial claims that gave rise to the Church of Jesus Christ of Latter-day Saints. But he sought to convey his history and beliefs in a way that would be palatable to the religious sensibilities of men and women in a country where mainstream Protestantism was the standard for acceptable religious beliefs. To a certain extent he succeeded. Matthew L. Davis, a former congressman who had transitioned to a career as a political correspondent for the London *Times* and the New York *Courier and Enquirer*, attended one of Smith's February lectures simply because his wife had expressed interest in the man and his new religious movement.[22]

In the lecture Davis attended, Smith stressed that none of the Mormons' beliefs were contrary to what was written in the Bible, and that they were more ecumenical than many perceived them to be. According to Davis, Smith remarked that the Book of Mormon "contained nothing inconsistent or conflicting with the Christian Bible, and he again repeated that all who would follow the precepts of the Bible, whether Mormon or not, would assuredly be saved." The next day, Davis wrote to his wife: "I have changed my opinion of the Mormons. They are an injured and much abused people. Of matters of Faith, you know I express no opinion."[23] Such moments were public relations victories for Smith and the Mormons. Davis was hardly chomping at the bit to join the religious group, but he was an influential member of the news media who began to sympathize with the Mormons as a direct result of having heard Smith speak.

Smith was clearly trying to normalize the Mormons. During his visit to the White House, he had told Van Buren that the only difference between the Mormons and other Christians was that they "differed in mode of baptism and the gift of the Holy Ghost by the laying on of hands," and that "all other considerations were contained in the gift of the Holy Ghost." This was a cryptic response to Van Buren's query, but Smith and Higbee explained in a letter home that they "deemed it unnecessary to make many words in preaching the Gospel to him."[24]

Americans had long held that certain groups were too fanatical—their belief systems too far outside the boundaries of mainstream Protestant Christianity—to be afforded the full rights of conscience celebrated in the country's constitution. This logic had justified discrimination and violent persecution of the country's Catholics and Jews, as well as several smaller groups, such as the Shakers.[25] If the targets were "fanatics," violent opposition was not bigotry; it was the protection of democratic society.

This notion was not merely implied. In 1812, John C. Calhoun, then a member of the United States House of Representatives, warned about the growth of fanaticism in the form of religious superstition. Unorthodox beliefs would lead to a "fearful retrograde in civilization" and "dreadful declension toward barbarism."[26] Given the prevalence of these sentiments, a focus on the peculiarities of Mormonism could irreparably harm the church's petitioning efforts. If the general public and elected officials in the federal government saw the Mormons as religious fanatics, they might deem the Missouri persecutions as a justified—even necessary—expulsion of a threat to American society.

With their public relations campaign in full swing, the Mormon leaders awaited their day in Congress. But the sluggish pace at which the legislature worked was trying Smith's patience. He had pressing business to attend to in Illinois, where his followers were laboring to rebuild their lives. He was needed in Nauvoo and longed to reunite with his family. Ultimately, Smith determined that he would return home and leave Higbee in the capital to represent the church before Congress. Smith would await word of the church's fate by letter.

"I THINK THEY WILL BE OBLIGED TO ACKNOWLEDGE THE JUSTICE OF OUR CAUSE"

The Mormons' memorial to Congress sparked controversy the moment it hit the Senate floor. Senator Young introduced the memorial on January 28, 1840, and Senator Lewis Linn, a Democrat from Missouri, immediately opposed it. "A sovereign State seemed about to be put on trial before the Senate of the United States," Linn declared. Several other Democrats rallied around Linn, including Senator John Norvell of Michigan, who immediately motioned that the Senate table the memorial, emphatically stating his intention that it "may lie there forever." Relentless, Young prevailed upon the Senate to hear the memorial read in its entirety before acting.[27]

When the memorial had been read aloud, Missouri senator Thomas Hart Benton joined Linn in opposition. At this pivotal moment, other senators came to the memorial's defense, most notably William Campbell Preston and Henry Clay. Following their respective speeches, Benton reduced his support for permanently tabling the memorial to a call for it to be tabled "only for a day or two." The motion passed.[28]

Two weeks later, the Senate once again took up the memorial. This time the response was much more subdued and the memorial was referred to the Judiciary Committee for further consideration. Finally, there was movement on the Mormons' petition, and, five days later, Senator Young submitted to the Judiciary Committee hundreds of documents in support of the Mormon case, chief among them an avalanche of affidavits itemizing property lost or damaged as a result of the Saints' expulsion from Missouri.[29]

Normally the Judiciary Committee would consider such matters behind closed doors. However, Elias Higbee requested that it hold a public hearing and the committee's chair, Senator Garret D. Wall of New Jersey, agreed.[30] The stage was set for dramatic political theater.

As Senator Linn had observed when the Mormons' memorial was first introduced on the Senate floor, it appeared that the state of Missouri was on trial. The state was not actually on trial—at least not yet. The committee was tasked with determining whether or not the Senate—and Congress generally—had jurisdiction in the case. Could they intervene in the conflict between Missouri and the Mormons? If the answer was "yes," there would be a full Senate hearing, replete with witnesses and evidence for both sides; otherwise, the Mormons would have to seek redress elsewhere. As Higbee prepared for his testimony before the committee, he was confident. "I think they will acknowledge the justice of our case," he wrote to Smith.[31]

With Smith on his way home to Nauvoo and Rigdon bedridden with an ongoing illness, Higbee was slated as the sole representative for the expelled Mormon community. But he had the voices of hundreds of his fellow refugees with him in the form of the affidavits.

Missouri, on the other hand, was represented by Senator Linn and one of its Democratic representatives in the House, Congressman John Jameson.[32] They came armed with years of experience navigating the policies and procedures of the United States Congress.

In addition to Senator Wall, the Judiciary Committee consisted of senators Thomas Clayton of Delaware, Robert Strange of North Carolina, John J. Crittenden of Kentucky, and Oliver H. Smith of Indiana. However, Crittenden and Smith were absent for the entire three-day event. No formal minutes of the hearing survive—if they were ever kept. But Higbee reported the details to Smith in a series of letters.

As the hearing commenced, Higbee addressed the committee members while the Missouri congressmen waited impatiently for their chance to rebut his claims. "I told them firstly that I represented a suffering people who had been deprived together with myself of their rights in Missouri," Higbee reported to Smith. But Higbee was quick to present his case as having far-reaching implications. The Mormons, he argued, were but one group of American citizens who "were deprived of the rights guaranteed to us by the constitution of the United States." He insisted that the federal government was their last recourse, as their previous appeals to state courts and elected officials had culminated in Governor Boggs's "extermination order." Future appeals were impossible because Boggs's order meant that Higbee, Smith, and Rigdon "had no ingress in the state of Missouri; nor could any [Mormons] have only at the expense of our lives."[33]

Higbee went on "to prove that the whole persecution from beginning to end was grounded on our religious faith" by providing "a brief history of the persecutions from the first settlement in the State to our final expulsion." Then came Higbee's fervent plea. The church's goal in petitioning Congress was to enlist its help in securing the Mormons' rights as American citizens, and inasmuch as those rights had been violated in Missouri, Higbee reported that he "demanded from them a restitution of all our rights and privileges as citizens of the United States, and damages for all the losses we had sustained in consequences of our persecutions and expulsion from the state."[34]

As soon as Higbee took his seat Missouri's representatives pounced. Representative Jameson declared that the Mormons had brought upon themselves the violent backlash in Missouri, including their ultimate expulsion under the threat of state-sanctioned extermination. He stated that he had "once been in the Mormon's favor; but afterwards learned that it was impossible to live among them," citing accusations of theft that the Missouri vigilantes had mixed with their disdain for the Mormons' religious practices when they justified their actions.[35]

"Making statements was one thing," Higbee shot back, "and proving them was another."[36] The verbal fray continued back and forth until it was time for the full Senate to reconvene and the committee was forced to adjourn for the day. The following day, it picked up right where it had left off. Jameson charged that the Mormons had total disregard for the laws of the United States and instead looked to Smith as a higher civil power.[37]

Higbee deflected the charges, citing the church's published statement on government as proof that they followed the Christian model of separating ecclesiastical and civil power—that the Mormons rendered "unto Caesar the things which are Caesar's, and unto God the things that are God's."[38]

On the hearing's third and final day, the Missouri delegation called as a witness a "Mr. Corwin," who had been a newspaper editor in St. Louis. He attempted to prove that "Jo Smith" led "the people altogether by revelation, in their temporal, civil & political matters, and by this means caused all the Mormons to vote the whole hog ticket on one side."

Higbee did not deny that the Mormons often voted together, but he offered an alternative explanation. It was "in consequence of the democratick principles having been taught us from our infancy," he stated, observing that the violent persecution had predated any accusations of bloc voting.[39] The committee wrapped up the hearing on a more mundane note, asking Higbee several questions about his religious beliefs and for data on the total amount of land church members had owned in Missouri.[40]

Higbee was hopeful. If the committee determined that the full Senate should consider the Mormons' case, the government would pay for dozens of witnesses to travel to the capital to testify. As he awaited the committee's decision, he wrote to Smith suggesting the names of several church members whose testimonies would be invaluable. Maybe the Mormons would have their property restored and their civil rights protected. Maybe the federal government would take the unprecedented action of ensuring religious liberty in individual states, particularly when one of the states had, in fact, been the egregious offender.

Higbee's hope was short-lived. Four days after the hearing concluded, Senator Wall privately informed him that the committee had unanimously decided that the Senate had no jurisdiction in the matter.[41] Congress would do nothing for the Mormons.

According to the official report written by the committee and published by the Senate, since "The wrongs complained of are not alleged to be committed by any officers of the United States, the Mormons should apply to the justice and magnanimity of the State of Missouri—an appeal which the committee feel justified in believing will never be made in vain by the injured or oppressed."[42] The United States Senate determined that it would continue to leave the protection of the citizenship rights of religious minorities to the individual states, even if the states were the ones infringing upon those rights.

When the dust settled, Higbee looked back on the committee hearing with fresh eyes. He started to see it as a sham orchestrated by Missouri's senators, a "trick" they used to kill the petition quietly in committee lest a full senate debate over the memorial's merits draw too much attention to the matter.[43]

Higbee was not the only one to adopt this view. Even Representative Reynolds concluded that the petition's fate was sealed by the political maneuvering of the Missouri delegation, which had sent the memorial to committee and then proceeded to attack it "with such force and violence that it could obtain scarcely a decent burial."[44] Perhaps the Missouri Senators thought that a committee hearing would give the Mormons the impression that their story had been heard and, in the wake of the committee's resolution, they would drop the matter altogether. Maybe this failed petitioning effort would end the state's saga with the Mormons once and for all. If this was, in fact, the hope of Missouri's elected representatives, they would be sorely disappointed.

"WE DEEM IT A GREAT INSULT"

Spring was in full bloom in and around Nauvoo, Illinois, when Higbee's final letter and the attached copy of the Judiciary Committee's report reached Smith at his home. In his absence, the Mormon refugees had made great strides in draining the city's swampy lowlands and starting construction on stout brick homes made from the clay they discovered beneath the mud. Indeed, the transformation of Nauvoo from an unhealthy swamp to a burgeoning settlement was well underway. But the news in Higbee's letter placed a damper on Smith's enthusiasm.

He brought the Senate Judiciary Committee's report before a general conference of the church. "We learn with deep sorrow, regret and disappointment," the minutes of that conference read, "that the committee on Judiciary . . . have reported unfavorable to our cause, to Justice and humanity."[45] The conference appointed several men to draft resolutions in response to the Senate's decision. In those resolutions sorrow, regret, and disappointment gave way to anger and disdain.

"We fondly hoped that in the Congress of the United States, ample justice would have been rendered us," the resolutions explained. "The exterminating order of Governor Boggs, is a direct infraction of the constitution of the U. States, and of the State of Missouri." Congress "in refusing to investigate . . . and turning a deaf ear, to the cries of widows, orphans, and innocent blood," was no less "than secondary the proceedings of that murderous mob, whose deeds are recorded in heaven, and justly calls down upon their heads, the righteous judgments of an offended God." They considered "the part of the report, referring us to the Justice and magnanimity of the State of Missouri for redress . . . a great insult to our good sense, better judgement, and intelligence" because they "could only go into the State of Missouri, contrary to the exterminating order of the Governor" and at the risk of their lives. Ultimately, the church conference deemed the Judiciary Committee's report "unconstitutional, and subversive to the rights of a free people."[46]

Smith was determined not to give up, but he was unclear on how to proceed. Over the next four years he sent petitions to Congress. Each and every time, those petitions fell on deaf ears. It became increasingly clear that a change in the power and authority of the federal government would be required for the Mormons and other religious minorities to receive anything resembling actual religious freedom. As Reynolds put it, "Smith returned to the State of Illinois a red hot Whig."[47]

Yet, Smith's reaction to the refusal of Congress to fully hear his case was deeper and less partisan than Reynolds could understand. It went beyond his disillusionment with Democrats. Smith's confidence in the American political system—his confidence in democracy—had been shattered. He could not count on the United States government to guarantee the citizenship rights of his people. The government had clearly stated that doing so was outside its jurisdiction. Accordingly, he directed more and more of his time and energy into building up the city of Nauvoo, transforming the swampy bend in the Mississippi River into a veritable city-state, designed to protect his people's rights of conscience.

3

. . . .

A CITY-STATE ON A HILL

SMITH WAS CERTAINLY JUSTIFIED IN EXPRESSING HIS discontent with American democracy. Its institutions had failed him. They had failed thousands of his followers. To them, the refusal of the Senate Judiciary Committee "to investigate the proceedings of the executive and others of the State of Missouri, and turning a deaf ear, to the cries of widows, orphans, and innocent blood," was comparable to "the proceedings of that murderous mob" that had inflicted the persecution in the first place.[1]

However, such disillusionment neither dampened Smith's resolve nor diminished his propensity to dream big. Convinced that the federal government was neither willing nor equipped to ensure the citizenship rights of religious minorities, Smith set out to construct a haven of religious freedom on the banks of the Mississippi River. His rejection by President Van Buren and the United States Congress seemed to have wounded him. By throwing himself fully into the work of designing and developing the City of Nauvoo, Smith sought both healing and a defense against future abuse.

In the long term, Smith also seemed determined to heal the nation. A presidential run was not on Smith's radar in 1840; he would not fix American democracy from the top down. Instead, taking a page out of his New England heritage, Smith began to conceive of Nauvoo as a metaphorical "city on a hill," the light of which would shine as an example for the rest of the country to follow. He would administer a healing balm at the local level and watch as it spread through the rest of the country.

"THE GREATEST CITY IN THE WHOLE WORLD"

Coincidentally, Smith set out to build his metaphorical "city on a hill" by building a literal city on a hill. "Nauvoo . . . is beautifully situated," one visitor wrote, "on a point formed by a broad and sweeping bend of the river."[2] The terrain was flat near that water's edge and gradually rose to a prominent bluff from which one could look west across the river and see deep into neighboring Iowa Territory.

Yet, in 1839, when Smith and the Saints first laid eyes on the land they were purchasing, it was hardly picturesque. The low-laying portions of the point were swampland. "The land was mostly covered with trees and bushes," Smith wrote, "and much of it so wet that it was with the utmost difficulty a footman could get through, and totally impossible for teams." The point contained only a scattering of buildings, many of them unoccupied, as the place was "so unhealthful, very few could live there."[3] Another Mormon described it as "a low marshy wet damp and nasty place."[4]

In a very real way, this scenario fit perfectly within the larger narrative of American history in which poor men and women on the margins of society were forced, through social and economic pressure, to reside on land disdained by the country's wealthier and better-integrated citizens. This impulse, present in every era of United States history, is central to the politically driven disempowerment of those who challenge conservative elements of society with new belief systems. Nineteenth-century Americans in the social and political mainstream had essentially deemed the Mormons "waste people" and relegated them to residing on wasteland.[5]

Even in their destitute and discouraged state, Smith and company saw potential in this undesirable tract of land. The church purchased nearly the entire parcel on credit and divided it into more than 150 city blocks, most of them subdivided into four lots. They started selling the lots to church members and other interested settlers. In the meantime, while

Smith and others journeyed to Washington, D.C., to petition the federal government, the Mormon refugees set to work draining their new, swampy home. The excess moisture was caused by several natural springs that flowed from the bluff above to the river below. By redirecting the run-off from these springs, the settlers allowed the low-laying portions of the peninsula to dry, leaving behind fertile soil. Below that soil they discovered rich red clay ideal for making bricks.[6] Brick homes represented prosperity and permanence. It was an almost poetic metaphor. The Mormons saw something in the land that wasn't clearly visible, and their vision was rewarded with the materials required to build a thriving society.

When Smith returned from the capital in the spring of 1840, he was pleasantly surprised by the progress his followers had made. "Our Church here is prospering," he wrote to a friend in Beverly, Illinois, "and many are coming into it. Our town is improving very fast. It is almost incredible to see what amount of labor has been performed here during the winter past. There is now every prospect of our having a good society, a peaceable habitation and a desirable residence here."[7]

The city he had planted the year before was sprouting up and appeared ready to blossom. The Latter-day Saints' "Zion" was still in Missouri, and they persisted in the belief that the version of the gospel of Jesus Christ that they preached would be heard throughout the world in the years to come. But in this moment, they believed that Nauvoo would prove a place of rest, a place for the growing number of Mormon converts to gather and practice their religion in peace. Indeed, as Smith explained to the city's earliest Mormon residents, the word Nauvoo "is of Hebrew origin, and signifies a beautiful situation, or place, carrying with it, also, the idea of rest; and is truly descriptive of this most delightful situation."[8]

Rest from persecution did not mean rest from labor. Prior to leaving for Washington, D.C., Smith and company had created a plat for the city, and church members who had purchased lots were quickly setting to work constructing their homes. This fueled a demand for building materials. Brickyards sprang up, as did mills for the processing of lumber. By May 1840, there were 300 homes in the city and every indication that the growth would continue unabated.[9]

Yet, the labor extended beyond the construction of homes. Smith was as ambitious as ever. He envisioned Nauvoo as more than just another young city hugging the banks of the Mississippi River. Its destiny, he believed, was much grander.

Standing before a gathering of church members on a hot and humid day in July 1840, Smith described his vision. "This is the principle place of gathering," he averred, "therefore as many as can come let the Brethren begin to roll in like clouds. We will sell you lots and if you can't pay for them you shall [have] them." The Latter-day Saints had settled in the area as poor refugees, and they were willing to accept the poor among them. "Whosoever will come let them come and partake of the poverty of Nauvoo freely," Smith continued, "and those who partake of our poverty shall be greatly blessed." But the city and its residents would not remain impoverished for long. Through their hard work, communal spirit, and a divine intervention that Smith was confident would follow, the city would soon be transformed. "Come brethren come all of you," Smith exhorted, "And I prophecy in the name of the Lord that the state of Illinois shall become a mighty mountain as a city set upon a hill that cannot be hid and . . . The City of Nauvoo also shall become the Greatest city in the whole world."[10]

While the fledgling city of Nauvoo seemed designed principally for the relief and protection of Smith and his long-suffering followers, in its future prosperity Smith predicted that it would offer the same to the rest of the world. With an eye on the prophesied last days that precede the Second Coming of Jesus Christ—and a mind still smarting from his snubbing by the president and Congress—Smith prophesied to his audience that at a future time the United States "will be on the very verge of crumbling to pieces and tumbling to the ground and when the constitution is upon the brink of ruin this people will be the Staff upon which the Nation shall lean and they shall bear the constitution away from the very verge of destruction." The Mormons would rescue the nation. And when that day came, the prosperity of Nauvoo would attract international attention, as kings, queens, and rulers would flock to the city to help build Zion.[11]

A lot would have to happen in the decades that followed if Smith's prophecy was to become reality. Smith's vision required resources. It required infrastructure. And so residents undertook large-scale building projects, with a temple and a boarding house chief among them. The temple would house large church meetings and sacred rituals that Smith would reveal in the ensuing years.[12] Built prominently atop the bluff overlooking the Mississippi River, Smith expected that passengers on steamboats would marvel at the structure and see it as a symbol of the faith of the men and women who constructed it.

The boarding house was slated for construction on the flats near one of the river landings. In a published revelation Smith deemed it just as important to Nauvoo's sacred mission as the temple. If kings, queens, rulers, and any number of other distinguished guests were to flock to the city in the years that followed, they would require suitable accommodations.[13]

Smith's ambitious plans also required more people—a lot of them. Earnest missionary efforts within the United States and Canada had swelled church membership to approximately 15,000.[14] There were branches of the church functioning throughout the country, including in major cities such as New York and Philadelphia.[15] Those domestic efforts would continue, but Smith's understanding of his role as a prophet included a duty to oversee the global spread of its message.

Mormon missionaries had first ventured overseas in 1837, when the church was still headquartered in Ohio. That mission was successful and signaled to church members that the metaphorical mission field was, indeed, "ready to harvest."[16] Accordingly, members of Quorum of the Twelve Apostles embarked on a mission to Great Britain at about the same time that Smith was completing his political mission to Washington, D.C. The church grew by thousands of members as the Mormon apostles experienced tremendous success, particularly among the poor, landless population, many of whom were consigned to extreme poverty as a result of the Industrial Revolution.

The Mormon apostles' message promised eternal salvation and their gathering together in the United States seemed to promise relief from their earthly plight. Apostle Heber C. Kimball wrote to Smith that "notwithstanding we have kept nothing back of the sufferings of the saints in America, yet it is astonishing to see the universal anxiety there is manifest amongst the saints here to get away to the land of promise and help to build up Zion." Kimball explained that, once baptized, the British converts "begin to want to go to America, for they declare that that is Zion."[17] By the end of 1840, there were more than 3,500 Mormons in Great Britain, and several groups had already immigrated to Nauvoo.[18]

For many Latter-day Saints, the rapid development of Nauvoo was a sign of divine favor. Their confidence soared. But many, including Smith, were keenly aware that such growth would not last—and ultimately not matter—if there were not laws and civic institutions in place to protect the rights and property of the city's citizens. After all, many of the Mormons rebuilding their lives in Nauvoo were doing so for the second, third, or even the fourth time since joining the church. They knew that expulsion and poverty could replace growth and prosperity in the blink of an eye.

"ONE OF THE MOST LIBERAL CHARTERS"

Seeking to avoid the tragedies that characterized the end of earlier Mormon efforts to build communities, Smith dedicated much of his time in 1840 to securing the legal rights and privileges for Nauvoo's city government. Smith had no legal training or experience in municipal affairs, so the prospect of drafting a city charter must have been somewhat daunting. Accordingly, he welcomed the help of John C. Bennett, a new member of the church who had influence with the state legislature in Springfield.

Bennett's religious conversion was not the result of Mormon proselytizing efforts. Instead, he sought out Smith and the church. The Quartermaster General in the Illinois state militia, Bennett learned of the Mormons' plight in Missouri and their flight to Illinois. In July 1840, he wrote to Smith that he desired to move to Nauvoo and to join the church. "I believe I should be much happier with you," he wrote.[19] He was so eager that he wrote what was essentially the same letter three times in the space of four days, perhaps to ensure that it arrived safely in Nauvoo.

"To those who have suffered so much abuse and borne the cruelties and insults of wicked men so long," Smith replied to Bennett, "a feeling of sympathy and kindness is something like the refreshing breese and cooling stream." He urged Bennett to move to Nauvoo and join with the Latter-day Saints as soon as he could, stating that "Were it possible for you to come here this season to suffer affliction with the people of God no one will be more pleased or give you a more cordial welcome than myself."[20]

Despite Bennett's station in the Illinois militia, there were rumors about him circulating throughout the state. Shortly after Bennett joined the church, Smith received a letter "from a person of respectable character" and residing in the vicinity where Bennett had lived. The letter warned Smith that Bennett "was a very mean man" who had abandoned a wife and children in Ohio. Smith later claimed that he had been unsure of the report's credibility at the time he had received it, and for that reason he had kept silent on the matter and continued to integrate Bennett into the church.[21] It is possible that Smith simply did not want to believe it.

Bennett was not a devoutly religious man. The thirty-six-year-old physician was an unabashed opportunist—and he recognized immense opportunity within the Mormon community. Bennett publicly lauded the statement of a phrenologist who had attempted to discern his character by measuring his skull. According to the pseudo-scientific reading, Bennett was ambitious, willing to "sacrifice money for fame and power."[22] The beleaguered yet determined Mormon community at Nauvoo seemed an avenue to both.

Like a shepherd who unwittingly let a wolf into his flock, Smith would one day regret elevating Bennett to a position of trust. But the prophet lacked such foresight in 1840. Bennett seemed genuine in his expressions of belief, and the eagerness of a well-connected outsider to help the Mormons must have seemed too good of an opportunity to pass up.

When Bennett arrived in the city, he did, in fact, bring with him some much-needed political acumen. Along with Smith and church member Robert B. Thompson, he quickly got to work drafting a legislative act for the incorporation of Nauvoo. In some ways the charters the men proposed in the act were quite typical for American cities. They specified the city's geographic boundaries and outlined the powers of its government. The mayor was to possess executive authority, and the city council was granted the legislative authority whereby it could pass ordinances and resolutions. In addition, the charter had provisions for the creation of a municipal court.[23]

Some of the chartered rights proposed in the act to incorporate Nauvoo were less universal, but not necessarily uncommon. The mayor would also possess judicial authority. The city could establish schools—including a university. To provide for the physical protection of the city's residents and their property, the charters would authorize the establishment of a militia.[24] For a group of Americans whose property had been destroyed or taken by force, this provision was especially appealing.

As for legal protection, the charters would authorize the city council to issue writs of habeas corpus to protect citizens from unlawful arrest. Though the language was clearly adapted from the charters of other cities, the inclusion of this power was undoubtedly prompted by the dubious arrest of Smith and others in Missouri and their prolonged imprisonment. Under this provision, should law officers from outside Nauvoo attempt to arrest a city resident, the city council could issue a writ of habeas corpus to the custodial officer, thereby granting the arrested individual release from custody until the legality of the arrest was considered in a court hearing.[25]

While each of the individual powers included in the act for the incorporation of the city of Nauvoo existed in the charters of other Illinois cities, what made Nauvoo's proposed charters unique was the aggregation of all of these powers. Whereas other cities adopted the powers and institutions that their founders thought were necessary at the moment of incorporation, Smith, Bennett, and Thompson essentially included all of the powers and institutions that were permitted by recent precedent.[26]

Would the Illinois legislature grant such concentrated power? Could the founders of Nauvoo convince the state that these powers were not excessive, but essential because of the dubious militant and legal actions taken against the Mormons in Missouri, actions that had driven them to Illinois in the first place? These questions loomed large as Bennett departed Nauvoo for Springfield in November 1840.

In the state capital Bennett set to work lobbying members of the state legislature. He found the work surprisingly easy. Despite the expansive powers set forth in the proposed charters, the Mormons were in a fortuitous position. With the state nearly deadlocked between the Whigs and the Democrats, members of both parties were eagerly courting the Mormon vote. As Thomas Ford recalled of the charter in his *History of Illinois*, "no one opposed it, but all were busy and active in hurrying it through."[27] The Mormons' civil rights were once again tied up in partisan politics. Only this time the political dynamics worked in the Mormons' favor.

Indeed, the charter practically sailed through the Illinois legislature. Introduced in the Senate on November 27 and read again on December 5 with minor revisions, both legislative chambers of the General Assembly approved the charter in the days that followed and, on December 16, a council consisting of the governor and the justices of the Illinois Supreme Court approved the bill. Effective February 1, 1841, Nauvoo would be an incorporated city, with all of the considerable powers and institutions set forth in its proposed charters intact.[28]

"Every power we asked has been granted, every request gratified, every desire fulfilled," an elated Bennett announced in a letter to the church's newspaper, the *Times and Seasons*.[29] Several of the state's elected officials were eager to congratulate Bennett on the charter's passage, including Whig senator Sidney Little (the bill's sponsor in the state Senate) and Illinois's Secretary of State and prominent Democrat, Stephen A. Douglas. Even up-and-coming Whig Abraham Lincoln approached Bennett and "cordially congratulated" him.[30]

News of the charters' passage arrived in Nauvoo to great celebration. A report in the Nauvoo *Wasp* trumpeted the charter as containing "the most liberal provisions ever granted by a legislative assembly."[31] For them, incorporation was not merely a necessary legal process. It meant that their literal and figurative city on a hill would have the powers of a veritable city-state.

"THOSE DAYS OF DARKNESS AND GLOOM HAVE GONE BY"

Smith was well aware of the exceptional nature of the city's charters. Yet, he demonstrated no hesitation in making the powers secured in the charters known to the wider public. He was either unaware or unconcerned that such a concentration of power in a city government controlled by a religious minority group might strike others as a risk to American democracy. In fact, in an open letter to the church he celebrated the charters and the protections they offered, declaring them a sign of the Illinois's goodwill toward the Mormons and its recognition that liberal powers were necessary to protect the community members' rights of conscience.

In that open letter, Smith and his counselors in the church's First Presidency celebrated the Mormons' resilience in the wake of their expulsion from Missouri and expressed gratitude for the welcome that church members had received in Illinois. In the state, the First Presidency declared, Mormons had "found an asylum, and were kindly welcomed by persons worthy of the character of FREEMAN." The state legislature "owned us as citizens and friends," the letter continued, "and took us by the hand, and extended to us all the blessings of civil, political, and religious liberty, by granting us . . . one of the most liberal charters, with the most plenary powers, ever conferred by a legislative assembly of free citizens, for the 'City of Nauvoo,' the 'Nauvoo Legion' and the 'University of the City of Nauvoo.'"[32]

Smith and company heaped even more praise on Illinois. As they saw it, the state had done more than merely protect a single religious minority group. "Illinois has set a glorious example, to the whole United States and to the world at large," the First Presidency's letter added, "and has nobly carried out the principles of her constitution, and the constitution of these United States, and while she requires of us implicit obedience to the laws, (which we ever hope to see observed) she affords us the protection of law—the security of life, liberty, and the peaceable pursuit of happiness."[33]

Smith's political education was bearing fruit. He was a religious leader first and foremost. Yet, he recognized that his religious vision for the redemption of the world was dependent on his ability to work within an existing political system. He needed Illinois to support and protect his fledgling community if it was to reach its full potential.

Feeling that they had laid the civic foundation for a peaceful community in which religious freedom was the order of the day, Smith invited his followers to once again gather together in a single place. Acknowledging that "a general gathering has heretofore been associated with most cruel and oppressing scenes," he nevertheless exuded confidence "that those days of darkness and gloom have gone by, and from the liberal policy of our State government, we may expect a scene of peace and prosperity, we have never witnessed since the rise of our church, and the happiness and prosperity which now await us, is, in all human probability, incalculably great."[34] This was a reiteration of Smith's prophecy several months earlier, that "the state of Illinois shall become a great and mighty mountain," and that "The city of Nauvoo also shall become the Greatest city in the world."[35]

Smith presented a highly triumphant and profoundly optimistic vision for the future, all in contrast to his recent past. Just two years earlier, in Missouri, he had experienced one of the lowest points of his life and religious leadership. Just months earlier, he had returned from Washington, D.C., disheartened by the federal government's inaction to relieve the plight of his community. Determined to safeguard against a repeat of the Missouri persecutions and convinced that state and federal governments were not up to the task, Smith and company designed and constructed their new community with the protection of their rights at the forefront of their minds. They were building a veritable city-state on a bend in the Mississippi River, the name of which signaled to all who would enter that it was a beautiful place, a refuge wherein the country's marginalized citizens could find safety. And Smith had invited the world to come to western Illinois to partake in this beauty and rest.

"THE NEW AND EVERLASTING COVENANT"

Thousands of people accepted Smith's invitation. As they flooded into Nauvoo following its incorporation in February 1841, the number of buildings filling the once swampy land grew rapidly. The British converts joined converts from all regions of the United States in changing not only their religious affiliations, but also their physical addresses. Nauvoo was booming.

The size and scope of Smith's power grew with the city. In the first municipal election in 1841, Smith was elected to the city council. When the city organized its militia, the Nauvoo Legion, Smith was appointed Lieutenant General, its highest rank.[36] From that time on and in keeping with common practices for those who served in the military or local militia units in the early American republic, many of his friends and associates addressed and referred to him as General Smith.

By the spring of 1842, Nauvoo's population had surpassed 10,000.[37] And the Legion counted more than 1,500 men in its ranks.[38] Smith was as powerful as ever.

Of course, Nauvoo faced the challenges that accompany any new and rapidly growing city. The ordinances passed by the city council during its first two years reflect a concerted effort to establish order amid the chaos that came with a surging population. They included the establishment of a police force, regulations on construction practices, procedures for eliminating standing water from city streets, and prohibitions against fighting.[39] While many of the new arrivals rejoiced that they had moved to such a beautiful city of promise, others were disappointed. The city and, in some cases, the prophet did not meet their expectations.

If new arrivals to the city expected Smith to be more than a man, they found instead a person who in his dress and demeanor appeared quite common. If they expected Nauvoo to have already grown into the society of Smith's prophecy, they found instead a fledgling city that on the surface looked like dozens of other American settlements then abutting the western frontier. The major visual exception to this was the temple under construction on the bluff—a dramatic sign of the city's ambitions—and of Smith's.

Smith tried to mitigate such disappointment by managing expectations. In one impromptu speech to a group of newly arrived converts, Smith "said he was but a man and they must not expect him to be perfect; if they expected perfection from him, he should expect it from them, but if they would bear with his infirmities and the infirmities of the brethren, he would likewise bear with their infirmities."[40]

Indeed, despite its unusual origins and its religiously laced ambitions, much of Nauvoo looked like any other American city. This was particularly true in its cultural institutions. The city established a weekly lyceum by 1841, both a Masonic lodge and a women's charitable society in the spring of 1842, and several schools.[41] Two newspapers set up shop in the city's printing office.[42]

Despite Smith's grievances with the federal government, on Independence Day Nauvoo displayed as much patriotism as any other American community. The day was filled with feasts and toasts. The city's band played as the Nauvoo Legion marched. People from surrounding areas filled the city to join in the festivities. "It was a beautiful sight," one spectator recalled years later, "to see the Prophet Joseph on his prancing black horse that seemed to keep time with the music of the band."[43] While Nauvoo was hardly a polished settlement, its residents were embracing many aspects of mainstream American life. They sought to create an exceptional city that protected their differences, but that did not necessarily separate them from the rest of the world.

In other ways, Nauvoo was pushing the boundaries of inclusivity in American society. Indeed, Smith did not waste his community's newfound peace and prosperity. While his own religious teachings were not always ecumenical, his experience as the leader of a religious minority group had impressed upon Smith the importance of the freedom of conscience and a strong sense that such freedom must be protected and fostered by governments. "We wish it likewise to be distinctly understood," Smith wrote in 1841, "that we claim no privilege but what we feel cheerfully disposed to share with our fellow citizens of every denomination, and every sentiment of religion." Nauvoo was "far from being restricted to our own faith," Smith averred, and he invited "all those who desire to locate themselves in this place" to come, promising that they would "hail them as citizens and friends and shall feel it not only a duty, but a privilege, to reciprocate the kindness we have received from the benevolent and kind-hearted citizens of the state of Illinois."[44]

This religious freedom was not limited to Christians. In a later discourse he declared: "Mahometans, Presbyterians, etc., if ye will not embrace our religion, embrace our hospitalities."[45] This liberal sentiment was codified by Smith and the rest of the city council in an ordinance guaranteeing "that the Catholics, Presbyterians, Methodists, Baptists, Latter-day Saints, Quakers, Episcopalians, Universalists, Unitarians, Mohammedans and all other religious sects and denominations whatever, shall have free toleration, and equal privileges in this city."[46] To Smith, religious freedom was more than a theoretical acknowledgment of the right of men and women to worship according to the dictates of their own consciences. Real religious freedom required the religious majority to defend—and even facilitate—the worship of others.

Another thing that set Nauvoo apart was that women could own property, as could free people of color.[47] While some were able to take advantage of such opportunities and voting rights were still restricted to the city's "free white male inhabitants who are of the age of twenty one years," the extension of property ownership to women and people of color was exceptional in the nineteenth-century United States.[48]

Smith also used the freedom and protection that Nauvoo seemed to offer to expand Mormon theology and ritual. The temple under construction in the city was the driver of this change. For instance, as early as 1840 Smith began to preach the doctrine of vicarious baptisms performed for deceased family members. The theological foundations for the practice were the teaching of Jesus that "Except a man be born of water and of the Spirit, he cannot enter the kingdom of God," and a less-direct reference of the apostle Paul, who, in arguing for the eventual resurrection of all men and women asked, "if the dead not rise at all, why are they then baptized for the dead?"[49]

Other doctrines and rituals destined for the temple that were revealed by Smith in Nauvoo included the endowment and sealing ordinances. The endowment consisted of instructions on the creation of the earth and mankind's purpose and symbolized entering the presence of God. During the ritual, participants covenanted to abide by various commandments, believing that keeping those covenants would allow them to dwell in God's presence in the next life.[50] Through the ritual of sealing, a husband and wife could be bound together for eternity. It was based in part on biblical references to the power that Jesus Christ gave to his disciple, Peter, that "whatsoever ye shall bind on earth shall be bound in heaven." In essence, Smith preached that marriages could extend beyond death and last for eternity.[51] While this was a common sentiment among Americans who believed in some form of an afterlife, Smith's introduction of the sealing ritual formalized it.

Connected to the ritual of sealing, but more radical—and potentially more explosive than any of Smith's other religious teachings—was the introduction of polygamy to a small circle of church members. According to Smith, the commandment to marry additional wives came from God and was more a restoration of past doctrine than a theological invention. It appears to have resulted from Smith's study of biblical prophets who practiced polygamy, including Abraham, Moses, and David. According to a revelation dictated by Smith to one of his clerks, at various times in the history of mankind God had authorized certain men to be married to more than one wife at the same time. Therefore, Abraham, Moses, and David were not under condemnation from God for their plural wives, so long as they married them with God's sanction. However, the revelation stated that if men and women strayed from the divinely authorized pattern for marrying more than one spouse, as David did, then they could expect harsh penalties from God. Explaining these biblical precedents in that way and declaring a fresh commandment from God, Smith instituted this practice. He deemed it a part of "a new and everlasting covenant" of marriage. Mormons eventually came to call it plural marriage.[52]

Historians disagree on when Smith first married a second wife, and surviving sources on these plural marriages in Nauvoo do not illuminate every aspect of the practice. Yet, the sources that have survived demonstrate that a small group of church members were engaged in plural marriage by 1841, but that the majority of Smith's followers were unaware of the practice. Indeed, the church's public position on marriage remained an unflinching insistence on monogamy.[53]

While the existence of plural marriages was radical, the way they occurred was not. A man who had been instructed by Smith on the doctrine would propose to a woman he wished to marry as a plural wife. If she accepted the proposed union, the couple was sealed for eternity and the union solemnized, not in a civil ceremony, but in a religious one. Plural marriages in Nauvoo did not typically result in households with one husband and multiple wives. Usually men practicing plural marriage continued to live with their first wife while their plural wives continued to live elsewhere, often in their parents' home if they had never married or in their own homes if they had previously been widowed. In some cases, Smith and others were sealed to women who were already married.[54]

The obvious critical explanation for plural marriage is that it was a doctrine Smith invented to justify sexual relationships outside of his first and only legal marriage. Sexual intercourse was certainly a component in many of these plural marriages, but not all. Several of the plural unions appear to have existed for purely religious reasons, namely, a way to ensure that all women who wanted to could participate in the ordinance of sealing and receive its benefits in the afterlife. Smith believed that through the sealing ritual he was binding families together for eternity, and that through plural marriage he was creating expansive eternal kinship networks. As historian and Smith biographer Richard Bushman explains, "The marriage revelation culminated the emergence of family theology . . . In Nauvoo, the family side of the priesthood came forward. Bonding families became the center of Joseph's doctrine."[55]

An accurate understanding of plural marriage also requires the perspective of the women who participated in it. "To understand the emergence of plural marriage in Nauvoo," historian Laurel Thatcher Ulrich writes, "we must attend to what these women and others like them cared about."[56] The motives of Mormon women for participating in plural marriage varied, as did their experiences as plural wives. However, many understood and embraced the theological aspect of the practice as taught by Smith, particularly that plural marriage created spiritual bonds that transcended the mere friendship or romantic attachment. Of course, this doctrinal acceptance was not universal in Nauvoo, but it was strong enough that several Mormon women who did not themselves participate in plural marriage were supportive of the practice.[57]

Recognizing that plural marriages were against state and federal anti-bigamy laws—as well as a major departure from what mainstream American society embraced as the only acceptable form of marriage—Mormon leaders did not publicize the practice.[58] Eventually, they seemed to believe, the millennial era would be upon the earth, and the laws and societal norms of the world would be supplanted by a higher, divine social order.

Plural marriage in Mormon Nauvoo is a complicated and controversial subject. Historians continue to pore over historical records to understand

the motives for the practice and its impact on participants.[59] Where Smith
and the events of his life that eventually brought him to a run for the presidency are concerned, the practice of plural marriage in Nauvoo signaled
both safety and risk. Only in the safe haven of Nauvoo could Smith have
introduced such a bold doctrine, and its practice suggests that in its early
days the safeguards weaved into the fabric of Nauvoo's charter were effective enough to allow for such a radical theological development. Yet,
the institution represented a serious risk for Smith and his community.
Monogamy was so ingrained in American society that the discovery of
plural marriage in Nauvoo would almost certainly invite disruption and
dissent within the community—and persecution from without.

Of course, only those who knew to look for something as unconventional as plural marriage were likely to find it in Nauvoo. To most
observers in the spring of 1842, the city appeared to be living up to its
promise. Hardly a perfect society, it offered a critique and correction to
many of the ailments of nineteenth-century American society. Yet, in the
very circumstances that empowered Smith and company to build their
haven on the Mississippi River also lay the impetus for the city's undoing.
By the summer of 1842, a series of events had renewed much of the same
hostility the Mormons had faced in Missouri. Would the charters and the
concentration of powers serve its intended purpose? Or would the specter
of the Missouri persecutions that haunted Nauvoo materialize into a new
set of problems?

4

. . . .

THE SPECTER OF MISSOURI

MAY 6, 1842, WAS A CHILLY NIGHT on the former Mormon land in Jackson County, Missouri. Rain streamed from the sky. Just three blocks from the site on which Smith and his followers had intended to construct a sacred temple stood a house whose owner had allowed mobs to drive the Mormons from that very land: former governor Lilburn W. Boggs.

Boggs had purchased his plot of land and built his home in the months immediately after he left office. Nearly two years later he was seated in his home reading a newspaper, oblivious to the impending danger that lurked in the dark, muddy streets outside. He did not notice the person approaching his window, positioning his pistol, and taking aim.

A shot exploded from the assassin's gun and buckshot sprayed into the home. Boggs was struck twice in the head, once in the neck, and once in the throat. His son rushed from another room to his father's side, as did neighbors who heard the shot. Despite the swift response, the prognosis was not good. The *Daily Missouri Republican* reported six days later that there were "no hopes of recovery by his friends, and but slight hopes from his physicians."[1]

News of the assassination attempt spread like wildfire in Missouri, and the flames soon jumped the Mississippi River into Illinois. Smith noted the news in his journal on May 14 and a published confirmation of Boggs's death the following day.[2] The May 28 issue of Nauvoo's *The Wasp* reported without sympathy that "Boggs is undoubtedly killed according to report; but who did the noble deed remains to be found out."[3]

Yet, the news of the death of the former governor and antagonist to the Mormons was premature. Boggs survived the attack and gradually regained his health. In his investigation of the assassination attempt, the Jackson County sheriff recovered a pistol at the scene, but the shooter's identity remained a mystery. Initial suspicion fell upon Boggs's opponents in his campaign for a seat in the Missouri Senate. However, before long the range of suspicion had expanded. "There are several rumors in circulation in regard to the horrid affair," reported one newspaper on May 21, "One of which throws the crime upon the Mormons."[4]

There was no substantial evidence linking the Mormons to the attempt on Boggs's life. Yet, it was well known that there was lingering animosity between the Mormons and the former governor. Revenge appeared as a likely motive. Though the Mormons had left the state, prejudice against them remained. Even after the Jackson County sheriff arrested another man for the crime, some Missourians suggested that Smith and his followers were somehow involved in the attempted murder. They looked for ways to tie the Mormons to the crime. They did not need to search for long. A disgruntled ex-Mormon saw an opportunity to exact revenge against Smith and the church.

"QUELL THE MORMON MONSTER"

John C. Bennett's rise to power and prominence in Nauvoo was meteoric. So was his fall. Or, at least it appeared to be.

Bennett's political acumen had been essential to Nauvoo's incorporation in the latter part of 1840, so it was no surprise that in February 1841 Bennett was elected the city's first mayor. That was only the beginning. The city council appointed him chancellor of the yet unorganized University of Nauvoo, and members of the Nauvoo Legion elected him Major-General. Perhaps most surprising of all, Smith tapped him to join the church's highest governing body, the First Presidency. By the Spring of 1842, Bennett was arguably the second most powerful person in Nauvoo. As the unabashedly ambitious physician later wrote, in early

1842 he "possessed power, wealth, and the means to gratify every passion or desire."[5] Then came the scandals. There is no evidence that Joseph Smith introduced Bennett to the practice of plural marriage. Nevertheless, Bennett caught wind of the practice and by early 1842 was engaging in his own form of it. Whereas Smith preached the spiritual reasons for the sealings to multiple women and the unions were solemnized with a religious ceremony, Bennett was decidedly more cavalier in his approach. He used the doctrine as a license for promiscuity. He proposed sex to several women, explaining that Smith was encouraging the liaisons. Some women consented; others resisted and complained to church leaders.[6]

According to later accounts, Bennett's promiscuity was a near constant problem in Nauvoo. Smith and other church leaders typically dealt with such matters privately. Bennett would confess his actions and apologize. Smith would then forgive him. To the casual observer, all was well in the First Presidency. However, at some point, Bennett's actions became too much for the city and the church to bear. Under intense pressure, Bennett resigned as mayor of Nauvoo on May 17, 1843, and withdrew his membership from the church at the same time.[7] He seemed set on remaining in Nauvoo, but as the church's leadership in the city further investigated allegations of immorality against Bennett and others, their discoveries prompted church leaders to excommunicate him on May 11, despite the fact that he had already voluntarily left the church. Smith testified against Bennett at a Nauvoo Legion court martial on June 30.[8]

In June, the *Times and Seasons* published a statement from the prophet. Smith deemed Bennett "one of the most abominable and depraved beings which could possibly exist" who "went to some of the females in the city, who knew nothing of him but as an honorable man, and began to teach them that promiscous [sic] intercourse between the sexes was a doctrine believed in by the Latter-Day Saints, and that there was no harm in it." Smith was careful not to publicly reveal the existence of plural marriages in Nauvoo. He simply claimed that Bennett was a man who used the public trust to prey on young women in order to gratify his "wicked, lustful appetites."[9]

Bennett was irate at the public attacks on his character. He did not see his relationships with other women as any different than those Smith maintained. Cashiered from the Nauvoo Legion, his power in the community was now entirely depleted. Unfortunately for Smith, Bennett was not one to leave quietly. Bent on redemption and revenge, Bennett immediately launched a campaign to discredit Smith and the church. The pen and the stage were his weapons of choice.

Cornered, his pride wounded, his character impeached, Bennett fought back ferociously. But fact and fiction, accuracy and embellishment are hard to separate in Bennett's attacks. His exposé, *The History of the Saints*—which he promoted with a national lecture tour—comprised an abundance of previously published materials. To his own letters to American newspapers Bennett added excerpts from an assortment of anti-Mormon editorials published over the previous fifteen years, so excessively that the *New York Tribune* described the book as "nothing more than a collection of all newspaper trash about the Mormons that has been published in the last few years."[10]

It was not all repurposed material, though. Bennett placed special emphasis on Smith's practice of plural marriage, dubbing it the "secret wife system." Then, taking a page out of the established anti-Mormon playbook, Bennett called Smith a charlatan who exploited the devotion of his followers for wealth and power. The ultimate goal of Smith "and his cabinet," Bennett claimed, was "temporal, as well as spiritual empire." Bennett warned that Smith had his eye on vast swaths of the West, which could "be licked up like salt, and fall into the immense labyrinth of glorious prophetic dominion, like the defenseless lamb before the mighty king of the forest!"[11]

Bennett was issuing a call to action. "I would commend to the candid and earnest attention of every patriotic and religious person the statement I have made," Bennett averred, entreating the public "to use all their influence and exertions to arrest and quell the Mormon Monster in his career of imposture, iniquity, and treason."[12]

If Americans did not quell their Mormon countrymen, Bennett warned, then "less than twenty years will see them involved in a civil war of the most formidable character. They will have to encounter a numerous and ferocious enemy, excited to the utmost by fanaticism and by pretended revelations from God." Much was at stake, Bennett concluded. If left unchecked, the Mormons would "deluge this fair land with the blood of her sons, and exterminate the results of the toil and the civilization of more than two centuries."[13] Bennett was advocating the violent suppression of a religious minority. But rather than acknowledge the apparent contradiction of such violence to the country's pretentions to religious freedom, he depicted it as a service to the country.

Smith acted promptly to mitigate the damage Bennett was doing to his reputation and that of the church. Smith denied the practice of plural marriage in Nauvoo as described by Bennett. But he left the denial at that, declining to publicly describe the plural marriage he and others were *actually* practicing in Nauvoo and how it differed from what Bennett charged.[14] Several Nauvoo citizens defended Smith's character in sworn affidavits. The Nauvoo *Wasp* published these affidavits in a special extra edition. Church leaders also dispatched more than 400 missionaries throughout the United States to counter Bennett's lecture tour with public addresses of their own.[15]

It is impossible to gauge with a high degree of precision the extent of the damage Bennett inflicted. There were certainly church members in Nauvoo who struggled with the claims put forth by Bennett, and many of them either left the church or diminished their level of activity. Some Nauvoo residents who had been aware of and uncomfortable with plural marriage were emboldened by Bennett, enough to become open critics of Smith.[16]

While many newspapers in Illinois and Missouri featured Bennett's letters, Bennett had greater difficulty finding a publisher for his book. New York publisher James Gordon Bennett rejected the book because of the dubious nature of some of its claims and the erotic nature of the illustrations Bennett had proposed to accompany the text. A church member in New York explained to Smith that James Gordon Bennett rejected the manuscript because "John C. Bennett designed to illustrate his proposed publication with so many obscene engravings . . . that it was as bad as the worst French books that were imported."[17] Many nineteenth-century Americans would have received with shock and disbelief the news that James Gordon Bennett had passed on publishing a book over concerns about decency. As an editor, he was frequently accused—and even sued—for dubious content published in his paper. He had vigorously defended the right of other publications to print indecent material.[18] Whether or not this was the reason he declined the book, John C. Bennett eventually found a publisher in Boston. But the book's seven illustrations were apparently not those he had originally chosen.

The reception of Bennett's public lectures was mixed and varied by location. While Bennett may have been able to turn some individuals against the Mormons, it appears more likely that he was primarily effective in solidifying existing prejudices. Those individuals and newspapers already suspicious of the Mormons were generally willing to broadcast and print Bennett's claims, even if they recognized that they were motivated by spite and that Bennett himself was a disreputable character. The editors of one Massachusetts newspaper reported that they were convinced by the claims against Smith, but that Bennett's "manner does not impress us, as that of one actuated by any very high and noble impulses," nor did they believe that "his original instigation to what he is doing, is the purest in the world."[19] The *New York Spectator* called Bennett "only not quite so bad" as Smith.[20] The *New York Herald* called Bennett a "pill-maker for purgatory."[21] In attempting to tear down Smith's reputation, Bennett was unable to redeem his own. Indeed, noted historian Hubert Howe Bancroft would eventually deem Bennett "a charlatan, pure and simple; such was he when he joined the Mormons, and before and after."[22]

However, there was one result of Bennett's actions that was immensely and immediately damaging to Smith. In a letter to a St. Louis newspaper, Bennett claimed that Joseph Smith was behind the attempted assassination of Lilburn Boggs and that Smith's close friend and bodyguard, Orin Porter Rockwell, had pulled the trigger. This was a claim that many in Missouri were especially eager to believe.[23]

"I AM NOW HUNTED"

Boggs and other Missouri officials pounced on Bennett's claim. Just six days after its publication, Boggs swore in an affidavit that Rockwell had been the gunman and Smith an accessory before the fact.[24] While he did not mention Bennett in the affidavit, the ex-Mormon's accusation was clearly a motivating factor.

For his part, Smith adamantly denied the allegations and attributed them to an embarrassed and spiteful Bennett. Evidence connecting Smith to the crime was scant and circumstantial. Rockwell had been visiting family in Independence, Missouri, at the time of the attempted assassination. Because the state's order that Mormons "must be exterminated or driven from the state" was still technically in effect, he used an alias. Beyond Rockwell's presence in the area, there was little else upon which to build a case against Rockwell and Smith.[25]

Nevertheless, Boggs's affidavit prompted Missouri's new governor, Thomas Reynolds, to request the cooperation of Illinois in extraditing

Smith to stand trial.[26] Weeks later, in August 1842, Illinois governor Thomas Carlin issued a warrant and offered a reward for Smith's arrest. He then dispatched the sheriff of Adams County to Nauvoo to apprehend the Mormon prophet.[27] This was precisely the kind of event that the Nauvoo charters had been designed to guard against. Its provisions were about to be tested.

On August 8, the sheriff arrived in Nauvoo and immediately arrested Smith and Rockwell. The legal machinery of Nauvoo jolted into motion. The habeas corpus sections of the city's charters—bolstered by a city ordinance passed a month earlier—authorized the municipal court to examine all outside arrest warrants. Acting as a court, the city council issued a writ of habeas corpus to Smith and Rockwell. The sheriff released his prisoners and went to consult with the governor on how to proceed. When he returned two days later, Smith and Rockwell had fled.[28]

Innocent or guilty, Smith knew that if he set foot on Missouri soil again he would be killed. While Rockwell fled to Philadelphia, Smith crossed the Mississippi River to hide out in his uncle's home in Iowa Territory. Suspecting that Smith would use the sparsely populated territory as his safety valve, Missouri officials lobbied the territorial governor to also issue a warrant for Smith's arrest.[29]

This news of potential problems in Iowa Territory prompted a new plan. Late at night on August 11, Emma Smith, accompanied by several other church leaders, discreetly met her husband on an island in the Mississippi River. There they planned a return to Illinois, but not immediately to Nauvoo. For the next three months, Smith worked hard to elude authorities.[30] For much of that time he hid in the homes of friends in the countryside north and east of Nauvoo. There were a few moments when he felt safe—or emboldened—enough to return to his city, but he kept a low profile while there. "I am now hunted," he lamented in a letter to a friend in New York.[31]

Meanwhile, church members in Nauvoo pleaded with the governors of Illinois and Missouri to relent in their pursuit of their mayor and prophet. The most adamant and impassioned pleas came from Emma Smith. In a series of letters to Governor Carlin of Illinois, she argued that the extradition attempt was unjust. Not only were the charges based on Bennett's dubious claims, but her husband had not even been in Missouri when the alleged crime had been committed. This mattered a great deal. Maintaining her husband's innocence, Emma Smith nevertheless asserted that even if he had helped plot the assassination of Boggs, if the plotting occurred in Illinois, then Missouri had no claim on him.[32]

In the face of Emma Smith's reasoning, Carlin remained intransigent. He was determined to turn the Mormon prophet over to Missouri.[33] Smith's best chance lay in remaining free until the governor-elect, Thomas Ford, was inaugurated in December.[34] The Mormons had voted overwhelmingly for Ford. Maybe he would be more reasonable. Maybe Ford's governorship would rekindle the hope among the state's Latter-day Saints that Illinois would, in fact, be the bastion of civil liberties they had celebrated it as nearly two years earlier.

Smith was, in fact, rewarded for his patience. Where Carlin had dismissed Emma Smith's arguments for the illegality of the extradition attempt, Ford was convinced. After several church leaders visited Ford in Springfield in December 1842, the newly installed governor wrote to Joseph Smith, urging him to come to the state capital for a hearing. Smith obliged, departing Nauvoo for Springfield on December 27.[35] Nathaniel Pope, a federal judge for the District of Illinois, heard the case on January 5, 1843, and ruled that Missouri's requisition was unenforceable. Since there was no evidence that Smith had committed the alleged crime in Missouri, Illinois was under no legal obligation to extradite him. The court did not declare Smith innocent, only that he was free to return home.[36] Once again Smith had successfully navigated political and legal processes. He was getting better at it.

His return to Nauvoo was triumphant. At elaborate dinner parties, Smith's friends and followers rejoiced in the court's decision. Toasts were made, and verses sung. "Our charter'd rights she has maintain'd, Through opposition great; Long may her charter champions, Still to protect the State," rang the verse of one song church members had written for the occasion. To the tune of "Auld Lang Syne," it concluded with the refrain,

> We'll have a jubilee, my friends,
> We'll have a jubilee;
> With heart and voice we'll rejoice,
> In that our Prophet's free.[37]

They were praising more than Smith's deliverance from the grasp of his enemies. Mormons in Nauvoo felt that their city-state on the Mississippi

River had been validated; its unusual legal powers had been tried and proved capable of protecting the Mormons' rights. Just days after Judge Pope's decision, apostle Willard Richards wrote to his brother that "President Smith & all the church never had so good a prospect before them as at the present time."[38]

5

....

MOBOCRACY

WHILE THE MORMONS CELEBRATED, THEIR OPPONENTS ACROSS the river regrouped and plotted their next steps. Missouri officials were determined to bring Smith back to their state, if for no other reason than to save face. Bennett and Boggs both convinced Governor Reynolds that they could not let Smith and the Mormons get the best of them. In this case, state pride won out.[1]

Pursuing Smith on charges related to the attempted assassination of Boggs had proven futile for Missouri leaders. They soon determined that their best chance of extraditing Smith lay in resurrecting the treason charges that had landed Smith in jail back in 1838 as his followers were being driven from the state. Smith and his fellow prisoners had eventually escaped and fled to Illinois in 1839. Their guards had allowed them to flee. Some suggested that they had done so with the blessing of authorities. With the Mormons out of the state and their case against Smith weak, the thinking went, state officials were happy to wash their hands of the affair. Whatever the circumstances of the escape, the treason charges had been officially dismissed in court.[2]

Missouri had attempted to resurrect the treason charges in order to extradite Smith once before. In June 1841, officers had arrested Smith in Nauvoo as a fugitive from justice. However, circuit court judge—and future United States Senator and presidential candidate—Stephen A. Douglas freed Smith just five days later, before he could be turned over to Missouri.[3] The fact that Missouri officials were returning to this original—and ultimately unsuccessful—plan suggests that their options in the pursuit of Joseph Smith were dwindling.

Missouri officials could not arrest Smith in Nauvoo; that much was clear. He was too powerful there; the municipal court would provide him legal cover, and the Nauvoo Legion stood armed and ready to protect the life and body of its Lieutenant General. Successful extradition would require catching him either off guard or far away from home.

"I WILL SHOOT YOU"

Their window of opportunity opened in June 1843 when the Smith family traveled approximately 200 miles northeast of Nauvoo to visit some of Emma's relatives who had settled near Dixon, Illinois. Possessing an arrest warrant they had quietly obtained from Governor Ford, a Missouri sheriff crossed the state line and was joined by an Illinois constable. The two men attempted to catch Smith by surprise. They posed as Mormon missionaries in search of their prophet. Believing them, the residents of Dixon unwittingly directed the law enforcers to the home Smith was visiting.

Once the lawmen had apprehended Smith, they unleashed years of pent-up frustration with the Mormon leader. At one point, Smith cried out for help. "God damn you I will shoot you," exclaimed the Illinois officer, gun drawn and pressed against Smith's head. Physical abuse and additional threats ensued. Perhaps trying to end the mistreatment by calling the officers' bluff, Smith finally faced the men, opened the front of his shirt to reveal his chest, and told them "to shoot away."[4]

When word of the surprise extradition attempt reached Nauvoo, church members William Clayton and Stephen Markham jumped on their horses and galloped as quickly as they could, worried that they would arrive too late. At the same time, the Nauvoo Legion began to mobilize.

Clayton and Markham arrived in Dixon to find their prophet still in custody. The two Mormons filed a complaint with Dixon authorities about the brutal treatment of Smith, which led to the arrest of the Missouri sheriff and Illinois constable. Both Smith and his arresters were issued writs of habeas corpus. The courts would have to sort matters out.

If the stakes were not so high, the scenario would have been quite comical. The Missouri and Illinois officers transported Smith south to Quincy for a hearing while they themselves were under arrest and escorted by their captors for the same purpose. Then, all of a sudden, a cloud of dust appeared on the road ahead of this traveling legal conundrum. Within that cloud were some 300 members of the Nauvoo Legion who had ridden to Smith's rescue.

Instantly relieved, tears welled up in Smith's eyes, then streamed down his cheeks. The Legion redirected the entire party to Nauvoo, where courts friendly to Smith ordered his release. The Mormon safeguards had worked again. Smith now appeared more untouchable than ever.[5]

While the event had ensured his safety for the time being, it left a sour taste in the mouths of many Illinoisans who had once been inclined to protect the Mormons. They believed that the Nauvoo Legion and the city's municipal court had overstepped their bounds. In this instance, the city had acted in such a way as to position itself as having greater authority than the state, and Smith, a mayor, seemed to claim that his authority superseded that of the governor.

"EVERYTHING CONNECTED WITH THE MORMONS BECAME POLITICAL"

The pressure that Bennett's lecture tour and the renewed tension with Missouri brought upon Smith and the Latter-day Saints at Nauvoo was compounded by frustration among Illinois partisans. Perhaps it was inevitable. After all, in addition to any genuinely humane concerns for the Mormons when they entered the state as destitute refugees, Illinois political leaders had seen opportunity in aiding Smith and company. As the Democrats and Whigs jockeyed for power, the Mormons were positioned to play the role of kingmaker. At some point, one of the parties would find itself on the losing side of a major election, and the all-important Mormon vote that they had unsuccessfully courted would be an easy scapegoat.

Indeed, while the Mormons had voted as a bloc in Missouri, in Illinois they were much more open about doing so. But they arrived at this transparency gradually. Shortly after returning to Nauvoo from Washington,

D.C., in 1840, Smith told a church conference that "he did not wish to have any political influence, but wished the saints to use their political franchise to the best of their knowledge."[6] By January 1842 Smith had come around to the benefits of voting openly as a bloc, but to do so independent of any singular political party. "We care not a fig for *Whig* or *Democrat*," he wrote in an editorial in the *Times and Seasons*, explaining that the Mormons at Nauvoo "shall go for our *friends*, our TRIED FRIENDS, and the cause of HUMAN LIBERTY, which is the cause of God."[7] Smith defended the practice in an 1843 discourse. It was "our duty to concentrate all our influence to make popular that which is sound and good," he explained, "and unpopular that which is unsound. Tis right politically for a man who has influence to use it as well as for a man who has no influence to use his." Smith was determined: "From henceforth I will maintain all the influence I can get. In relation to politics I will speak as a man in religion in authority. If a man lifts a dagger to kill me, I will lift my tongue."[8]

Americans had a complicated history with bloc voting, particularly when those voting blocs were directed by religious leaders. Clergymen had long been active in American politics. During the Revolution the Continental Congress explicitly invited clergymen to preach Revolutionary politics from their pulpits. Clergymen subsequently remained active in the political sphere, but such activity was never universally accepted. While present-day Americans debate what the country's founders believed to be the proper place of religion and religious leaders in their political system, the reality is that the debate itself is one of the most enduring traditions of the founding era. Indeed, the historical pattern is that Americans welcomed clergymen using their power to direct their congregations to vote one way or another—so long as the clergymen were agreeing with their positions. The moment a clergyman preached politics that a sizeable group of Americans disliked, that group was quick to cry out and insist that men of the cloth restrict their speech to spiritual matters.[9]

This American tradition of mixing religion and politics while disagreeing on how they should mix certainly applied to Mormon bloc voting, but perceptions of the practice were also influenced by a long tradition of anti-Catholicism and a fear of religious fanaticism. American Protestants had deemed Catholics unfit for full participation in republican government. They reasoned that Catholics' devotion to the Pope, "another Prince" of "a foreign Jurisdiction," prevented them from voting independently and placed the fledgling American republic at risk of subversion by a religious "empire."[10] Similarly, the nineteenth century brought about increased hostility toward religious groups that Protestants deemed too fanatical. Protestants argued that they could not trust anyone who believed in visions of the deceased, miracles, and continuing revelation from God to help determine the political course of the country. While visions, miracles, and revelation were all at one time key tenets of Protestant Christian theology, Protestants in nineteenth-century America disagreed on the nature and extent of such supernatural occurrences in their own time. While Protestants debated the cessation of visions, miracles, and revelations between their various denominations, they could generally agree that certain groups took their supernatural claims too far.[11]

However, the Mormons did not view bloc voting as a means of exerting control over their countrymen or of subverting democratic norms. Rather, they saw it as a means of self-preservation, a point of leverage that tied their desire to live and worship peacefully in Nauvoo to the interest of the state's non-Mormon power brokers. It was a way of protecting themselves since the government had failed to do so. Even if their voting practices alienated one half of the Illinois electorate, they would preserve the protection they received from the other half.

For the first few years, Illinois partisans welcomed—and courted—the Mormon bloc vote. That is, they accepted and sought to benefit from the practice until the Mormons muddied their electoral strategy and drew the ire of Democrats and Whigs alike. The deterioration of this electoral safeguard occurred across two different elections.

The first was the 1842 Illinois gubernatorial election. Former governor Joseph Duncan, a Whig, sought to reclaim the office after a four-year absence. His Democratic opponent was Adam Snyder. Smith and the Mormons pledged their support to Snyder. Then, when Snyder suddenly died mid-campaign, they transferred that support to his replacement on the ticket, Thomas Ford.[12]

The Whigs had known since December 1841 that the Mormon vote was not in their corner.[13] Accordingly, Duncan incorporated a vigorously anti-Mormon plank into his platform. He used a campaign event in Edwardsville, Illinois, on May 4 to decry what he called "the dangerous and alarming powers which were granted to the Mormons, in various charters passed at the last session of our Legislature." Accusing the Mormons of seeking to become "a privileged sect over all other religious denominations and classes of our citizens," he claimed that they were enabled by "the corruption of a Legislature . . . solely for the purpose of obtaining political support." Duncan declared that if elected he would repeal "All extraordinary anti-republican and arbitrary powers" from the Nauvoo charters.[14]

Duncan's vitriol only made the Mormons more committed to Ford, the ultimate winner of the race. Duncan had revealed himself an unabashed anti-Mormon, who in his criticism of Nauvoo's unprecedented civic power implied that such power was all the more dangerous because of the unconventional religious beliefs of the city's citizens. In response, Smith named his horse "Jo. Duncan," and the citizens of Nauvoo cast 1,038 votes for Ford against 6 for Duncan.[15]

Still, the Mormons' support of the Democrats in such a consequential election drove many Illinois Whigs to Duncan's anti-Mormon position. Nowhere was this more evident than in the partisan press. At a time in American history when many newspapers openly aligned with a political party or cause, several of the influential Whig papers in western Illinois assumed decidedly hostile stances in their reporting on the Mormons. For examples, the editors of Springfield's *Sangamo Journal* dedicated most of the June 10, 1842, issue to trying to expose "the CORRUPT BARGAIN" between the state's Democrats and "Joe Smith, the Mormon prophet, by which they have formed a league to govern the State." Column after column sought to prove "such a nefarious PLOT AND LEAGUE."[16] Duncan and his attacks on the Mormons would eventually fade from the public eye. The state's Whig newspapers, on the other hand, were institutions with devoted readerships willing to hold grudges against their political enemies.

Remarkably, a year later a Whig–Mormon reconciliation appeared on the horizon. That year's congressional race pitted Whig Cyrus Walker against Democrat Joseph Hoge. Both candidates courted the Mormon vote, taking the position that Nauvoo's controversial use of writs of habeas corpus was, in fact, legal. An attorney, Walker eventually gained the upper hand during the June extradition attempt in Dixon when he represented Smith in court pro bono. Apparently in return, Smith pledged his vote to Walker, implying that the rest of the Mormons in the congressional district would follow suit.[17]

The Mormon vote seemingly in hand, the Whigs could smell victory. But any celebration was premature. On the day before the election,

Hyrum Smith second-guessed his brother's choice. "Bro Hiram tells me this morning," Joseph Smith announced to a public meeting in Nauvoo, "that he has had a testimony that it will be better for this people to vote for [H]oge, and I never knew Hiram to say he ever had a revelation and it failed."[18]

In a dramatic turn, Joseph Smith kept the letter of his deal and voted for Walker. However, he abandoned the apparent spirit of the promise. The majority of the Mormons in the district voted for Hoge. The influence of the church's leadership on Nauvoo's vote was staggering. In the city's final vote count, Walker received just 90 votes to Hoge's 1,083. Hoge won the congressional district by a mere 574 votes. In this election, the Mormons had, indeed, played the role of kingmaker.[19]

Whereas the Smith brothers explained the last-minute change as the result of revelation, others saw it as the product of a more calculated strategy. In the recent extradition attempt, the Nauvoo municipal government had acted in defiance of Governor Ford's order. Now they feared that a frustrated Ford would send the state militia to Nauvoo to reassert his authority by arresting Smith, a move that would almost certainly lead to violence. Perhaps the Mormon leaders in Nauvoo determined that pooling their votes for the Democratic candidate would stave off the ire of the state's Democratic governor.[20]

Whatever the thinking behind this switch, the election turned even more Illinoisans decidedly against the state's Mormon population. Smith and company had used their concentrated electoral power as a tool to preserve their rights and safety. Yet, in many ways they botched their bloc voting to the extent that it had the opposite effect. They had alienated themselves from both parties. Spurned once again, the Whig editors of the *Sangamo Journal* vented that the Mormons had "discarded a man [Walker] who had always been their friend—and to whom they were under many obligations—and gave their votes to an individual [Hoge] to whom they were a stranger and under no obligation."[21]

If the Mormons had been consistent and predictable in their voting, they might have maintained the support and protection of at least one party. But the fickleness they demonstrated in August 1843 made both parties wary. According to Ford, the unpredictability of the Mormon vote "arrayed against them in deadly hostility all aspirants for office who were not sure of their support, all who have been unsuccessful in elections, and all who were too proud to court their influence."[22]

Indeed, when Ford wrote his *History of Illinois* in 1847, he pointed to the events of the summer of 1843 as the beginning of the end for the Mormons in Illinois. "From this time forth," he recalled, "the whigs generally and a party of the democrats, determined upon driving the Mormons out of the state; and everything connected with the Mormons became political."[23]

"PEACEFULLY, IF WE CAN, BUT FORCIBLY, IF WE MUST"

While Ford identified the events of summer 1843 as the moment when it all went south for the Mormons in Illinois, one group of citizens had turned against them years earlier. Many of the non-Mormon residents of Hancock County had watched with grave concern as Mormon refugees flooded the area. Any sympathy they may have expressed for the plight of these beleaguered families vanished in the wake of the Mormons' rise to power. Their large and seemingly ever-increasing numbers, coupled with their penchant for living in tight-knit communities, made them a threat to take over the county's political and economic structures.

The leader of Hancock County's anti-Mormon movement was Thomas Sharp of Warsaw, Illinois. A lawyer by training, Sharp moved to Warsaw in September 1840 at the age of twenty-two to open his legal practice and soon after his arrival started working as the editor of the town's newspaper, the *Western World* (later renamed the *Warsaw Signal*).[24] By the Spring of 1841, he was a devoted critic of Smith and the Mormons. In May 1841, he warned the readers of his paper that should the Mormons "step beyond the proper sphere of a religious denomination, and become a political body, as many of our citizens are beginning to apprehend will be the case, then this press stand pledged to take a stand against them."[25] Sharp framed his opposition to the Mormons as a way of preserving democracy, but his prejudice against their religious beliefs frequently peeked out from that thin facade. He called Mormonism "the vilest system of knavery that has ever yet seen the light of heaven" and Smith "a more consummate impostor and a more impious blasphemer than any whose acts *disgrace* the annals of villainy or hypocrisy."[26]

The anti-Mormon invective that Sharp and others wove into the pages of the *Warsaw Signal* was unceasing. The editors did not mince words.

When the Nauvoo Legion failed to use force to protect Smith during the extradition attempt in August 1842, the newspaper lamented a wasted opportunity. If Smith had resisted, the editorial bemoaned, "we should have had the sport of driving him and his worthy clan out of the State *en masse*."[27] During the early 1840s, the paper frequently called for anti-Mormon meetings throughout the county, urging residents to "lay aside former party feelings and oppose, as independent freemen, political and military Mormonism."[28]

Following the August 1843 congressional election, a second hub of anti-Mormon activity arose in Hancock County, this one in the county seat of Carthage. In September, a meeting of Carthage citizens adopted a set of resolutions pertaining to the county's Mormon population. Smith, the resolutions stated, "has evinced, in many instances, a most shameless disregard for all the forms and restraints of Law." Concern about the increase in Mormon power in the county was at the heart of the resolutions. "We have had men of the most vicious and abominable habits, imposed upon us," the group of citizens complained, "to fill our most important county officers, by [Smith's] dictum . . . that he may the more certainly control our destinies, and under himself . . . as absolutely a despot over the citizens of this county, as he now is, over the serfs of his own servile class." The Carthage anti-Mormons resolved to organize themselves and non-Mormons in surrounding communities to resist any future "wrongs" committed by the Mormons, "peacefully, if we can, but forcibly, if we must."[29]

The phrase, "Peacefully, if we can, but forcibly, if we must" was eerily familiar to the Latter-day Saints. Similar language had preceded the mob violence that drove them from Jackson County, Missouri, in 1833 and then from the entire state of Missouri in 1838.

"Peacefully, if we can, but forcibly if we must" might as well have been the motto for nineteenth-century American vigilantism. It was a key component in a common pattern. A majority population (often the "old settlers" of an area) would dub minority groups who looked, thought, believed, or lived differently than they did a threat to democracy. They would meet and resolve that extralegal action was necessary for the preservation of democracy, often committing their resolutions to writing as if doing so justified any subsequent mobbing. They would then unleash violence on the population in question. Sometimes these mobs targeted religious minorities. Other times they unleashed their violence upon racial minorities, abolitionists, or immigrants.[30]

If the use of violence was quintessentially American, then Illinois was as American as any other state in the union. Men in the state had long prided themselves on their ability to suppress unwanted minority groups in order to gain or maintain land and power. They had done it to the Sac and Fox Indians in the Black Hawk War of 1832. Illinois mobs had attacked abolitionists in the 1830s, attacks that culminated in the lynching of the prominent abolitionist clergyman Elijah Lovejoy in 1837. Indeed, the pattern was so well established that Illinoisans wishing to rise to power in the young state knew that the quickest and surest way to make names for themselves was to excel in violently putting down unwanted minority groups. Governor Ford had first risen to political prominence through his militia service in the Black Hawk War. So had Abraham Lincoln.[31]

Those who participated in or condoned mob violence against undesirable minorities showed little remorse. In their view, the victims of mob violence had brought it upon themselves through their fanaticism and disregard for the established social order. If the government and the courts would not force minority groups into submission, then the majority would take matters into its own hands. Many vigilantes perceived mobs as part and parcel to a democratic society.[32]

Elected officials acknowledged as much. Even if they opposed mob violence, they believed that there was nothing they could do about it. "Where large bodies of the people are associated to accomplish with force an unlawful but popular object," Ford wrote, "the government is powerless against such combinations." Had the Mormons "Scattered through the country" instead of congregating "in one great city," Ford reasoned, "they might have lived in peace."[33] Violence was regrettable, but unavoidable.

News of the Carthage anti-Mormon meeting reached Smith in Nauvoo on September 15.[34] Smith saw the "Mobocracy" of the county's anti-Mormons as driven by prejudice, jealousy, and resentment. Four days later, Smith wrote to Governor Ford, enclosing a copy of the Carthage meeting's resolutions "to show your excellency to what an unjustified pitch disappointed ambition, malignance, and ungoverned persecution may be carried."[35]

Indeed, both sides of the brewing conflict justified their respective positions by appealing to freedom and democracy. The Hancock County anti-Mormons saw a correlation between the decline in their power and the rise of Mormon power. Perhaps they recognized that such a transition was a natural result of the recent shifts in the county's demographics. But the disgruntled citizens fixated on the seemingly undemocratic practices that they believed were the true cause of their loss of authority.

The Mormons, on the other hand, saw their actions as consistent with the laws of the democratic society in which they lived. They viewed their liberal use of writs of habeas corpus—unusual in American jurisprudence—as in keeping with the charter a democratic government had granted to Nauvoo in 1840, and as absolutely necessary to protect Mormon citizens from unjust arrest. The same went for bloc voting. As a statistical minority in the state, voting as a bloc offered Mormons the chance to tip the scales between the factions of the white Protestant majority. They viewed that leverage as essential to the protection of their citizenship rights. Perhaps the Mormons were aware that many of their actions were unprecedented in the still relatively young democracy. But the Mormons felt that their unprecedented actions were only necessary because of the shortcomings of the very democracy they were accused of undermining.

Even as the Mormons celebrated the Constitution and the Revolution that preceded it, they were painfully aware of the myriad ways that the country was failing to live up to its founding ideals. Democracy could be good, but the Mormon experience in the United States revealed that it was not inherently so. As Smith proclaimed in a speech to the people of Nauvoo in August 1843, "All our wrongs have arisen under the power and authority of democracy." The Mormons of Nauvoo were certainly among what historian Benjamin Park has called "democracy's discontents."[36]

While the increasingly powerful Mormons and their increasingly hostile neighbors fought over the rights and duties required in a democratic society, one thing was abundantly clear to Smith: the prospect of mob violence was now a clear and present threat. The safeguards that city and church leaders had installed against its return were stressed, desperate for reinforcement. The Mormons' city, their rights—and maybe even their lives—were at stake.

6

. . . .

PRESIDENTIAL HOPEFULS

THINGS WERE GETTING WORSE FOR THE MORMONS in Illinois in November 1843. They faced opposition from both the Democrats and the Whigs. Anti-Mormons in their own county were organizing to expel them from the state, and Illinois officials were poised to condone the action and perhaps participate in it themselves. A repeat of the Mormons' expulsion from Missouri seemed likely. The Mormons' need for federal intervention was more acute than ever. So, in addition to their annual petition to Congress, Smith and the Mormons began to strategize for the approaching presidential election.

The election of 1844 was a year away, but there were already five men positioning themselves to run for the White House. The incumbent, John Tyler, was essentially a non-factor in the race. He had ascended to the presidency following the death of the first Whig president, William Henry Harrison. However, after Tyler repeatedly clashed with his own party by thwarting its legislation, the Whigs expelled him from their ranks. He was a president without a party—and thus with only the bleakest prospects for re-election.

For the country's Whigs, there was a clear choice to replace Tyler: Henry Clay of Kentucky. There is perhaps nobody in United States history who wanted to be president more than Clay did—he made three failed bids for the presidency, in 1824, 1832, and 1840. And there was perhaps no one more qualified. The 66-year-old Clay, whose tall, slender frame belied his political prowess, had already served six terms in the House of Representatives (including three separate stints as Speaker of the House) and been a Senator three different times. In addition, he had served as Secretary of State to President John Quincy Adams.[1]

Clay was also the architect of the Whig Party, which he built by forming a coalition of disparate groups. In the early 1830s, the principal thing these groups had in common was their opposition to Andrew Jackson. But Clay gave that coalition shape and platform, molding it into a potent force in American politics. [2]

Indeed, in December 1839 Clay had lost the Whig nomination to William Henry Harrison by a razor-thin margin.[3] Tyler's betrayal of the party's platform when he ascended to the executive chair had left many Whigs with buyer's remorse. If they had nominated Clay in the first place, they reasoned, then they would never had experienced the fallout from Tyler's expulsion from the party. As early as January 1842 several Whig newspapers had already started printing endorsements of Clay in an election almost three years away.[4]

In the Democratic Party, the apparent front runner was former president Martin Van Buren. He had challengers, though. Richard M. Johnson of Kentucky, who had served as Vice President in Van Buren's administration, was also preparing for a campaign. Johnson had proven a liability for the Democrats, in large part because of his interracial relationships, including his connection to Julia Chinn, a free woman of color. Laws prohibited marriage between the two, but he treated Chinn as his wife and had children with her. In fact, Johnson's familial situation was so controversial that the Democrats refused to place him on the ticket for Van Buren's re-election in 1840, and the president campaigned without a running mate.[5] Nevertheless, Johnson was persistent in his desire to remain a player on the national political stage.

John C. Calhoun of South Carolina was also openly weighing his prospects. He had been a national political figure for nearly three decades. A short career in the House of Representatives was followed by a seven-year stint as Secretary of War under President James Monroe and two terms as Vice President, one under John Quincy Adams and the other under Andrew Jackson. He had tested the waters for a presidential run in

1824 but withdrew when it became apparent that he had no traction in a crowded field.[6] Calhoun's presidential prospects had since been hampered by the ways he had used his role as vice president to subvert both Adams and Jackson. In Jackson's administration, Calhoun had contradicted the president by advocating for the right of states to nullify federal legislation. This controversial position made Calhoun a favorite son in South Carolina but harmed his national reputation.[7] Smith had met Calhoun in Washington, D.C., in 1839, but the senator had declined to advocate for the Mormons' petitioning efforts.

Then there was Lewis Cass. A former governor of Michigan Territory who subsequently served as Andrew Jackson's Secretary of War—and was thus charged with carrying out the president's controversial Indian removal policy—Cass had served as the country's minister to France until 1842. Upon his return, his eyes were set on a much higher office. Cass and Calhoun represented the biggest threats to Van Buren's nomination.[8]

The election of 1844 was shaping up to be a contest between some of the most experienced politicians and statesmen in American history. Each of these prospective candidates had been born during the American Revolution and came of age in the nation's formative years.[9]

Joseph Smith and the Latter-day Saints had dealt with at least three of these presidential candidates during the preceding decade. Of course, Smith had met with Van Buren in the White House in 1839. But his interaction with Cass predated that meeting by six years. After the Mormons' expulsion from Jackson County, Missouri, in 1833, church leaders in that state had written to Andrew Jackson, who then passed the letter to Cass to handle as the Secretary of War.[10] Cass had responded dispassionately. "The President cannot call out a military force to aid in the execution of the state laws," he wrote, "until the proper requisition is made upon him by the constituted authorities."[11] Without a formal request for federal intervention from a state government, Cass would send no help.

Clay had been the most responsive. Smith had met with the Kentuckian in Washington, D.C., in the days following his unsuccessful 1839 appeal to Van Buren. Clay had been sympathetic to the Mormons' plight and had signaled a willingness to advocate for their quest for redress and reparations. Indeed, the Whigs' preference for a strong national government was in line with Smith's hope for federal intervention on his behalf. But Clay had also suggested that the Mormons move west to Oregon in order to avoid future persecution.[12]

While the Mormons' best bet seemed to lie with Clay, Smith did not put all his eggs in one basket. He was not bound to the platform or ideology of either party. At a meeting with some of his closest advisors on November 2, 1843, the men resolved to "write a letter to the five candidates for the Presidency to enquire what their feelings were or what their course would be towards the saints if they were elected."[13]

"SHOULD FORTUNE FAVOR YOUR ASCENSION TO THE CHIEF MAGISTRACY"

On the evening of November 4, 1843, church apostle and Nauvoo newspaper editor John Taylor called on Smith at his home. He was accompanied by Smith's scribe, Willard Richards. They carried with them the draft of a letter written in Smith's voice, intended for the five presidential candidates.[14]

"As we understand you are a candidate for the presidency at the next election," the letter opened, before explaining that the Latter-day Saints had come to "constitute a numerous class in the school politic of this vast republic." Even though they had "been robbed of an immense amount of property, and endured nameless sufferings by the State of Missouri, and from her borders have been driven by the force of arms, contrary to our national covenants," their efforts to obtain "redress by all Constitutional, Legal and honorable means" had been unsuccessful. As a result, the letter concluded that Smith had "judged it wisdom to address you this communication, and solicit an immediate, specific and candid reply." In underlined text, Smith's question was simple and straightforward: "What will be your rule of action relative to us as a people, should fortune favor your ascension to the chief magistracy?"[15]

Smith's question implied that the Mormon vote was at stake, and that it would go to the candidate willing to commit to supporting the Mormons by offering them redress for past persecutions and by safeguarding their rights in the future. Declaring the Mormons "a numerous class in the school politic of this vast republic" was certainly an overstatement in national terms. But when it came to Illinois and its nine electoral votes, the Mormons wielded significant political clout. They held the balance between the Whig and Democratic parties. In a close national race, the

Mormons could provide a candidate with the electoral edge he needed to win the presidency.

Smith approved the letter, and Richards proceeded to write five copies, one to each candidate. They were identical letters, with one exception. The letter Smith sent to Van Buren included additional text. Following the underlined question, Smith asked Van Buren whether his "views or feelings have changed, since the subject matter of this communication was presented you, in your then official capacity . . . and by you treated with a coldness, indifference and neglect bordering on contempt."[16]

The letters departed Nauvoo in different directions. As Smith waited for the candidates' responses, he attended to his business as Nauvoo's mayor, the church's president, and the lieutenant-general of the Nauvoo Legion. Some of it was fairly mundane: hearing cases in the mayor's court, examining the fringe intended for the pulpits of the temple, and managing the ongoing sale and distribution of city lots.[17]

Yet, life was hardly ordinary for Smith and his followers in Nauvoo. Much of Smith's focus was on taking proactive measures in case further hostilities broke out between the Mormons and their enemies in Illinois or Missouri.[18] Danger seemed to lurk around every corner, and it was not mere paranoia. The day after Smith approved the letters to Calhoun, Cass, Clay, Johnson, and Van Buren, he sat down to dinner. Before he could finish his meal, he arose with a start and scrambled to the door, where he vomited so violently that he dislocated his jaw. According to Smith's journal, in the pool of vomit on the ground below was "fresh blood" and "every symptom of poison."[19] Had someone tried to kill the Mormon prophet in his own home? Or, was it merely illness? The answer is unclear, but in such a charged atmosphere people feared the worst.[20]

Smith was not the only one who felt that his life was in danger. On separate days in late November and early December, two Mormons living outside Nauvoo's city limits were kidnapped and taken to Missouri. The abducted men, Daniel Avery and his son, Philander, had been accused of stealing horses in Missouri three years earlier.[21] There is no clear evidence that the Avery kidnappings were connected to Missouri's unsuccessful efforts to extradite Smith. However, the kidnappers' choice of this moment and such brash, illegal methods to seek justice for the alleged crimes of the Avery men unnerved Smith and the Mormons. The echoes of their Missouri persecutions reverberating in their ears, the Nauvoo Legion and the city's police force were placed on high alert—mobilized and ready for war.[22] Although Smith hoped the uneasy peace would hold until the tension could be permanently relieved, he also worried that in the event of violence the forces at his command would be insufficient. He needed reinforcement.

Since 1833, Smith had expressed frustration with those in the federal government who used a strict interpretation of states' rights to justify their inaction in response to anti-Mormon violence. More particularly, Smith bristled at the repeated claim that the president could not deploy federal troops to intervene in intrastate conflicts without a formal request from a state's governor. Amid the heightened animosity from anti-Mormons in western Illinois during the final months of 1843, Nauvoo officials threw the legal equivalent of a Hail Mary pass.

Prompted by the Avery kidnapping, on December 8, the city council approved a plan to petition Congress to designate Nauvoo a federal territory. In such a scenario, the city would effectively secede from Illinois and fall under the protection and direct authority of the federal government. Months later Smith would explain that such an arrangement would "set us everlastingly free, and give us the United States troops to guard us and protect us from any invasion."[23]

Petitioning for a city that was already a part of a state to be granted territorial status was unprecedented in the history of the United States. Indeed, the petition was a commentary on Smith's dissatisfaction with the American political system. The United States Constitution protected the free exercise of religion, but if an individual state denied some of its citizens that very right, the federal government was powerless to come to their aid. Smith and company determined that if they were denied federal protection—and defense by federal troops—because a barrier of states' rights prevented it, they would simply remove that barrier by becoming a federal territory.

There was essentially no chance that Congress would grant such an unusual request. Smith and his fellow church leaders must have suspected as much. Still, the fact that they would make the request in the first place demonstrates just how desperate they were. It also speaks to the plight of religious minority groups in nineteenth-century America. With a political system seemingly designed to keep them marginalized, sometimes all they could do was throw whatever they could against the metaphorical wall to see what stuck.

The petition's slim chances notwithstanding, Smith stuck to his plan of seeking federal intervention on the Mormons' behalf while taking aggressive steps in the municipal sphere that he controlled. Citing the three unsuccessful attempts to extradite Smith to Missouri, the intolerability of the seemingly constant harassment, and the legal costs associated with the repetitive prosecutions, the city council made it illegal for anyone to try to arrest Smith on charges related to "the aforesaid Missouri difficulties." The punishment for such an act: "imprisonment in the City Prison for life." Such convicts could "only be pardoned by the Governor with the consent of the Mayor of the said city."[24]

This was bold. The Avery kidnappings had placed Smith on edge, a feeling compounded by rumors that had reached Nauvoo two days earlier suggesting that the kidnappings were but a prelude to yet another attempt by Missouri to apprehend Smith.[25] The Mormons clearly intended the ordinance to protect Smith from further extradition attempts. However, declaring that a governor's pardon was subject to a mayor's review came across as brash. It was fodder for the Mormons' critics and appears to have increased their numbers. "What beautiful legislation!" a letter to the editor of the *New York Tribune* exclaimed, "The pardoning power taken from the Governor!—and life imprisonment under a city ordinance!!"[26] Although Nauvoo would eventually rescind the ordinance, the damage was done.[27]

Smith and his fellow church leaders were availing themselves of every possible avenue for redress and protection. But experience had made Smith wary of putting his faith in government protection alone. "A burnt child dreads the fire," Smith wrote to Governor Ford, "and when my old friends, men women and children look to me in the hour of danger for protection and the wives of kidnapped men beg with tears for Justice and protection I am bound by my oath of office and by all laws human and divine to grant it."[28] To cover all their bases, the Mormons paired their municipal ordinances with appeals to the federal government and the men seeking control of its executive branch. They went further still when they sent pleas for help directly to their fellow Americans.

"TO THE GREEN MOUNTAIN BOYS"

Dozens of Nauvoo citizens crowded into the assembly room on the second floor of Joseph Smith's store on November 26. The primary purpose of the meeting was to collect signatures on the petition drafted earlier that week. However, Smith had bigger plans for those in attendance.

Standing before the packed room, Smith urged "every man in the meeting who could wield a pen" to "write an address to his mother country," meaning the state of his birth.[29] Smith was prepared to follow his own directive. A week earlier, he had assigned his clerk, William W. Phelps, to write on his behalf "an appeal to the citizens of Vermont," where Smith had been born nearly 38 years earlier.[30]

Titled *General Smith's Appeal to the Green Mountain Boys*, the brief pamphlet invoked Vermont's celebrated Revolutionary heritage. In the 1770s, Ethan Allen led a military company that protected land grants in the part of New Hampshire that would eventually become Vermont. The armed group subsequently joined the fight for American Independence, seizing Fort Ticonderoga for the patriots. Allen was a legend in Vermont, and the state's residents relished this part of their heritage. In recounting stories of Allen and his famed "Green Mountain Boys," they prided themselves as being ever ready to defend "liberty, property, and life."[31]

Smith and Phelps put this legendary Vermont pride to the test. They portrayed the Mormon persecutions in Missouri as a violation of the basic tenets of the American Revolution, a blatant disregard for the principles for which Allen and company had once fought. The pamphlet even went so far as to identify Smith himself as a "Green Mountain Boy." Without specific details, the pamphlet called on Vermonters to once again rise up, rekindle the "patriotism of '76," and protect the rights and liberties of the Mormons—their fellow Americans, led by a native of their state. "Whenever a nation, kingdom, state, family or individual has received an insult, or an injury . . ." the pamphlet declared, "it has been the custom to call in the aid of friends to assist in obtaining redress." In confiscating the Mormons' property and expelling Smith and his followers from its borders, Missouri had brought disgrace "upon constitutional liberty." If Vermont and the rest of the country eschewed its Revolutionary principles by declining to assist the Mormons, then "Vermont is a hypocrite—*a coward*—and this nation the hot bed of political demagogues."[32]

General Smith's Appeal to the Green Mountain Boys was read publicly in Nauvoo and then printed as a pamphlet. Copies were sent to Congress and given to Mormon missionaries, who would carry it to towns throughout Smith's native state.[33] Even if Vermonters did not rush to the side of

Smith and the Mormons, the public readings of the pamphlet in Nauvoo electrified many of the city's residents.[34]

Several of these Mormons followed Smith's lead. Over the following weeks and months, seven Latter-day Saints wrote to the people or governments of six different states. Each of these printed addresses asserted the Mormons' American identity. The mistreatment of the Mormons and other religious minorities, these documents argued, was incongruent with the liberal principles that nineteenth-century Americans associated with the birth of the United States. The Mormons maintained that for Americans to stand idly by while religious minorities were denied their basic rights was to deny their shared revolutionary heritage.[35]

Of course, this was an idealistic interpretation of the American Revolution. In reality, the Revolution had amounted to a violent transfer of power from England's ruling elite to an aggrieved colonial elite. Still, some groups saw increased rights as a result of American victory; others did not.[36] To many Americans in the late eighteenth and early nineteenth centuries, religious freedom was never intended to be universal. Instead, it was largely designed by Protestants for Protestants. Varying degrees of toleration were granted to Catholics, Jews, and other non-Protestants, but they did not receive equal rights and protection under the law. Depending on whom one asked, some would even argue that not all Protestants deserved full citizenship rights.[37]

Still, decades of public celebrations and dozens of published histories had pushed to the front of public memory a more romantic version of the Revolution, one that was ultimately self-serving for the generations of Americans who struggled with a sense of inadequacy as the inheritors of their forefathers' experiment with republicanism.[38] American-born Mormons were no exception. While their appeals to states, laced with celebratory rhetoric about their shared past, may have seemed a flimsy gimmick to some, the Mormons genuinely hoped that their appeals to this sense of the United States as an exceptional bastion of freedom and an asylum for the oppressed would resonate with the general public. With enough public outcry on their behalf, the Mormons believed, they would receive not only redress for past persecutions but defense from future ones.

Joseph Smith and the Mormons in Nauvoo were acting on multiple fronts while awaiting responses from the five presidential hopefuls. They must have watched the city's post office intently. When would their responses arrive? Would one or more candidates pledge their support for a religious minority struggling to maintain its rights? Or would the Mormons have to explore still other options?

"THE STATES RIGHTS DOCTRINES ARE WHAT FEED MOBS"

Considering the way Smith's 1839 meeting with Van Buren had ended, and the harsh statements Smith had made in campaigning against his re-election, it should come as no surprise that Smith received no response from the former president. Perhaps for similar reasons, Johnson—who had been Van Buren's Vice President—also sent no response. Smith apparently assumed that their reticence signaled a total lack of interest in helping the Mormons. But Smith did receive written responses from the other three candidates.

Clay responded first. "If I ever enter into that high office," he wrote from his home in Ashland, Kentucky, "I must go into it free and unfettered, with no guarantees but such as are to be drawn from my whole life, character and conduct." Yet, in an effort to demonstrate to Smith that he was no enemy to the Mormons, he continued: "It is not inconsistent with this declaration to say, that I have viewed, with a lively interest, the progress of the Latter day Saints; that I have sympathised in their sufferings under injustice, as it appeared to me, what has been inflicted upon them." In conclusion, Clay asserted that the Mormons, "in common with all other Religious Communities . . . ought to enjoy the security and protection of the Constitution and the Laws."[39]

This was textbook political deflection. Clay refused to commit to support the Mormons in their ongoing struggles, but he was careful not to slam the door on such a possibility, lest he lose the Mormon vote, and Illinois's electoral votes with it. Smith did not immediately respond to Clay, but several months later he would publish an open letter to Clay making it clear that he and his people were no longer interested in vague assurances.[40]

The responses from Cass and Calhoun both reached Smith on December 27. No longer the Secretary of War, Cass was now able to express his personal opinion rather than recite the official position of the Jackson administration. "I think that the Mormonites should be treated as all other persons are treated in this Country," Cass wrote, "That is they should be protected in their rights." Yet, there were limits to how far Cass was willing to go to guarantee those rights. "I am bound however, in candor to add, that if your application for the redress to which you consider yourselves entitled has been, as you say rejected by the Constituted authorities of the State of Missouri, and by Congress, I do not see what power, the President of the United States can have over the matter, or how he can interfere in it."[41]

Much like Cass, Calhoun opened his letter diplomatically. "If I should be elected," he wrote, "I would strive to administer the government according to the Constitution and the laws of the Union; and that they make no distinction between citizens of different religious creeds, I should make none." Calhoun explained that "As far as it depends on the Executive department, all should have the full benefit of both and none should be exempt from their operation."[42]

This opinion must have sounded promising to the Mormons. That is, until they read the rest of the letter. Calhoun transitioned from the theoretical to the practical. "But as you refer to the case in Missouri," he explained, "candor compels me to repeat what I said to you at Washington, that, according to my views, the case does not come within the jurisdiction of the Federal Government, which is one of limited and specific powers."[43] Calhoun declared himself free of religious prejudice, but a staunch devotee of the doctrine of states' rights.

Smith had received these replies with consternation. He asked his clerk and trusted associate William W. Phelps to draft responses that would show Cass and Calhoun "the folly of keeping people out of their right and that there was power in government to redress wrongs."[44] The reply to Cass has, alas, disappeared from the historical record. However, on January 2, 1844, Phelps finished the letter to Calhoun. Three days later, he and Smith read through it together, making sure it accurately conveyed Smith's feelings.[45]

Smith was indignant. He chided Calhoun for adopting such a narrow view of the United States Constitution and accused him of not considering—or worse, not caring—about the ramifications of such a rigid and intransigent constitutional interpretation. According to Smith, by insisting that the federal government had no jurisdiction in the Mormons' case, Calhoun and like-minded officials were essentially signaling to other religious minority groups that "a 'sovereign State' is so much more powerful than the United States, the parent Government, that it can exile you at pleasure, mob you with impunity, confiscate your lands and property, have the Legislature sanction it—yea, even murder you as an edict of an emperor, and it does no wrong; for the noble Senator of South Carolina says the Federal Government is so limited and specific, that it has no jurisdiction of the case!" This is what states' rights amounted to for Smith.[46]

Smith did not stop there. "If the General Government has no power to reinstate expelled citizens to their rights," he declared, "there is a monstrous hypocrite fed and fostered from the hard earnings of the people. In Smith's opinion, "Congress, with the President as Executor, is as almighty in its sphere as Jehovah is in His."[47]

Smith was calling into question the founding generation's constitutional theory, particularly where the protection of individual rights was concerned. Many of the men who drafted the Constitution, who advocated for its ratification by the American people afterwards, and who assisted in drafting the Bill of Rights, identified state governments as those best equipped to protect the individual rights of American citizens. Even more, one of the chief concerns of those who opposed the new constitution was that it established a large and distant government. This was, in part, a reaction to the imperial crisis that gave rise to the Revolution, in which aggrieved American colonists protested the abridgement of their rights as freeborn Englishmen by a government on the other side of the Atlantic Ocean. Based in part on this experience, Congress adopted the Bill of Rights to prevent a "distant" federal government from violating individual rights.[48]

By the 1840s, however, the constitutional landscape had changed. While the Bill of Rights was designed by Congress to keep the federal government in check, Smith was acknowledging that no effective apparatus existed to do the same for state governments. Smith's letter to Calhoun declared—and his earlier petitions had implied—that where the abridgement of individual rights was concerned, American citizens had more to fear from state governments than from the federal government. Not only were state governments ill equipped to address violations of individual rights, they were themselves among the most egregious offenders of those rights. While the constitutional theory of the founders made sense in the 1780s in the aftermath of the Revolution, the pragmatic experience of the ensuing fifty years illuminated a key flaw therein: when state governments denied a minority group of its citizens their rights to life, liberty, and property, there was no clear, well-established avenue at the federal level by which such rights could be restored.

Joseph Smith and the Mormons are not the people whom scholars often think of when discussing theories behind Constitutional law and its application. Indeed, Smith surely never anticipated taking on this role when he founded the church in 1830. But the role was thrust upon him in his desperation to combat a system that fostered religious intolerance and, at times, violent persecution. This desperation brought him to contribute to the growing movement toward popular constitutionalism in the country, arguing passionately for the adaptation of the Constitution to the needs of the citizenry. Or, in the words of the modern legal scholar Hendrik Hartog, "the Constitution must be a recognition and an expression of legitimate aspirations" of the living and not a "conservatorship" of the past.[49]

To Smith and his fellow Mormon leaders, the writing was on the wall. Clay *might* assist the Latter-day Saints if he was elected president, but they could not count on it. Cass and Calhoun had openly declared that they would not help. Inasmuch as the efforts to obtain redress for their losses in Missouri and to prevent a repeat of such persecution in Illinois were the most important political questions facing their community, the Mormons needed a candidate firmly committed to helping them if elected president. Not one of these five men fit the bill.

"THAT JOSEPH SMITH BE A CANDIDATE FOR THE NEXT PRESIDENCY"

Almost one month later, on January 29, 1844, the Quorum of the Twelve Apostles and a few other church leaders filed into Smith's office. It was a particularly cold day—the mercury sank well below zero—but the mood in Smith's office was warm.[50] News of the responses of the presidential candidates had almost certainly spread throughout town. Frustrated with politicians unwilling to protect religious minorities, the Mormon leadership convened to chart a different course.

It is unclear if this pent-up frustration was discussed at length in the meeting or if the men arrived determined to take action. Either way, at some point in the meeting, apostle Willard Richards motioned that Nauvoo's electors in the Electoral College would act independently of the

Whig and Democratic parties, "that Joseph Smith be a candidate for the next presidency," and that church leaders "use all honorable means to secure his election."[51] With no apparent signs of hesitation, the men unanimously approved the motion.

Just like that, Joseph Smith was a candidate for president. It is unlikely that he had foreseen such a turn of events when he visited Van Buren in the White House four years earlier. The move was a sign of desperation. With none of the candidates willing to take up their cause, Smith and company accepted that they would need greater influence within the federal government, and there was no greater influence within the federal government than the President. Smith threw his hat into the ring because he believed his people's quest for religious freedom—and, by extension, religious freedom for all other American religious minorities—required a political revolution in Washington, D.C.

7
. . . .

A POLITICAL TRACT

ON THE SAME DAY HE DETERMINED TO run for president, Joseph Smith met with one of his scribes, a former newspaper editor named William W. Phelps. He instructed Phelps on "an address to the people" that expounded his "views on the powers & policy of the govmct [government] of [the] United States."[1] Phelps would employ his literary flair in service of Smith's political ideas.[2]

In twelve pages, *General Smith's Views on the Powers and Policy of the Government of the United States* set forth a platform heavy on social and political reform. The issue of religious freedom had pushed Smith into the presidential race, but he was hardly a one-issue candidate. He had ideas on a range of issues, from slavery and prison reform to immigration and the size of Congress.

In some ways, the pamphlet demonstrates just how little traction the issue of religious freedom had on its own. It was difficult for Americans who were not themselves affected by religious discrimination to rally to the cause of universal religious freedom. To win American voters to his side, Smith packaged his arguments for greater equality—guaranteed by a stronger federal government—in a radical political tract.

Still, it would be a mistake to dismiss Smith's campaign platform as mere political opportunism. While each of the planks in his platform was controversial nationally, many of them were also deeply personal to Smith and, in a sense, reactions to seminal and trying events in his life. The pamphlet was at once politically ambitious and, for Smith, personally poignant.

"THE FREEST, WISEST, AND MOST NOBLE NATION OF THE NINETEENTH CENTURY"

Throughout the history of presidential politics, it has been common for candidates to lament the decline of the United States and promise to restore the country to its supposed greatness. What is uncommon, however, is for candidates to acknowledge a specific moment when the country ceased to be great, to identify the high-water mark when American greatness began to recede. This was not the case for Joseph Smith. In his mind, the decline of the United States started on March 4, 1837, the day Martin Van Buren became president.[3]

To emphasize this turning point, Smith opened *General Smith's Views* with a brief history of the United States as seen through its presidents, quoting extensively from presidents' inaugural and annual addresses. In fact, a few days before Smith launched his presidential campaign, he had assigned Phelps "to write a piece on the situation of the nation . . . referring to the Presidents messages &c."[4] Phelps apparently worked that piece into the pamphlet. The resulting four-page history was superficial and celebratory. There was no nuanced examination of what actually transpired during the administrations of the first seven presidents, only a ready acceptance that their rhetoric in official addresses to the public was reflective of reality in the daily lives of average Americans.

Such a glossed-over history was in keeping with the way Americans of this era wrote about their own past. They almost universally paid homage to their Revolutionary origins. They deified the founders and, in the process, made the country's birth a quasi-religious event.[5] Yet, this was not mere nostalgia; it had a pragmatic purpose. As historian Andrew Burstein writes, this devotion to an idealized Revolutionary heritage "promised to preserve a language of unity and harmony and pure motives in an era of widely divergent tastes and purposes."[6] In the fractious and fractured political climate of the 1840s, political actors drew on these narratives to differing ends. Selective and skewed portrayals of history are not a twenty-first-century phenomenon. Nineteenth-century politicians generally molded their country's past to fit one of two narratives: keeping American greatness uninterrupted or restoring greatness that had recently been lost. Smith was no exception.

Pointing to a perceived tradition of American religious freedom, Smith quoted James Monroe's first inaugural address, wherein the fifth president asked the American people, "Who has been deprived of any right of person and property? Who restrained from offering his vows on the mode he prefers, to the Divine author of his being? It is well known that all these blessings have been enjoyed to their fullest extent."[7] Of course, Monroe's claim of religious freedom was inaccurate. The histories of Jews, Catholics, and some evangelical Christian denominations in the early American republic are rife with examples of discrimination and persecution. By emphasizing Monroe's language of religious freedom, Smith made treatment of the Mormons seem like an aberration in American history.

But there was no room for ambiguity in Smith's account of the nation's first seven presidencies. The eighth was another story.

"At the age, then, of sixty years, our blooming republic began to decline under the withering touch of Martin Van Buren!" Smith declared. When Van Buren ascended to the presidency, Smith claimed that "Disappointed ambition; thirst for power, pride, corruption, party spirit, faction, patronage; perquisites, fame, tangling alliances; priest-craft and spiritual wickedness in *high places*, struck hands in midnight splendor." Van Buren and his political allies were the embodiment of "hypocritical pretensions, and pompous ambition" who claimed to serve the people but were, in fact, "luxuriating on the ill-gotten spoils of the people" while destroying the people's rights and prosperity across the country "like a tornado." Van Buren's policies did not differ substantially from those of his immediate predecessor, but Smith had clearly taken personal insult at Van Buren's refusal to help him and his followers. Even though the Mormons' troubles had started years before Van Buren had assumed the presidency, Smith insisted that the decline of the United States had commenced with the eighth president.[8]

It had continued, according to Smith, under Van Buren's successors. William Henry Harrison, who had held the office for only thirty days, "died before he had the opportunity of applying one balm to ease the pain of [the] groaning country." The tenure of his replacement, John Tyler, had been "three years of perplexity and pseudo whig democrat reign," which had compounded the country's problems. "No honest man can doubt for a moment," Smith declared, "but that the glory of American liberty, is on the wane; and that calamity and confusion will sooner or later destroy the peace of the people."[9] Smith believed that he was the man to right the ship and used the final three pages of his campaign pamphlet to describe the actions he would take to restore America to greatness.

"REDUCE CONGRESS AT LEAST ONE HALF"

Reform of the federal government was a major focus of Smith's platform. When he had traveled to Washington, D.C., in 1839, he did so with high hopes. However, he had returned to Nauvoo in 1840 frustrated and convinced that the ideals of religious equality enshrined in the Constitution and other founding documents would not be realized until Congress was competent enough to enforce them.

Part of Smith's proposed solution to this problem was to decrease the size of Congress. "Frustrate the designs of wicked men," Smith wrote, "Reduce Congress at least one half. Two Senators from a state and two members to a million of population, will do more business than the army that now occupy the halls of the National Legislature." According to the Constitution, the number of representatives from each state "shall not exceed one for every thirty Thousand, but each State shall have at Least one Representative."[10] Accordingly, Smith's plan constituted a major reduction of the House of Representatives.

However, reducing the number of men in Congress was not enough for Smith. He also advocated for a reduction in pay for representatives and senators alike. "Pay them two dollars and their board per diem; (except Sundays)," Smith declared, "that is more than the farmer gets, and he lives honestly."[11] The source of this average daily profit for farmers is unclear, but since 1818, members of Congress had received $8 per day for their service in the federal government.[12] Congressional pay was hardly exorbitant, but it was more than most Americans made. Perhaps Smith hoped to tap into the country's class divide to portray Congress as an elite institution built upon the backs of average Americans.

Through such calls for congressional reform, Smith positioned himself as a populist of sorts. No other presidential candidate was focused on the ratio of representatives to population; no other candidate was calling for a decrease in compensation for representatives and senators. This was the rhetoric of political outsiders. It was the rhetoric of men who believed their interests were ignored and their rights of little consequence to those who controlled the federal government. Common in populist movements throughout the history of the United States, this rhetoric aimed to mobilize voters who felt the government was out of touch with "the people." Smith certainly felt this way, and his position on congressional reform was a clarion call to other like-minded voters to rally around his candidacy. "Curtail the offices of government in pay, number and power," Smith concluded, "for the Philistine lords have shorn our nation of its goodly locks in the lap of Delilah."[13]

Smith bolstered this populist position by calling for bipartisanship. He argued that politicians' devotion to party over the needs of average Americans had contributed to the country's decline. "Democracy, Whigery and Cliquery, will attract their elements and foment divisions among the people," he explained, "to accomplish fancied schemes and accumulate power." But while politicians conducted partisan power struggles, average Americans suffered. "Poverty driven to despair, like hunger forcing its way through a wall, will break through the statutes of men, to save life and mend in the breach in prison glooms." *General Smith's Views* introduced the country to a turn of phrase that encapsulated Smith's advocacy for bipartisanship, and one that Smith would return to repeatedly in the months that followed the pamphlet's publication. "We have had democratic presidents: whig presidents; a pseudo democratic whig president," Smith wrote, "and now it is time to have *a president of the United States*."[14]

Of course, an expansion of federal power was a key part of Smith's reform platform. Even as he called for a smaller federal government, he wanted to empower that leaner government to better protect the rights of minority groups. In practical terms, he focused on the ability of the president to dispatch federal troops to individual states to protect minority groups who faced violent opposition at the hands of the majority. "Give every man his constitutional freedom," Smith averred, "and the president full power to send an army to suppress mobs; and the states authority to repeal and impugn that relic of folly, which makes it necessary for the governor of a state to make the demand of the president for troops, in cases of invasion or rebellion." Smith justified this position by alluding to Lilburn Boggs of Missouri. "The governor himself may be a mobber and, instead of being punished, as he should be for murder and treason, he may destroy the very lives, rights, and property he should protect."[15] In essence, the states themselves could be—and had been—complicit in violence against minority groups. Only the federal government could stop them.

"LET THE UNION SPREAD FROM THE EAST TO THE WEST SEA"

While federal power was Smith's top concern, a different issue had polarized the country ahead of the election: westward expansion. The country's first major territorial expansion occurred in 1803 through the Louisiana Purchase. That transaction secured for the United States 530 million acres of land in the geographic center of North America. But by 1844, Americans had set their gaze on land further south and west— land that was essential to their vision of a United States that stretched from the Atlantic to the Pacific Ocean.

The majority of Americans favored westward expansion, regardless of their partisan affiliations. They believed in their country's "manifest destiny" to control and settle most of North America, displacing the nonwhite men and women who already occupied those lands. However, they fundamentally disagreed on the way such expansion should occur. As historian Amy Greenberg writes, "through the early decades of the nineteenth century, most Americans believed that expansionism would spread progress and enlightenment to all mankind and that through the power of influence and persuasion America's manifest destiny would be revealed." But by the 1840s, more and more Americans were advocating for aggressive expansion by military means.[16]

In 1844 these rival visions of American expansion collided in debates over Oregon and Texas. The United States had long claimed the Oregon Country—thousands of Americans had moved there—but that claim was contested by Great Britain. While some expansionists considered compromises that would divide the territory in two, others were insistent that the United States must control the Oregon Country in its entirety, even if that meant another war with the British.[17]

The conversation surrounding Texas was similarly fraught. Since the 1820s, thousands of planters had moved out of the Southern United States to Texas, which was then a part of Mexico. In 1836, the Republic of Texas declared its independence and elected Sam Houston its first president. However, there were many Texans who saw independence as merely a step toward annexation by the United States, hoping that the process could occur peacefully if Texas was an independent state. In their minds, Texas would enter the Union as a slave state, a prospect that thrilled the proslavery states of the South and worried the free states of the North.[18]

Indeed, there were multiple racial dimensions to the expansion of the United States that factored into political debates during the 1840s. At the heart of the very idea of the country's "manifest destiny" was a belief in white Americans' racial superiority to the Native Americans and mixed-race peoples who occupied much of the land west of the Mississippi and south of United States territory. So many white Americans accepted such a dubious racial taxonomy that it factored little in the debates over the timing and means of the country's westward expansion.[19]

However, race was a more prominent factor in conversations about westward expansion, as it pertained to the expansion of slavery. This was particularly the case when it came to the proposed annexation of Texas. Slaveholders in the South, as well as abolitionists in the North, recognized that if the institution of slavery did not expand, it would die. The death could come by one of two means. If the territorial expansion of the United States continued without an accompanying expansion of slavery, slave states would soon be outnumbered and overpowered in the federal government, opening the door for the abolition of slavery through political channels. In addition, if slavery did not expand westward, the slave populations in the South would continue to grow until they were large enough to revolt against the white societies that had enslaved them for generations.

Slaveholders saw Texas as a safety valve for the institution of slavery. And so the question of annexation became a flashpoint in the heightening sectional debate over slavery. Even as Joseph Smith was preparing his campaign platform, President John Tyler had dispatched his Secretary of State, Abel P. Upshur, to negotiate the peaceful annexation of Texas. Even if those negotiations proved successful, any treaty would face an uphill climb in the United States Senate.[20] And the annexation of Texas would bring the country closer to war with Mexico.

Beyond considerations related to slavery, many Americans worried that if the United States did not annex Texas, a European power might. Specifically, they worried about Great Britain. Rumors spread throughout the country that British agents were bribing officials in Texas to affect a British annexation.[21] While the British do not appear to have actually made serious overtures, they recognized the immense value that a political and economic alliance with Texas would bring. With Britain in the throes of the Industrial Revolution, its textile manufacturers desperately needed cotton grown in North America. This put the United States in a strong position with regard to its trade relationship with Great Britain. An independent Texas could provide an alternative source for cotton and swing the balance of power back toward Britain. Historians continue to debate the degree to which Great Britain represented an actual threat to American power and trade. However, the fears of British interference were real enough for many politicians from Northern states to overcome their objections to annexation.[22]

The status of Texas was poised to become the most important issue in the election of 1844. Henry Clay was in favor of acquiring Texas but insisted that it must be done peacefully. During the 1820s, while serving as John Quincy Adams's Secretary of State, Clay had twice tried to purchase Texas from Mexico. In 1837, just two years after he wrote that he did not oppose annexation, he cautioned that he "would not for one moment consent to involve this country in war to acquire that country."[23] Still, Clay recognized that the sectional considerations tied up in the Texas question might require him to take a clearer position on the issue. Accordingly, in early 1844 he embarked on a listening tour of the Southern United States, hoping to discover a stance on the annexation of Texas that could help him win the presidency later that year.[24]

Van Buren similarly approached the Texas question with trepidation. Many of his supporters in the North opposed the action because it would strengthen slavery as well as the political power of the Southern states. Van Buren feared losing their votes. Still, one of his most trusted political allies warned him that open opposition to annexation would prove a "mill stone" that would "sink" his candidacy.[25] Could Van Buren successfully navigate the debate and emerge unscathed?

Van Buren's opponents for the Democratic nomination were more squarely in favor of annexation. As the American minister to France in the 1830s, Lewis Cass had urged King Louis Philippe to stymie British pretensions in North America, most notably in Texas. He was also a devoted expansionist. So, while a formal declaration of his position on Texas would not come until March, when he tried to differentiate himself from rivals Van Buren and Clay, his general opinion on the matter was never a mystery.[26] As for Richard M. Johnson, Van Buren's former vice president, he had declared in 1843 that while he hoped that the annexation of Texas could occur peacefully, he preferred "a little war and Texas along with it, to no war and no Texas."[27]

Meanwhile, President John Tyler used the Texas question as a desperate attempt to win Democrats over to his side. His Secretary of State, John C. Calhoun, also believed that annexation was necessary. In fact, Calhoun was engaged in annexation negotiations with the Texas government even as Smith was working with Phelps to draft his platform.[28]

Smith added his opinion on expansion. "Oregon belongs to this government honorably," he contended, "and when we have the red man's consent, let the union spread from the east to the west sea." As for Texas, Smith wrote that if that republic were to formally petition "Congress to be adopted among the sons of liberty," the United States should "give her the right hand of fellowship." But Smith did not stop there. Congress should "Refuse not the same friendly grip to Canada and Mexico." He maintained that such expansion would effectively prevent "foreign speculation."[29]

Smith was an ambitious expansionist, but the language in his pamphlet suggested a primarily restrained approach. The United States should assert its right to its claim of the Oregon Country but only populate the territory with white settlers after Native Americans consented to such settlement. Where the annexation of Texas was concerned, that should occur only if the independent Republic of Texas requested it. As for Smith's vision of a scenario in which Canada and Mexico similarly requested annexation, it revealed Smith's optimism that the United States would someday occupy nearly the entire North American continent. In all of this, however, Smith insisted that expansion occur at the informed request of the sovereign people whose territory was being consumed. Most of his countrymen were not as accommodating.

"BREAK OFF THE SHACKLES FROM THE POOR
BLACK MAN"

Support for westward expansion—and the annexation of Texas in particular—was usually tied to the expansion of race-based slavery. But not for Smith. In the same pamphlet that envisioned annexation of Texas, Smith called for the immediate and total abolition of slavery.

Since the founding of the United States, slavery had increasingly polarized the country. As Northern states gradually abolished the institution, Southern states grew more committed to it. By the 1840s the country was deeply divided on the issue.

Although there were more Americans opposed to slavery in the 1840s than in any previous decade, the movement was as splintered as ever. One of the fault lines was abolition. Not all anti-slavery Americans were abolitionists; many were content to advocate for the containment of slavery to the states in which it already existed. Yet, even the abolitionists did not agree on whether their goal should be immediate or gradual emancipation of slaves. Nor were they able to find consensus on what should become of former slaves, some advocating for integration in American society while others argued for resettlement in Africa. And, of course, opponents of slavery did not necessarily believe in the political and social equality of the races. The movement split into rival camps.[30]

Smith's personal opinions on race and slavery varied over the course of his life, and in such a way that precludes any clear judgments. In the 1830s Smith had expressed concern that the total abolition of slavery would "set loose upon the world a community of people who might peradventure, overrun our country and violate the most sacred principles of human society—chastity and virtue."[31] Yet, years later in Nauvoo, Smith dismissed a racial taxonomy that argued that people of African descent were naturally inferior to whites. He countered that this perceived inferiority was not the product of genetics; it was merely the result of environmental circumstances. "They come into the world slaves mentally & phy[s]ically," Smith stated. "Change their situation with the white & they would be like them." In addressing his flock, Smith was adamant that people of color "have souls & are subjects of salvation."[32]

In several instances Smith discouraged the mixing of races. As mayor of Nauvoo he fined two black men for trying to marry white women. In a political speech he would deliver in the months following the publication of his platform, he would suggest colonization of freed slaves as a viable option. Yet, Smith sold land in Nauvoo to free black men and permitted some of them to be ordained to the priesthood.[33] Like so many other nineteenth-century Americans, Smith's views on race were often contradictory, if not evolving.

As for the institution of slavery, Smith and the church had sought a middle ground in the conflict. Perhaps because missionary efforts had yielded new converts in the Southern states that included slave owners, the church had not prohibited slaveholding among its members. A notice in a church-owned newspaper in 1835 declared: "We do not believe it right to interfere with bondservants neither preach the gospel to, nor baptize them, contrary to the will and wish of their master."[34] While several Protestant denominations split over slavery during the 1840s and 1850s, the Church of Jesus Christ of Latter-day Saints Church remained intact. Some of the slaveholding converts to Mormonism moved to Nauvoo and appear to have brought their slaves with them, although such instances were rare, and Smith encouraged slaveowners who relocated to the city to free their slaves.[35] After the mob violence church members had experienced in Jackson County, Missouri, Nauvoo newspapers took great pains to avoid the appearance of advocating for free people of color to move to Nauvoo.[36] Yet, those who did settle in the city were allowed to own property.[37]

Smith's pamphlet pitched a pragmatic solution to the problem of slavery. "Petition also, ye goodly inhabitants of the slave states, your legislators to abolish slavery by the year 1850, or now, and save the abolitionist from reproach and ruin, infamy and shame," Smith wrote. He had little patience for the extreme measures of American abolitionists but similarly repudiated the inhumanity of slaveholders. In describing the failure of the United States to live up to the lofty ideals of its founding documents, Smith had opened his pamphlet by lamenting that "some two or three millions of people are held as slaves for life, because the spirit in them is covered with a darker skin than ours."[38] Six pages later he summarized his plan for emancipation. "Pray Congress to pay every man a reasonable price for his slaves out of the surplus revenue arising from the sale of public lands, and from the deduction of pay from the members of Congress."[39]

Paid emancipation was not a new concept in the United States, but the scale at which Smith was proposing it—and the idea of federal administration of the process—was unprecedented. Abolitionists had regularly purchased the freedom of slaves and then aided their resettlement in the North or in Africa. Yet, this occurred at the individual or family level. Smith was proposing that the federal government purchase the freedom of all slaves, thus granting universal freedom to people of color in the United States, but compensating slave owners for their loss. "Break off the shackles from the poor black man, and hire him to labor like other human beings," Smith concluded before quoting Joseph Addison's famous play, *Cato*, "for 'an hour of virtuous liberty on earth, is worth a whole eternity of bondage!'"[40]

Pragmatic as Smith's proposal may have been, it was ideologically problematic. Most antislavery Americans agreed that one human should not be allowed to own another human. Similarly, many American slave owners justified their peculiar institution by dehumanizing their slaves and treating them as property, not as fellow humans. Smith's proposal for the abolition of slavery ran contrary to both views. He argued that the souls of black Americans were equal to those of white Americans and, therefore, that they should be free. Yet, his proposal to purchase their freedom validated the idea that these men, women, and children were actually property. Whether Smith recognized the contradiction is impossible to say. Either way, neither the committed abolitionists nor the determined slave owners were likely to accept such a proposal.[41] In this Smith was unexceptional. The impasse over slavery would only be broken by war.

"THE MOTHER BANK"

The nation's system of banking was a polarizing issue in the politics of the early American republic. Ideological battles over national banking institutions were at the heart of many of these debates. But Smith approached the issue from a pragmatic—and populist—angle.

The First Bank of the United States was chartered in 1791 by the federal government, but it was largely under private control, with its officers appointed by its principal stockholders. Secretary of the Treasury Alexander Hamilton and the emerging Federalist Party championed the bank as necessary for the country's economic development. Republicans such as Thomas Jefferson opposed it as unconstitutional and claimed that it was designed for the profit of merchants and speculators but not average Americans. When the bank was up for renewal in 1811, opponents of the bank won a slim victory and allowed the charter to expire.[42]

A second national bank, modeled after its predecessor, was established by the federal government in 1816. However, in 1829 President Andrew Jackson placed the Second Bank of the United States in his crosshairs. He continued to question its constitutionality despite the fact that the Supreme Court had affirmed it. Furthermore, he distrusted paper currency and preferred "hard money." Several years ahead of the expiration of the bank's charter, Jackson waged a war against the institution. Eventually, he won. By the mid-1840s, banking and the country's economic health remained important political topics, but the discussion had moved away from the chartering of national banks.[43]

But Smith supported the re-establishment of a new national bank "For the accommodation of the people in every state and territory . . . with branches in each state and territory." He maintained that this bank would be different from its two predecessors. The new national bank would be public instead of private, and its "officers and directors . . . elected yearly by the people with wages at the rate of two dollars per day for services." No men would build private wealth from the national bank and its branches, but the public would. Smith envisioned a profitable public bank with the net gains of the "mother bank . . . applied to the national revenue" and to those of the branches "to the states and territories' revenues."[44]

To allay fears of paper currency, Smith explained that the bank and its different branches would "never issue any more bills than the amount of capital stock in her vaults and the interest." Furthermore, Smith claimed that the currency would "be par throughout the nation, which will mercifully cure that fatal disorder known in cities, as *brokerage*; and leave the people's money in their own pockets."[45] It would be a bank focused on the financial needs of American citizens and not the profits of its investors.

There was more to Smith's call for a new national bank than the resurrection of the partisan feuds of past decades. Smith and his followers—like hundreds of thousands of other Americans—were trapped in an economy slowed by a shortage of reliable currency. The anti-banking backlash that fueled Jackson's "Bank War" and that grew further amid the widespread failure of state-chartered banks during the depression of 1837–1842 hindered the founding of new government-backed banks throughout the United States. One consequence of this development was a dearth of reliable bank notes in circulation throughout the country. In 1837, President Martin Van Buren sought to alleviate the financial panic spreading across the country by proposing a system of subtreasuries, or government-owned vaults for housing money, so that the federal government did not have to rely on banks to serve as depositories for federal funds. Under Van Buren's plan, the federal government would issue bills backed by coins or precious metals in its subtreasuries that would function as currency. The plan was debated for years. In 1840, Congress established the Independent Treasury to protect the federal government's specie in subtreasuries from which the government could draw to pay its expenses. However, contrary to Van Buren's initial plan, the Independent Treasury would not issue bills, and the plan's critics claimed that the Independent Treasury actually restricted the country's money supply further.[46]

This currency shortage was particularly acute in western states, where most men's wealth was tied up in the land they purchased on credit—often as speculative ventures. Even advocates of "hard money," or coins made of precious metals, struggled in the economy of the 1830s and 1840s because of a national shortage of such specie. With currency and specie both in short supply, men found it difficult to transact routine business and resorted to stopgap measures such as bartering, trading with promissory notes, and patronizing so-called wildcat banks.[47]

In Illinois, the crisis was compounded further by the failures of the state-chartered bank in 1842 and the state legislature's refusal to charter any new banks to replace it.[48] Smith's proposed bank was designed to alleviate these practical concerns more than it was to rehash ideological clashes. He was proud of this fact. Amid the drafting of his political platform, an entry in Smith's journal kept by one of his clerks read: "I was the first one who publicly proposed a national Bank on the principles I had advanced."[49]

"PARDON EVERY CONVICT"

In 1838, Smith had spent six months in a damp, crowded jail cell in Liberty, Missouri, the conditions of which were inhumane by any standard. He had been denied a fair and timely trial and considered himself fortunate to have been able to escape prior to standing before a rigged court for a final verdict.[50] It should come as no surprise, then, that Smith campaigned for prison reform. Yet, his call for reform extended beyond the treatment of the accused and the convicted; he questioned the very philosophy of crime and punishment that underlay the burgeoning American penitentiary system.

When the first American penitentiary opened in Philadelphia in 1790, advocates for social reform hailed it as a major step toward creating a moderate and rational form of punishment. Their goal seemed noble. They believed that prisons should do more than punish criminals through isolation and a restriction of their freedom; the penitentiary would reform convicts and prepare them to re-enter society as virtuous citizens.[51]

However, in the decades that followed, the country's penal system consistently fell short of its lofty ideal. Living conditions in many American penitentiaries were poor, and the treatment of prisoners by their guards often reprehensible. Published reports from organizations dedicated to prison reform laid bare this inhumanity before the American public. Many were outraged, but the growth of the penitentiary system continued unabated.[52]

Objections to penitentiaries extended beyond the poor conditions in which prisoners lived and the practices they were subjected to within prison walls. To many nineteenth-century Americans, the penitentiary had become a tool of social control. Visitors to the United States such as Alexis de Tocqueville observed that the criminal justice system that so often incarcerated the poor while the wealthy remained free by paying fines was an "aristocratic institution in the midst of a complete Democracy."[53] Furthermore, as historian Jen Manion argues, American elites "used the penal system to discipline and punish citizens in ways that advanced social hierarchies rooted in race, gender, class, and sexual differences."[54] The men and women disproportionately incarcerated in penitentiaries—free people of color, immigrants, and the poor—clearly recognized what was happening. They understood that the system was designed to keep them down. This group included Joseph Smith.

"Petition your state legislature to pardon every convict in their several penitentiaries," Smith urged in his pamphlet, "blessing them as they go, and saying to them in the name of the Lord, *go thy way and sin no more*." Smith proposed that the civil penalties prescribed for "larceny, burglary or any felony"—with the exception of murder— should consist of "work upon the roads, public works, or any place where the culprit can be taught more wisdom and more virtue; and become more enlightened."

He argued that "Rigor and seclusion will never do as much to reform the propensities of man, as reason and friendship." Looking beyond punishment for crime, Smith argued that penitentiaries would become obsolete if Americans did a better job of educating rising generations. "Let the penitentiaries be turned into seminaries of learning, where intelligence, like the angels of heaven, would banish such fragments of barbarism."[55]

Above all else, Smith condemned "Imprisonment for debt" as "a meaner practice than the savage tolerates with all his ferocity."[56] In the early nineteenth century, debtor prisons continued to punish the poor while keeping them poor. Even a small debt left unpaid could land a man in a locked workhouse where he had to remain until he had worked off the amount owed. Meanwhile, the family of the incarcerated debtor was left to languish without his labor and income.[57]

Detention of debtors was at the discretion of the lender and often arbitrary. Lenders could use the debt as a means of punishing a man who was not well liked, or who represented a challenge to social norms, such as those who embraced controversial religious movements.

Smith could certainly relate to the punitive nature of the laws regulating debtors and the effect it had on keeping poor Americans poor. In 1830, Joseph Smith Sr. was incarcerated in a New York debtor's prison for his inability to pay a fourteen-dollar debt. Despite the elder Smith's attempt to pay part of the owed sum when the creditor called and to arrange for the payment of the balance shortly thereafter, a constable arrested and held him until his family could settle the debt and arrange for his release.[58]

Not only had Smith been raised in the cycle of poverty associated with tenant farming, he had for several years lived under the burden of heavy debts. When he traveled to Washington, D.C., in 1839–1840, Mormons in Ossining, New York, invited him to visit and preach. Yet, Smith had to decline the invitation as he owed heavy debts to creditors in that state. As the president of the Ossining Branch of the church warned in his December 1839 letter to Smith, "I am aware that you could not visit [in] the City without laying yourself liable to imprisonment . . . I mention these things so that you may not be brought into bondage unawares; perhaps by those, who may feel a disposition to persecute the saints."[59] Because of the fear of prison—and the almost inescapable poverty that was bound to follow—Smith was unable to travel as freely in his own country.

Individual states had already started to reform their debtor laws. Since 1820, many states had restricted imprisonment for debt to those found guilty of gross fraud.[60] In 1841, Congress had passed a bankruptcy act that provided financial relief to thousands of Americans.[61] But such reform was not universal, and, for Smith, it was not enough. In his campaign platform, Smith made it clear that as president he would use his influence to champion a nationwide reform of the criminal justice system generally and debtor laws specifically.

"THE VOTE WAS UNIVERSAL IN THE AFFIRMATIVE"

Phelps finished the initial draft of *General Smith's Views* by February 5, apparently with the help of another clerk. Smith made a few minor revisions to the text before approving of the whole by signing his name at the bottom of the final page.[62]

Three days later Smith convened a meeting in the upper room of his general store. The room had been the site of several momentous occasions in the history of the church. Smith had organized the women's Relief Society here. It was also where he had first introduced the rituals that would be performed in the temple. It was fitting that he would launch his presidential campaign in the same room.

Phelps read the finished draft of *General Smith's Views* aloud. Those assembled found it "in the highest degree interesting" and watched eagerly as their prophet arose to address the room. "I would not have suffered my name to have been used by my friends on any wise as president of the United States or candidate for that office," Smith explained, "If I & my friends Could have had the privilege of enjoying our religious & civel rights as American Citizens even those rights to which the Constitution guarantees unto all her citizens alike."[63]

Smith lamented the circumstances that had brought him and his people to this point. "Persecution has rolled upon our heads from time to time from portions of the United States like peels of thunder because of our religion & no portion of the government as yet has stepped forward for our relief." As a result, he declared, "I feel it to be my right & privilege to obtain what influence & power I can lawfully in the United States for the protection of injured innocence."[64]

Closing his remarks dramatically, Smith invoked the possibility that he may not survive the campaign. "If I lose my life in a good cause I am willing to be sacrificed on the alter of virtue righteousness & truth in maintaining the laws & constitution of the United States if need be for the general good of mankind."[65] If the country could not guarantee religious freedom, the Mormon prophet was prepared to die a martyr to that cause.

Following Smith's speech and remarks by two other church leaders, "a vote was taken whether the views of Gen Smith would be maintained by the assembly or not." According to apostle Wilford Woodruff, "The vote was universal in the affirmative."[66] Smith ordered 1,500 copies of the pamphlet printed, and approximately two weeks later his order was ready.[67]

On February 25 a prayer meeting convened in the upper room of Smith's store. Those in attendance prayed "that 'Gen Smiths views of the power & policy of the United States' might be spread far and wide—& be the means of opening the hearts of the people."[68] Smith directed fellow church leaders to mail copies of the pamphlet to President Tyler and his entire cabinet, all nine Supreme Court justices, prominent congressmen, the governor of every state, and the country's principal newspapers.[69] Conceived and commenced in Nauvoo, Smith's candidacy was going national.

8

....

THE POLITICAL
KINGDOM OF GOD

GENERAL SMITH'S VIEWS **WAS NOT THE SUM** of Joseph Smith's political vision. Smith barely *had* a political vision. His political activity was a matter of necessity. His policy positions were probationary, they were designed to protect the civil rights of minority groups in the United States until the Second Coming of Jesus Christ made all debates over human governance irrelevant.

Smith approached politics from the perspective of an American prophet: both the Constitution and God's law needed to be maintained. However, should the Constitution—or the United States government— prove detrimental to God's law, then they were expendable. Smith and other Latter-day Saints revered the founding; American institutions were not necessarily worthy of veneration.[1]

In March 1844 Smith established a political auxiliary to the church called the Council of Fifty. The name referenced the approximate number of the council's members. Smith declared that the Council of Fifty was a preliminary step toward millennial government, or a government that would rule following the Second Coming of Jesus. Accordingly, clerk

William Clayton titled the first entry in the council's minute book, "Record of the Council of Fifty or Kingdom of God."[2]

The Council of Fifty would play a key role in managing Smith's presidential campaign. But Smith's vision for the Council extended beyond 1844. It was far grander in scope and more radical in its implications.

"PRINCIPLES WHICH THE CONSTITUTION OF THE UNITED STATES LACKED"

"At early candlelight" on March 10, the first meeting of the Council of Fifty commenced.[3] However, the immediate impetus for the gathering was not Smith's campaign. It was Smith's receipt of two letters from Mormons who had gone off to the Wisconsin Territory to obtain lumber for the temple and boarding house in Nauvoo. They suggested that Smith consider relocating the church's central gathering place outside the United States, to the Republic of Texas.[4] They had written their letter before reading Smith's campaign platform in which he called for the annexation of Texas. Nevertheless, Smith was willing to consider the matter.

Clayton read the letters to the men assembled. Smith then rose to speak. He solicited the opinions of those present on the prospect of leaving Nauvoo—and the United States. But before the discussion commenced, Smith told the men that "he wanted all the brethren to speak their minds on this subject and to say what was in their hearts whether good or bad." He did not want to be surrounded "by a set of 'dough heads.' "[5] There was no room for sycophants where such important matters were concerned.

The men conversed late into the night. Clayton did not record what each individual said, but in his personal journal wrote that "many great and glorious ideas were advanced."[6] When the meeting reconvened the following morning, it became apparent that church leaders in Nauvoo were open to exploring relocation beyond the borders of the United States. However, the men participating in these discussions were not ready to make such considerations public. They unanimously passed a motion that "every member of [the council] be bound to eternal secrecy as to what passed here, not to have the privilege of telling anything which might be talked of to any person even to our wives, and the man who broke the rule 'should lose his cursed head.' "[7] Council members appear to have used such stark language to emphasize the importance of confidentiality. When word of the council eventually leaked to the public, no heads were lost.

It was in this second meeting that the council assumed the structure of a formal, standing organization. The council appointed a committee "to draft a constitution which should be perfect and embrace those principles which the constitution of the United States lacked."[8] Smith had long been a champion of the United States Constitution but had rarely refrained from criticizing its blatant shortcomings. "There is only two or three things lacking in the Constitution of the United States," he would tell the Council of Fifty. "If they had said all men [are] born equal, and not only that but they shall have their rights they shall be free, or the armies of the government should be compelled to enforce those principles of liberty."[9] Apparently, he believed that this committee could draft a corrective document.

The group reconvened on March 13. More church members had joined the group, and much of the meeting was dedicated to apprising them of what had already transpired. Then, on March 14, Smith declared a revelation from God naming their new organization. "Verily thus saith the Lord," Smith declared, "this is the name by which you shall be called, The Kingdom of God and his Laws, with the keys and power thereof, and judgement in the hands of his servants."[10] For men well versed in the Bible as Smith and company were, the implication of the council's revealed name was clear. They were establishing the political kingdom of God, the very kingdom that the biblical prophet Daniel had prophesied would "fill the entire earth" during the millennium and "never be destroyed."[11]

Council members were not surprised by Smith's millennial language. Thousands of Americans were awaiting the end of the world when Smith launched his presidential campaign in 1844.[12] Some groups, including the Shakers, believed that the millennium had already started.[13] However, typical Christian fervor for the Second Coming of Christ was heightened by reformed Baptist William Miller, who had published a series of lectures in which he predicted that Christ would return between March 1843 and March 1844. Thousands of Americans were convinced by Miller's lectures. Called Millerites or Adventists by their neighbors, they prepared their personal affairs for the imminent millennial era. But when that year passed without incident, Miller revised his prediction to April 18, 1844.[14]

Joseph Smith and the Mormons were among the American Christians who scoffed at William Miller and his predictions. Throughout 1843 and 1844 Millerites lectured in Nauvoo on the end of the world. Responding in February 1843, Smith preached "that Miller is in want of information" and that his calculations were incorrect in part because they were based on a faulty translation of the Bible.[15] That same year Mormon elder Noah Packard published a pamphlet dismissing Miller's biblical calculus.[16] Smith, Packard, and their coreligionists did not deny that the Second Coming might occur in 1844 or soon thereafter, but they did not believe that the timing of the long-watched-for event would be discovered through dubious biblical calculus. They insisted that God would not make the precise moment of the Second Coming known to humankind but that a divinely appointed prophet such as Smith could help men and women recognize the warning signs described in the Bible.[17] According to Smith, Miller and others predicting the precise date of Christ's return were "false prophets."[18]

Like those belonging to many other Christian denominations, Mormons believed that in the millennium earthly governments would be replaced by the Kingdom of God. In calling his newly formed political council the Kingdom of God, Smith was not declaring to church members that the millennium had commenced. Instead, he seemed to suggest that it was time for them to lay the framework for the divine government that would rule after the second coming. They were getting a head start.

This belief was connected to the most radical element of the Council of Fifty. Its members had not yet resolved to leave the United States. They were merely discussing the possibility. But when they talked about such a prospect, they were not talking about becoming citizens of another country, of moving from one democracy to another. They were contemplating political independence. They were looking "to some place where [they could] go and establish a Theocracy either in Texas or Oregon or somewhere in California &c."[19]

"THEODEMOCRACY"

What would a Mormon-made theocracy look like and how would such a government function? Some members of the council pointed to ancient Israel—a nation that was governed by its ecclesiastical leaders, beginning with Moses and Joshua—as their model. Yet, "Moses's government" was more of a rhetorical tool than an actual blueprint, a way of justifying the form of government with a historical example deemed noble by most Christian and Jewish Americans.[20] On the question of what their theocracy would look like, consensus eluded the Council of Fifty.

Disagreement among council members was often centered on the relationship between church and state. Some members expressed extreme visions of a theocratic future that bordered on authoritarianism. For example, apostle Brigham Young stated that he "cannot see the difference between a religious or political government."[21] On a separate occasion, he insisted that "No line can be drawn between the church and other governments, of the spiritual and temporal affairs of the church. Revelations must govern. The voice of God, shall be the voice of the people."[22] Such claims foreshadowed some of Young's tactics in future roles of ecclesiastical and political leadership.[23]

Like Young, other council members saw Smith's prophetic role as essential to government by God. Smith was the council's standing chairman, but in one momentous meeting council members anointed him the council's "prophet, priest, and king."[24] There may have been some council members amenable to life under a prophet-king, but Mormon religious beliefs help contextualize this curious anointing. Smith had encouraged Mormons in Nauvoo to participate in temple rituals in which they were similarly anointed kings and priests and queens and priestesses unto God. He explained that these anointings had "nothin[g] to do with temporal things" but were instead designed to elevate men and women in their respective "kingdoms," or spheres of stewardship.[25] Furthermore, despite Smith's anointing in the Council of Fifty, he and others tempered the more authoritarian impulses of some council members with collegial but emphatic opinions of their own.

Indeed, Smith had one of the more moderate political voices in the council, and he described an approach to theocracy that was far more democratic than Young's approach. "There is a distinction between the Church of God and kingdom of God," Smith explained. "The laws of the kingdom are not designed to effect our salvation hereafter. It is an entire, distinct and separate government." In an ideal government, Smith saw the church and state as having complementary, but ultimately separate, functions. "The gifts of prophets, evangelists &c never were designed to govern men in civil matters," he stated, adding that, similarly, "The kingdom of God has nothing to do with giving commandments to damn a man spiritually. It only has power to make a man amenable to his fellow man."[26]

Smith advocated for "theodemocracy." In April 1844, Smith published an editorial in a church newspaper in which he declared, "I go emphatically, virtuously, and humanely, for a theodemocracy, where God and the people hold the power to conduct the affairs of men in righteousness."[27] Back in the Council of Fifty he expanded on this notion. Theodemocracy, he explained, "consisted in our exercising all the intelligence of the council, and bring[ing] forth all the light which dwells in the breast of every man." Accordingly, a governing council would use their knowledge of God and his will to make policy decisions and then seek divine approval of their decisions through revelation. Theodemocracy was "for the people to get the voice of God and then acknowledge it, and see it executed." In such a government, the common democratic phrase, *Vox populi, Vox Dei*, would take on a different meaning than the conventional "the voice of the people is the voice of God." According to Smith, in a theodemocracy it would be translated, "The voice of the people assenting to the voice of God."[28] Whereas a simple theocracy might appear as the law being dictated from above, a theodemocracy would raise its citizens to new revelatory heights where they could experience a stronger connection to God and a deeper understanding of his plan for the moral redemption of humankind.

In addition, Smith was emphatic that such a theocracy must not privilege Mormons over other citizens. In a speech before the Council of Fifty, Smith observed that three non-Mormons had been admitted to the council "to show that in the organization of this kingdom men are not consulted as to their religious opinions or notions in any shape or form . . . and that we act upon the broad and liberal principal that all men have equal rights, and ought to be respected." Smith apparently worried that, if placed in charge of the civic government, his coreligionists might themselves become the perpetrators of religious discrimination. Accordingly, he issued a warning: "Let us henceforth drive from us every species of intollerance . . . Hence in all governments or political transactions a mans religious opinions should never be called in question. A man should be judged by the law independant of religious prejudice."[29]

If the details of this proposed theocracy appear vague, it is because the council never fully set them forth. The committee Smith had tasked with drafting a new constitution struggled with their assignment. On April 18 the committee presented a partial draft of their constitution to the entire council. "We, the people of the Kingdom of God," the document commenced, appropriating the language of the United States Constitution. Following several biblical allusions and references to the failure of the United States government to protect the Mormons, the draft constitution consisted of three articles. The first article established God as the "rightful lawgiver to man." The second article declared God's prophet as the person through whom God's law would be revealed. The third article afforded the people the right to elect other government officers.[30]

This draft of the constitution was hardly a blueprint for a functioning government. Furthermore, it was more authoritarian in tone than the vision Smith had set forth in his council speeches. But that is as far as the constitution progressed. On April 25, Smith counseled the committee to abandon the project and declared a revelation from heaven. "Verily thus saith the Lord," the revelation read, "ye are my constitution, and I am your God, and ye are my spokesmen. From henceforth do as I shall command you."[31] The Council of Fifty itself would comprise a living constitution.

This was welcome news to Young, who had questioned the need for a written constitution. "We may say we will have a constitution because it is fashionable," Young had stated after first hearing the draft read in council. He explained that he preferred instead "to have the revelations to form a constitution from, than anything else we can get."[32]

In addition, the question of where the Mormons could establish such a theocracy was never settled in the Council of Fifty while under Smith's leadership. Texas was a favorite choice of many council members. In March, Smith had dispatched council member Lucien Woodworth to the Texas Republic to enter secret negotiations with President Sam Houston about establishing a Mormon colony along the Rio Grande.[33] Such a colony could help Houston and Texas with some of their own problems. Mexico and Texas were engaged in a border dispute over the ownership of the strip of land between the Nueces River to the north and the Rio Grande to the south, commonly called the Nueces Strip. At stake for Texas were navigation rights on the Rio Grande. In the nineteenth century, the quickest solution to border disputes was often territorial occupation, for one country to establish permanent settlements on the land in question. In theory, the Mormons could create such settlements. As a bonus for Houston and Texas, the Mormons came with their own militia unit.[34]

Still, not everyone in the council was convinced that Texas was their best option. Some council members continued to push for settlement in Oregon. Others argued in favor of California. No matter the eventual location, the ideal setting would be an isolated one where the Mormon community could govern itself in peace. "We will hunt a spot somewhere on earth where no other government has jurisdiction," Sidney Rigdon declared to his fellow council members, "and cannot interfere with us and there plant our standard."[35]

Despite the Council of Fifty's ongoing debates over what a theodemocracy would look like, how it would operate, and where it should commence, such conversations remained theoretical. Outside the council room, church members continued to function as citizens of a democracy. Furthermore, even after all their bold declarations that the United States was a fallen nation, many council members—including Smith—still believed the country could be redeemed.

Indeed, fleeing the United States was a worst-case scenario for Smith and the Mormons in Nauvoo. It was an avenue designed to escape extermination if mobs comprised of their fellow Americans once again determined to wage war against them. Even as conversations about Texas, Oregon, and California continued in the Council of Fifty throughout the spring of 1844, council members focused intently on devising plans that would allow the Mormon community to remain in the country. An independent theocracy may have been inevitable in Mormons' millennialist views, but such a government could wait if they could get adequate protection from American democracy.

"BREAK DOWN TYRANNY AND OPPRESSION"

Like Smith, the Council of Fifty recognized that the major obstacle to ensuring the Mormons' rights as American citizens was the doctrine of states' rights. It was the primary and repeated excuse that federal officials cited in denying the Mormons protection. Just as the Nauvoo City Council had petitioned Congress for the city to become a federal territory in December 1843, the Council of Fifty explored unconventional legal and political strategies for circumventing states' rights.

One of these ideas centered on the United States Army. On March 19, 1844, apostle Willard Richards motioned that a "communication be made immediately to the General Government" petitioning for Smith to be an officer in the United States and placing him at the head of an army of volunteers to protect western territories, including Oregon, from foreign invasion. The council unanimously approved Richards's motion on March 21 and appointed a committee to draft a petition to Congress.[36]

On March 26 the council considered the petition. It set forth a long list of reasons for raising an army to protect the country's vast territory west of the Mississippi River. These reasons included preventing "quarrel and bloodshed on our frontiers," protecting "the inhabitants of Oregon from foreign aggression and domestic broils," and preventing "the crowned nations from encircleing us as a nation on our western and Southern borders." Such an army, the petition claimed, would increase "equity, liberty, justice, humanity, and benevolence" throughout the west and "break down tyranny and oppression, and exalt the standard of universal peace." To accomplish such goals, the petition requested that Congress authorize Smith "to raise a company of one hundred thousand armed volunteers" and to lead the army he raised, presumably as a general. The council unanimously approved the petition and determined to submit it to both Congress and President John Tyler.[37]

While the petition focused on the protection of western lands and Americans settling thereon, the council's ulterior motives are easy to detect. Smith had long complained that the federal government could not dispatch the United States Army to individual states to protect groups of citizens from mobs. Such an action required a formal request from a state's governor.[38] However, if Smith was a general with a large army at his command, he could personally ensure the protection of the Mormons—and all other religious minority groups living on or near the western frontier.

The petition was an audacious move, and one that stood virtually no chance of succeeding. The size of the proposed army was absurd. The petition called for 100,000 volunteers at a time when the entire United States Army consisted of approximately 8,000 enlisted men and officers.[39] Furthermore, while there was precedent for officers in local militias receiving commissions as officers in the army, a jump from local militia officer to general in the army would be inconceivable to many in Congress, especially because of the public controversy that surrounded Smith.

The council dispatched apostle Orson Hyde to Washington, D.C., to submit this petition to Congress. Hyde left Nauvoo on April 4 with plans to join fellow apostle Orson Pratt, who was already in the capital managing the latest effort to secure reparations for the Missouri persecutions. Together, Hyde and Pratt would work with the Illinois delegation in Congress to make inroads with the national legislature. Eventually apostle Heber C. Kimball traveled to Washington to aid the lobbying efforts.

However, Hyde, Pratt, and Kimball recognized that a military commission for Smith was not the only potential solution to the Mormons' problem and used their time in the capital to conceive of additional avenues for protection. In June, Hyde and Kimball drafted a petition requesting that Congress give the Mormons "a liberal grant of land, in one of the Territories of the United States, to be located in such a manner as not to deprive any previous actual settler of any just right or claim." Should Congress find such a grant inconsistent with its duties, the petition urged the legislative body to sell the Mormons the preemption rights to such a tract of land "with the privilege of paying the money at the periods of ten, fifteen and twenty years in such a manner as your Honorable Bodies shall prescribe."[40]

A federal grant of land in the western territory was likely a more palatable option for Congress—and certainly a more probable one—than making Smith a general in the army. Indeed, it was in keeping with the advice of one of the country's most prominent senators and presidential candidates, Henry Clay. Clay had apparently advised Smith and the Mormons to move west to Oregon or some other sparsely populated area in the western territory where they could live in peace. Smith and company had initially received Clay's suggestion as an insult. It was yet another refusal by government officials to address the violent and bigoted behavior of the majority and placed the burden of maintaining peace on the back of the persecuted minority.[41]

Still, the Council of Fifty appeared open to the idea of moving west and saw merit in the isolation—and relative independence—it would provide them. At the very least, in a federal territory they would not have to worry about states' rights as a political obstacle to any future problems with their non-Mormon countrymen. To Mormon leaders such a plan was more attractive than Clay's suggestion because it would occur on their own terms and the land would be free or available for purchase at a favorable price.

Mormon apostles in Washington recognized that their petitions' prospects were slim, but they were determined. "We intend to tease [Congress] until we either provoke them or get them to do something for us," Hyde wrote in a letter home.[42] One bill could keep the Mormons in Nauvoo; the other could potentially pave the way to something approaching political independence and theocracy. Or, Congress could ignore both petitions, and the Council of Fifty would continue to explore additional options to secure the Mormons' citizenship rights.

"FREE TRADE AND SAILORS' RIGHTS"

Of course, the Council of Fifty recognized that Smith's presidential candidacy was another option for securing Mormons' rights and continued residence in the United States—as well as an important step in redeeming the country. Accordingly, the council played an integral role in managing Smith's campaign.

One of the council's functions was to craft a consistent campaign message. In April, council members adopted a "name," or slogan, for their electoral enterprise. At Smith's suggestion, their choice was a string of political buzzwords: "Jeffersonianism, Jeffersonian Democracy, free trade and Sailors rights, protection of person & property."[43] Smith and company did not expound on the slogan, nor did they attempt to clarify seeming redundancies therein. Each of these phrases already existed in the American political lexicon. Most were associated to some degree with individual liberties. For example, "Free Trade and Sailors' Rights" had been a patriotic rallying cry for Americans during the War of 1812 but had since evolved into a generic and malleable phrase denoting personal liberty.[44] And that seemed to be at the heart of such a clunky and unwieldy campaign slogan. Smith and the Mormons were promoting the kind of patriotic liberty associated with celebratory accounts of the country's past.

Council members also discussed the coordination of nominating conventions throughout the country and deliberated on potential vice-presidential candidates. In addition, they willingly participated in an ambitious plan to canvass the entire country as electioneering missionaries. Such canvassing was at the heart of Smith's electoral designs.

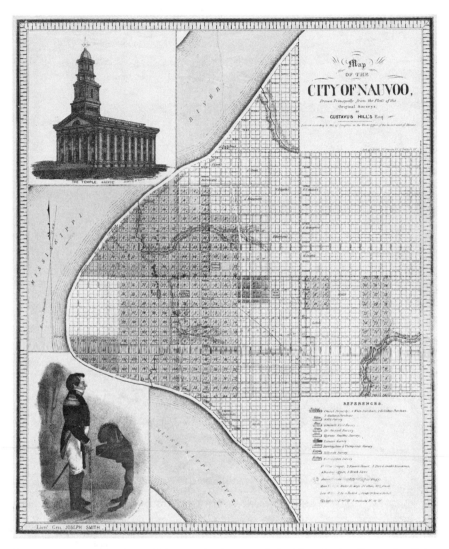

Figure 1. Map of the City of Nauvoo (1842). Joseph Smith and other Latter-day Saint leaders took on the role of urban planners as they designed a city to accommodate a rapid influx of converts to Nauvoo. (Courtesy of the Church History Library, Church of Jesus Christ of Latter-day Saints.)

Figure 2. Painting of Joseph Smith (1842). In 1842 Joseph Smith sat for a portrait with artist David Rogers. (Courtesy Community of Christ Archives.)

MARTIN VAN BUREN.

Eighth President of the United States.

Figure 3. Martin Van Buren, lithograph, circa 1840. In December 1839, Joseph Smith met with President Martin Van Buren at the White House, where he asked the president to aid the Latter-day Saints' petition to Congress for redress and reparations. Van Buren declined to help. (Library of Congress, Prints & Photographs Division.)

Figure 4. John C. Calhoun, photograph, circa 1850. In 1843–1844, Joseph Smith and John C. Calhoun exchanged letters on the plight of the Latter-day Saints and the role that the states' rights doctrine played in enabling the persecution of religious minority groups. (Library of Congress, Prints & Photographs Division.)

Figure 5. Lewis Cass, photograph, circa 1855. Cass was the primary challenger to Martin Van Buren for the Democratic nomination in 1844. Like Calhoun, Cass wrote to Joseph Smith in 1843 explaining that he believed the federal government could do nothing to redress the persecution of religious minorities by a state. (Brady-Handy photograph collection, Library of Congress, Prints & Photographs Division.)

Figure 6. Henry Clay, lithograph, circa 1844. The Whig nominee for president in 1844, Henry Clay had expressed sympathy for the Latter-day Saints but declined to publicly declare his support for redress for the religious minority if elected president. (Library of Congress, Prints & Photographs Division.)

Figure 7. "For President, Gen. Joseph Smith" (1844). Issues of *The Prophet*, a Mormon-owned campaign newspaper published in New York, featured this endorsement of the Smith-Rigdon ticket. (Courtesy of the Church History Library, Church of Jesus Christ of Latter-day Saints.)

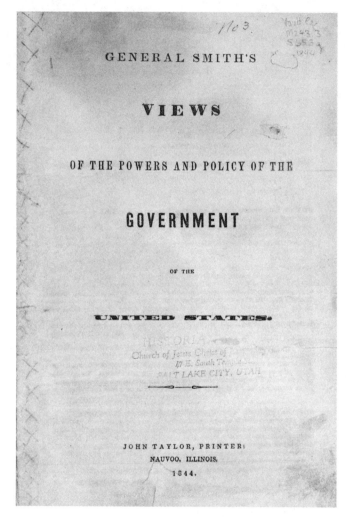

Figure 8. General Smith's Views (1844). In February 1844 Joseph Smith published a
pamphlet that contained his campaign platform. Among other political positions,
Smith called for a stronger federal government, the territorial expansion of the
United States, the re-establishment of a national bank, and the abolition of slavery.
(Courtesy of the Church History Library, Church of Jesus Christ of Latter-day Saints.)

Figure 9. Carthage Jail, lithograph, 1853. On June 27, 1844, a mob assassinated Joseph Smith and Hyrum Smith at the jail in Carthage, Illinois. (Courtesy of the Church History Library, Church of Jesus Christ of Latter-day Saints.)

Figure 10. Nauvoo, photograph (1846). One of the earliest surviving photographs of Nauvoo, featuring the recently completed temple on the bluff overlooking the city. (Courtesy of the Church History Library, Church of Jesus Christ of Latter-day Saints.)

9

. . . .

ELECTIONEERING
MISSIONARIES

JOSEPH SMITH HAD AN ADVANTAGE OVER OTHER Americans who might have thought about launching a presidential campaign without the support of an established political party. He had an experienced corps of missionaries. Since even before the formal founding of the church in 1830, Mormon men had embarked on proselytizing missions. Now it was time for Smith and the Council of Fifty to apply that experience to their political goals.

This had been part of the plan since Smith had accepted the nomination of his fellow church leaders in January. "There is oratory enough in the church to carry me into the presidential chair the first slide," Smith had stated in the same meeting in which he had accepted the nomination of the Quorum of the Twelve Apostles to enter the race.[1] While he was certainly overstating his chances for electoral success, he was not exaggerating the persuasive speaking skills of his followers or their ability to endure months on the road.

Mormon leaders notified members of the church of the impending mission assignments on April 9, 1844, during the final day of a special conference of the church in Nauvoo. As president of the Quorum of the Twelve Apostles, Brigham Young addressed the congregation of nearly 1,000 men. "We are acquainted with the views of Gen. Smith, the Democrats and Whigs and all factions," Young asserted. "It is now time to have a President of the United States. Elders will be sent to preach the Gospel and electioneer."[2]

Hyrum Smith spoke next. "We engage in the election the same as in any other principle," the prophet's brother explained, "you are to vote for good men, and if you do not do this it is a sin." He exhorted the elders not to fear "man or devil," but to "electioneer with all people, male and female, and exhort them to do the thing that is right. We want a President of the U.S., not a party President, but a President of the whole people . . . a President who will maintain every man in his rights." If the electioneering missionaries would "Lift up [their] voices like thunder," he concluded, then "there is power and influence enough among us to put in a President."[3]

The speeches were effective, and 244 men volunteered for electioneering missions. Church leaders compiled a list and made assignments of the states they would canvass. In the week that followed, the list of electioneering missionaries grew to include 339 men.[4] It would grow further still once the missionaries got to campaigning, with additional men joining the canvassing effort in the states where they lived. But 339 from Nauvoo was a good start and church leaders were optimistic.[5]

"LET US HAVE DELEGATES IN ALL THE ELECTORAL DISTRICTS"

By late April, the Council of Fifty had determined it was time to mobilize the army of electioneering missionaries that the church had assembled. At a meeting of the council on April 25, Smith "suggested the propriety of passing some resolutions, saying that those in the council who could, should go forth immediately to electioneer &c." Smith appeared as worried about the suspicion that frequent council meetings might raise in the area as he was about the upcoming election. "We must suspend our meetings for the time being and keep silence on the subject," he told the council, "lest by our continual coming together we raise an excitement. We can call the council together again when necessary."[6]

Electioneering was the priority. "Let us have delegates in all the electoral districts and hold a national convention in Baltimore," Smith continued, adding "that the easiest and the best way to accomplish the object in view is to make an effort to secure the election at this contest."[7] This was a grandiose plan for Smith and his fledgling grass roots campaign. They would canvass the country, hold conventions in each state to select electors, and then convene in Baltimore in the late spring to formally nominate Smith.

National presidential nominating conventions were relatively new on the American political scene. Prior to the 1830s, a party's presidential and vice-presidential candidates were typically chosen by a caucus comprised of the party's members in Congress. Change came in 1831 when the upstart Anti-Masonic Party, determined to effect greater transparency in national politics, held a national nominating convention so that the entire country would understand the process by which its candidate for the election of 1832 was selected.[8]

The Anti-Masons were never more than a minority party and would soon thereafter be largely subsumed by the Whigs, but their convention was a popular innovation. Within eight months of the Anti-Masonic convention, both the National Republicans (later the Whig Party) and the Democrats held national nominating conventions of their own.[9] In many ways, the relatively extreme transparency of a public convention exhibited by the Anti-Masonic Party made the traditional party caucuses appear elite and disconnected from the voters. Even though much of the American democratic system had been crafted behind closed doors, the metaphorical dark, smoky back rooms—and the literal versions, too—now appeared undemocratic. It was an image that both Whigs and Democrats wanted to avoid.

Each of those first national nominating conventions was held in Baltimore, largely due to its geographic centrality on the East Coast, the city's proximity to Washington, D.C., and its accessibility by land and sea. The different parties liked Baltimore enough that they held their nominating conventions in that city ahead of nearly every presidential election in the 1830s and 1840s.[10] Both major parties were scheduled to convene in Baltimore in May. Smith planned to gather his supporters in the same place shortly thereafter, signifying to the general public that he was determined to play on the same national political stage as his opponents.

Smith was entering a political arena that was undergoing significant transformation. The democratization of American society in the early 1800s led to greater participation in elections by a wider array of American men than ever before. This, in turn, led to changes in the way politicians sought public office. The founding generation had assumed an air of disinterest in their public service. They were ambitious men, but they disguised their ambition. Instead of openly seeking office, they worked behind the scenes, coordinating the activity of surrogates who campaigned on their behalf. This way, when they were elected they could claim they were accepting the position as the will of the people and not as an honor they had sought.[11]

By the 1840s, Americans had mostly moved beyond this culture of affected disinterest, although many still considered it inappropriate for a candidate to openly campaign by traveling the country making stump speeches. To work around this, presidential candidates in the 1840s expanded the use of cultural politics to create and grow active bases of political support. These cultural politics carried a candidate's message to Americans through pamphlets, printed broadsides, and political cartoons. Campaigns also used music. They published and distributed songbooks so that supporters would be able to join together in support of their candidate at public events. Auxiliary organizations such as reform societies or the Freemasons also proved essential for creating support and mobilizing voters. In some cases, local clubs were formed expressly to manage the affairs of a national campaign in a specific location. In essence, while presidential candidates still limited their direct interaction with voters, they had no qualms about expanding the ways their surrogates electioneered, nor did they pretend to be uninvolved in campaign planning.[12]

Even in an age of political experimentation, Smith's decision was unprecedented. No presidential candidate had ever dispatched hundreds of electioneers, much less hundreds of electioneering missionaries. This was largely a result of Smith's unique circumstances: his political base was centralized and localized. If Smith was going to stand a chance in that fall's election, he and his supporters had to look beyond the conventional.

"WE GO FOR STORMING THE NATION"

Throughout April, May, and June of 1844, the electioneering missionaries departed Nauvoo in droves. They ranged in age from sixteen to sixty-six. Their occupational backgrounds were diverse; so was their place in the Mormon priesthood—the high-ranking apostles served alongside other male church members ordained to the priesthood offices of seventy, elder, priest, teacher, and deacon.[13] Years later, one of the electioneering missionaries, George Miller, recalled that "at no period since the organization of the church had together been half so many elders in the vineyard, in proportion to the number of members of the church."[14]

Enthusiasm radiated from those who accepted the assignment to campaign for their prophet. "All things are going on gloriously at Nauvoo," Brigham Young and his fellow apostle Willard Richards wrote to a church member serving a mission in England, adding that "We have already received several hundred volunteers to go out electioneering and preaching and more offering. We go for storming the nation."[15]

There was no group more optimistic about Joseph Smith's chances to win the presidency than the hundreds of men who electioneered for him. Perhaps living in Nauvoo made many of them unaware of the challenges awaiting them, the hostility or indifference with which most Americans would respond to Smith's candidacy. Alternately, many of them were experienced missionaries who knew the public's general opinion of the Latter-day Saints, but they believed that God approved of their political actions and that they would prosper as a result. In either case, these electioneering missionaries were Smith's political base. They were so committed that they were willing to put their lives on hold for several months to campaign for their prophet.

Many of these groups of departing missionaries channeled their zeal and got to work the moment they left Nauvoo. For example, one group of nearly sixty missionaries boarded a steamboat in Nauvoo and immediately began preaching politics to their fellow passengers. Steaming southward toward St. Louis, apostle Lyman Wight delivered a speech that "produced some sensation among the passengers." Wight's speech was followed by a straw poll "for the different candidates for the next presidency." Unlike the actual presidential election, the women onboard cast votes alongside their male counterparts. Sixty-three men and four women declared their preference for Smith, although this total may have included the approximately sixty missionaries on the steamer. Henry Clay was second, with the votes of twenty-seven men and six women. Van Buren was the choice of thirteen men and two women, Lewis Cass the preference of one man, and the Liberty Party's James Birney the favorite of two.[16]

There were established patterns to Mormon missionary work. Missionaries typically followed the biblical precedent of traveling without "purse or scrip."[17] Often, they worked in pairs. Missions varied in duration—some lasted for years while others lasted mere weeks—and in distance—some missionaries remained in their state of origin while others crossed oceans and international borders. In many cases, missionary assignments brought Mormon men to areas where they had family connections. Indeed, much of the church's early growth occurred through kinship networks. Many of Smith's most trusted associates, including Brigham Young and Willard Richards, only joined the church after other members of their family had done so.[18]

Most of the Mormon electioneering missionaries followed these same patterns—and thus endured the same challenges as more traditional proselytizing missions. Traveling without purse or scrip meant that that after each long day of walking to and speaking at public meetings, the missionaries were dependent on the kindness of strangers to give them room and board. Often, they were denied both. In such instances, the men slept outdoors. "We lay out under a pine tree," Henry G. Boyle recorded in his journal while campaigning in his home state of Virginia, "because no one would keep us over night."[19] Some of the electioneering missionaries were natural campaigners, while others lacked confidence in their ability to preach politics. Yet, church leaders did not seem to mind if some of the missionaries focused on proselytizing instead of campaigning. After all, enlarging Smith's religious support in the United States would simultaneously enlarge his political support.

Several electioneering missionaries focused their efforts on members of their extended families. In many cases their relatives' homes became bases for their electioneering operations. When missionaries Daniel Hunt and Lindsey Brady preached in the home of Hunt's family in Kentucky, they baptized twelve of Hunt's relatives and several others in the community.[20]

Some of this electioneering missionary work looked more like visiting family than public speaking. The lone woman electioneer, Nancy Tracy, accompanied her husband to western New York and apparently joined him in preaching and campaigning to their family. "We ended our visit for this time with my relatives," Tracy wrote, "not forgetting to preach for them the Gospel and give them Joseph's views on the policy of the government."[21]

Yet, in the western United States, finding one's family was sometimes easier said than done. Assigned to campaign for Smith in Maryland, a miner in Nauvoo named Jacob Hamblin determined that he would first visit his family in Wisconsin Territory before heading east, "to see if I could convince my father's folks of the gospel." It was only after making the approximately 350-mile journey that he discovered that his family had moved to Iowa Territory and were living just 30 miles from Nauvoo.[22]

Mormons also canvassed their relatives by mail. For example, Dwight Harding mailed an earnest appeal to his father and other non-Mormon family members in Southbridge, Massachusetts. But his father was un- persuaded. "You wrote to me that you want Calvin Palmer and I and all the rest of your connections should vote for Jo Smith for president of these United States," he replied, noting that he had received the copy of *General Smith's Views* enclosed in that letter. "Dwight, I don't thank you for that the people here aint such fools as to vote Jo Smith for president," he wrote, adding that he did not condemn Mormonism but that he thought they were "in an error."[23] Conversion was off the table, as was voting for the man they viewed as the imposter who had deluded their son.

Even non-Mormons living in Nauvoo described the campaign in let- ters to family members. In a routine letter to friends and family, Nauvoo resident Sally Randall wrote, "Now I want to know what father and the rest of the people thinks of Joseph Smith being president. If they want a righteous man at the head let them vote for him."[24]

Thirty-year-old Daniel H. Wells struck a playful tone when he wrote his staunch Whig family in Oneida County, New York. "We still live and have our being and not having anything very pressing on hand," he quipped, "thought we would bring out a candidate for President as you will see by the papers I send you." He explained that publicizing Smith's candidacy did not mean that they had "anything against our own loved 'Harry of [the] West' but who would live in a city that could not have at least one candidate for President." Wells was a friend to Smith and the Mormons—and eventually joined their church himself. Yet, while he was willing to publicize Smith's presidential ambitions, he still hoped that the Mormons would eventually vote for Henry Clay.[25]

As for the general public, reaction to the electioneering missionaries varied by location. Some missionaries spoke to enthusiastic crowds. In southeastern Pennsylvania a group of these missionaries held a camp meeting "in the woods" that was attended by hundreds of people and lasted for two days.[26] Another campaign camp meeting in Pittsylvania County, Virginia, attracted an audience of more than 500 men and women.[27]

Other missionaries found far less public interest in their political message. After a measure of success in nearby Cincinnati, Amasa Lyman had high hopes for a meeting he scheduled across the river in Newport, Kentucky. His spirits quickly sank, however, when he arrived to find a sparse crowd consisting of "no ladies and some half dozen men and two pigs."[28] Some Americans were interested in Smith's political message, but not Smith himself. "I would just say that the people in Chicago are aroused . . .," read a report to the editors of the *Times and Seasons* in May 1844, adding that "Joseph's views and measures are liked very much, though many are opposed to the man."[29]

Sometimes the electioneering missionaries had to contend with rowdy crowds. Such was the case when Brigham Young and six other apostles attended the Mormons' Massachusetts nominating convention in Boston in July 1844. Delegates and curious onlookers crowded into one of the city's concert halls, The Melodeon, where they were "addressed with much animation and zeal" until "the well dressed rowdies of Boston assembled en masse to 'rout the Mormon humbugs.'" A convention attendee who anonymously reported the experience to a newspaper identified the interlopers as "Whig young gentlemen" and nativists. When the police arrived at the hall to restore order, fighting broke out, and the officers "were assaulted and beaten badly by a set of desperadoes." The police eventually dispersed the crowd, ending the convention for the day. To apostle Wilford Woodruff, the entire event was "a disgrace to Boston" that showed "the spirit of the times."[30]

Still, no one opposed the electioneering missionaries and Smith's candidacy as intensely as anti-Mormons in western Illinois. According to missionary reports, some responded to their campaign with sneers that Smith and the Mormons should not be allowed to vote, let alone run for office.[31] Others threatened violence if it ever appeared that Smith stood a chance to win the presidency. "Joe Smith will never occupy the presidential seat," a man flatly told a seventeen-year-old missionary campaigning near Warsaw, Illinois, "before he gains the election he will be killed."[32]

People living outside Illinois and Missouri could easily dismiss or mock Smith's presidential ambitions. But those Americans who lived closer to his seat of power took the campaign more seriously. To them Smith was a real and proximate threat.

"CALCULATED TO EXCITE DISCONTENT,
INSURRECTION, OR REBELLION"

There was a certain segment of the American population that saw a threat in Smith's campaign that had nothing to do with religion or bloc voting. The threat they saw was to the institution of slavery. Despite Smith's apparent belief that he had found a pragmatic solution to the problem of slavery that would appeal to Northern and Southern states alike, the call for the total and immediate abolition of slavery met a stout wall of resistance.

The clearest example of this occurred in Tennessee. A group of campaign missionaries found some initial success in converting Tennesseans in Dyer County to their religious and political causes. Consequently, one of the missionaries, Abraham Smoot, contracted with a local printer to print 3,000 additional copies of *General Smith's Views* for distribution in the area. Yet, when he returned days later to pick up his order, he was confronted by a local attorney who threatened to prosecute him for violating a state law that prohibited "any publications to be made in this state or circulated there in that was calculated to excite discontent, insurrecttion or rebellion amongst the slaves or free persons of coular [color]."[33]

Just nine days earlier, the same band of electioneering missionaries had faced angry opposition elsewhere in the state. The men had assembled in the Dresden, Tennessee, courthouse to coordinate their campaign efforts in the area when they were interrupted by 150 of the town's residents. The local sheriff "began to hold fourth in frunt of the courthouse in a most abuseave maner," and "commanded his followers to forme around [the missionaries] at each door." The sheriff then assumed a place at the judge's bench. "Fello citizens," he exclaimed, "you see that these men are come amongst us to raise insurrection and pasing abolishaun principles amongst our slaves." The townspeople blocking the exits shouted their agreement with the sheriff, and the electioneering missionaries exited the building "throu the midst of the rable."[34]

The reaction to Smith's candidacy and position on slavery was presumably similar in most Southern states. Whether electioneering missionaries found themselves at risk of legal prosecution for distributing copies of *General Smith's Views* is unclear, largely because there are few surviving records from those assigned to campaign in the Deep South. Ultimately, church leaders dispatched far fewer electioneers to the Southern states, perhaps because they recognized that Smith's position on slavery would be a nonstarter for most Southern voters.[35]

However, in slave states situated along the Mason–Dixon Line, Mormon electioneering missionaries seemed to find pockets of the population more open to Smith's views on slavery. At least, this was the case in Kentucky. "I found my friends willing to listen and conversed on the political situation although I was in a slave state," an electioneering missionary and native Kentuckian, William Watkins, recalled years later. "The question of slavery as advocated in the views of the document I carried found great favor."[36]

Yet, states such as Kentucky were special cases. Their populations were much more divided on the issue of slavery, a division that often depended on geography and terrain and its suitability for planting. Many Kentucky slave holders even prided themselves on what they perceived as the mildness of slavery in their state relative to that of the much larger slaveholdings in states to the south. Yet, the reality was that slave life was not necessarily better in lighter concentrations, as small slaveholdings brought unique suffering to enslaved men, women, and children. Nevertheless, Kentuckians were generally more open to conversations about the abolition of slavery than the white populations of other Southern states. Indeed, during the Civil War that engulfed the country nearly fifteen years later, Kentucky was numbered among the border states, or slave states that did not secede from the Union.[37]

Despite these pockets of support in the South for Smith's plan to abolish slavery, the chances of gaining a sizable political following in the region were slim. While Smith's plan for compensated manumission was a pragmatic attempt at compromise, this mattered little in a political climate where slavery was becoming increasingly central to each successive election cycle. As the country slowly fractured along sectional lines, the appetite for compromise disappeared.

"MANY THINK THIS IS A HOAX"

Smith did not rely on electioneering missionaries alone to spread the news of his presidential campaign. Since the 1790s, newspapers had played a key role in elevating candidates to public office.

The two church-owned newspapers in Nauvoo—the *Times and Seasons* and the *Nauvoo Neighbor*—naturally covered *General Smith's Views* and other aspects of Smith's campaign in an extremely positive manner. The editors of these papers rarely acknowledged any conflict between Smith's position at the head of a rapidly growing church and his ambition to hold the highest elected office in the United States. When they did engage in the controversy over the combination of church and state, they simply wrote off their opponents' misgivings to a misguided understanding of the political nature of Christianity. Such a stance was epitomized in a letter to the editor of the *Times and Seasons* from "A Friend to the Mormons." This anonymous writer insisted that in praying that God's "Kingdom come, thy will be done on earth as it is in heaven," Christians were essentially asking God "to destroy the distinction of Church and State on earth; for that distinction is not recognized in heaven."[38]

Yet, while church-owned newspapers read primarily by church members might have roused Mormons to action in support of their prophet's presidential ambitions, these papers were insufficient to reach non-Mormon voters in the rest of the country. Mormon leaders acknowledged this and informed church members of their responsibility to aid in the church's electioneering efforts. In an editorial that appeared in both the *Times and Seasons* and the *Nauvoo Neighbor*, Mormon apostle John Taylor wrote that "The step we have taken is a bold one, and requires our united efforts, perseverance, and diligence . . . Mr. Smith is not so generally known personally as are several of the above-named candidates, and although he has been much spoken of as man, he has been a great deal calumniated and misrepresented, and his true character is little known." It was therefore up to church members to "take away this false coloring; and by lecturing, by publishing, and circulating his works, his political views, his honor, integrity, and virtue, to stop the foul mouth of slander, and present him before the public in his own colors, that he may be known, respected, and supported."[39] Mormon leaders clearly cared about the public perception of Smith—at least, where their petitioning efforts and his presidential campaign were concerned—and called upon the entire church in the United States to help influence that perception. The country's thousands of newspapers were essential to this effort.

Smith sent his campaign pamphlet to hundreds of newspaper editors throughout the country. He knew that not all of them would like his candidacy or his platform, but surely some positive press would result.

Certainly, Mormon leaders were not so naïve as to think that the country's non-Mormon newspapers would respond to Smith's candidacy as positively as their own publications did. But it is unlikely that they anticipated that so few papers would be willing to seriously consider the planks of Smith's campaign platform on their own merits. Instead, nearly every newspaper that mentioned Smith's presidential bid mocked his political ambitions, or, if they took them seriously, focused almost exclusively on what they perceived to be a dangerous blending of church and state.

As the electioneering missionaries canvassed the country, published responses to *General Smith's Views* began to make their way back to Nauvoo. Several editors reported on Smith's candidacy, but few commented on the merits or faults of his political positions. Instead, most of these newspapers focused on Smith as a leader of a rising religious group that mainline Protestants deemed "fanatical" and on how that ecclesiastical position might influence the way the American public viewed his candidacy. Other newspapers used Smith's campaign as a source of political humor or as a foil to the agenda of their long-standing political or ideological rivals.

On the surface, the press did not take his candidacy seriously. Yet, underlying the mockery in many instances was a sense that Smith and his political ambitions represented a dangerous combination of church and state. Whether viewed by these commentators as a joke, a threat to democracy, or some combination of the two, the country's newspapers did not offer any serious consideration of his unique campaign platform. Instead, they presented Smith as unfit for the presidency and irrelevant to the election.

The jokes at the expense of Smith and his campaign came quickly. On March 2, *Niles' National Register* relayed reports to its readers of "the encroachments and usurpations of Jo Smith, the despotism of the Nauvoo corporation, and the hostilities of the Mormon legion." Then, a few column inches later, the paper announced Smith as a candidate for president and declared: "Stand out of the way—all small fry."[40] On May 23, The *New York Herald* reported that the Mormons "claim possession of from two hundred thousand to five hundred thousand votes in Nauvoo and throughout the Union, and with that calculate that they can hold the balance of power and make whoever they please President." The *Herald* then mockingly advised "the Mormon delegates—if they can't do the business in the ordinary way of private sale—to hold an auction, and let the Mormon vote go to the highest bidder," before adding that "It seems by this movement that Joe Smith does not expect to be elected President, but he still wants to have a finger in the pie, and see whether something can't be made of it."[41]

Other newspapers weaved into their satirical prose serious critiques of the potentially dangerous combination of religious and political power in a single person. Again, such reasoning invoked much of the same rhetoric employed by those who opposed extending religious freedom—and, by extension, full participation in political processes—to American Catholics. The *People's Organ* of St. Louis reported that "Gen. Joseph Smith, priest, prophet, military leader (we had almost said king) among the Mormons, is out as candidate for President of the United States. There is no joke in the matter—Gen. Jo received seven votes for President on board of a steamboat the other day; shouldn't wonder if he beat [John] Tyler."[42] Indeed, while the *People's Organ* jokingly referred to the concentration of Smith's power in Nauvoo as bordering on that of a king, it reflected very real concerns among non-Mormons in Illinois and Missouri over the adverse effects of mixing church and state.

Two East Coast newspapers co-opted Smith and his platform in their own ongoing political endeavors. On May 15, the *Boston Investigator*, a newspaper dedicated to free thought and strongly in favor of the abolition of slavery, complimented Smith on "a plain philosophical discourse, entirely free from cant, and full of the very best advice." The paper briefly listed the main points of *General Smith's Views* before recommending Smith's "opinions on the subject of Abolition" as "worthy of attention. He goes for a liberal and generous policy, and advises Government to use its surplus revenue for the purchase of the freedom of the slaves. He thinks the slaveholders would agree to this, and that no other measure of emancipation is just."[43]

Three days later, the *Working Man's Advocate* of New York City reprinted the *Boston Investigator*'s piece and added its own commentary. The *Working Man's Advocate* had long prioritized the plight of the poor white laborer in the North over that of the captive black slave in the South and accordingly argued that "Gen. Smith's plan of taking the surplus revenue to purchase the freedom of the slaves would never do. Before the Working Men of the North can pay taxes to free the Southern slaves, they must *emancipate* themselves from the dominion of land-*Lords*."[44]

Interestingly, the National Reform Association, the organization that sponsored the *Working Man's Advocate*, had written to Smith a month earlier, asking his opinion on their plan to end the sale of public lands in favor of the free distribution of lots as a means of giving white men a way to work free of wage labor and landlords. Smith had replied that he could support such a proposal, but only after the larger problems of slavery and government excesses had been addressed. In essence, he reversed the National Reform Association's priorities.[45]

The National Reform Association had not received Smith's letter by the time the *Working Man's Advocate* printed its editorial. While neither the *Boston Investigator* nor the *Working Man's Advocate* mocked Smith, they certainly did not depict him as a serious contender for the presidency. Rather, they saw in his independent run for the White House an opportunity to reiterate their own long-held positions.

Of course, there were a few exceptions to the prevailing skepticism of Smith's presidential ambitions and general disregard for his political positions in the non-Mormon press. Notable examples among these rare instances include the report of a correspondent published in the *New-York Tribune* as "Life in Nauvoo." In describing Smith's candidacy for president, the correspondent warned the paper's readers that while "many think this is a hoax—not so with Joe and the Mormons. It is the design of these people to have candidates for electors in every State of the Union; a convention is to be held in Baltimore, probably next month." While he did not state an opinion on Smith's prospects in the presidential race, he did caution readers not to "sneer at [the Mormons], or deem them as of little consequence for good or for evil. They are becoming a potent influence to the people of the State of Illinois."[46]

Whereas the *New-York Tribune* article was relatively neutral, positive press for Smith's campaign came in a letter published in a newspaper in Belleville, Illinois, from one of the town's physicians, Dr. William Goforth. Following an interview with Smith in Nauvoo occasioned by the dedication of the Masonic Hall in that city, Goforth wrote the editor of the *Belleville Advocate*. "The name of Joseph Smith, of Nauvoo, is now before the people as a candidate for President of the United States," Goforth explained. "With this name is proclaimed . . . Jeffersonian Democracy, and free trade and sailors' rights, and the protection of persons and property. The interview on this occasion was satisfactory, & I know not of hearing a sounder policy designed for public inspection and American prosperity."[47] The letter was published on April 18, 1844, a strong endorsement for Smith and his presidential ambitions. While Mormons certainly read Goforth's endorsement with great satisfaction, this and other such endorsements were outliers.[48]

Why would the nineteenth-century print media mock some marginal candidates and completely ignore others? What purposes does comedic criticism of office seekers serve? It appears that the decision of these different newspapers to satirize Smith, or criticize him in a humorous fashion, had deeper ramifications than mere comic relief for a country that was increasingly divided over serious policy issues. In many ways the mockery of Smith's presidential ambitions served to ward off undecided voters, men without strong allegiances to candidates in either of the two major parties who might seriously consider Smith as a viable candidate. Those who already disliked—or at least distrusted—Smith and the Mormons would almost certainly feel validated by such satirical coverage of the Mormon prophet's candidacy. Those already committed to a Whig or Democratic candidate might simply be amused by it. But those who did not harbor anti-Mormon prejudices and did not retain a partisan allegiance might read such newspaper articles as a warning that publicly supporting Smith would draw similar criticism upon themselves.[49] In essence, mocking and satirical coverage of a political candidate such as Smith could reasonably be interpreted as a strategy designed to get potential supporters to dismiss him before ever seriously considering his positions.

Much of the print media's response to Smith and his presidential ambitions also belied deeper political concerns. Ultimately, they were analyzing a marginal candidate who stood virtually no chance of being elected. Indeed, the mockery of Smith's campaign was at times little more than a thin veil designed to cover profound discomfort with the fragile state of democracy in the country and deeply rooted fears that the American political experiment would not survive the challenges coming from Smith and others like him.

"A FAITHFUL ADVOCATE AND DEFENDER OF THE CONSTITUTION"

Smith and the Council of Fifty quickly realized that they could not count on the newspaper media to cover Smith's campaign—at least, not without prompting. During the same April 25 meeting in which the council determined to dispatch electioneering missionaries, Smith's brother, William, "motioned that the Eastern Cities be advised to establish a weekly periodical in each, to advocate the claims of . . . Joseph Smith for the presidential chair." Sidney Rigdon amended the motion to expand its geographic scope by replacing "Eastern Cities" with "every where in the United States." Ultimately, Joseph Smith concluded that the motion should advise Latter-day Saints to establish political newspapers in "all other principle cities in the East, West, North and South and every other place practicable."[50]

The impetus of William Smith's motion in the Council of Fifty was almost certainly a conference of Mormons in New York City earlier that month. William Smith had presided at this meeting on April 2–3, in which those assembled considered the publication of a newspaper in support of Smith and his campaign. The conference approved the plan and appointed a four-person committee to oversee the operation.[51] William Smith returned to Nauvoo, and the committee promptly went to work. Henry J. Doremus, a physician and member of New York City's Mormon congregation, purchased a press and the type. The committee then secured a space for their printing operation on Spruce Street in Lower Manhattan, a street nicknamed "printers row" for the abundance of newspapers produced on it. On May 18, just six weeks after the campaign newspaper was first discussed, the first issue of *The Prophet* came off the press.[52]

The editors wrote in *The Prophet*'s prospectus that the paper was "an advocacy and herald of the Church of Christ of Latter Day Saints." While published content would also include reports on "Agriculture, Commerce, and Manufacture, as well as to the Foreign and Domestic News of the Day," the political goals of the paper were front and center. *The Prophet* would "be a faithful advocate and defender of the Constitution of the United States."[53] Of course, a cursory perusal of the newspaper's columns would reveal to readers that by advocating and defending the Constitution, the paper's editors meant promoting the candidacy and platform of Joseph Smith.

The Prophet was initially edited by committee, but after releasing the first few issues, financial trouble necessitated a change in the newspaper's ownership. New York–based church member Sam Brannan assumed control of the printing operation and its debts. With the help of William

Smith and others, Brannan ensured that the paper's weekly issues continued uninterrupted.[54]

For Brannan, owning and editing *The Prophet* combined his religious devotion with his professional ambitions. In the annals of American history Brannan is best remembered for his role in the California Gold Rush of 1848. Among other things, he was the founder and proprietor of the *California Star*, the first newspaper to publish news of the discovery of gold near Sacramento.[55] However, the path to Brannan's notoriety began with his work as a Mormon printer.

Born in Maine in 1819, a teenaged Brannan had moved to Ohio in 1833 just as the Mormon community in that state was beginning to flourish. He joined the church and, with dreams of spreading important news stories throughout the country as the editor of his own newspaper, started an apprenticeship in the church's printing office in Kirtland, Ohio. During at least part of his apprenticeship, he boarded in Joseph Smith's home.[56] After Smith and many other Mormons left Kirtland in 1838, Brannan traveled the country working as a journeyman printer, eventually moving to New York City.[57] If Brannan had doubted the trajectory of his career during the years between Kirtland and New York, he must have felt reassured to find himself the owner and editor of a newspaper that promoted the presidential candidacy of the man he followed as a prophet. Life seemed to be working out.

Brannan and company filled the columns and pages of *The Prophet* with campaign literature. Much of it originated with Smith in Nauvoo. For instance, they reprinted *General Smith's Appeal to the Green Mountain Boys* and *General Smith's Views*.[58] Political editorials from the Nauvoo newspapers typically appeared in *The Prophet* within a few weeks of their initial publication.[59] Furthermore, *The Prophet* reported on political meetings held throughout the country by Smith's electioneering missionaries and publicized plans for the Mormon state and national nominating conventions.[60] The New York newspaper also provided a forum for countering criticism of Smith's presidential campaign. When eastern newspaper editors mocked or dismissed Smith's candidacy, Brannan and company would quickly respond in print, much faster than their media counterparts in Nauvoo could.

The fourth and subsequent issues of *The Prophet* during the campaign featured a formal endorsement of Smith for president accompanied by a dramatic graphic. Above a stormy sea a burst of light breaks up dark clouds. Imposed on the image is a Latin phrase: "*Error vis veritas frustra*," meaning "O power of truth, frustrate error." A second Latin phrase appeared below the image: "*Super hanc petram aedificabo*," or "I will build upon this rock." This latter phrase alluded to Jesus saying of Peter that "upon this rock I will build my church." Mormons interpreted this phrase to mean the "rock" of revelation. These two phrases invoked the theodemocracy espoused by Smith in his campaign platform. Below all this, in large letters appeared the newspapers official endorsement, "FOR PRESIDENT, GEN. JOSEPH SMITH, OF NAUVOO, ILLINOIS. A Western Man with American Principles."[61]

No reliable estimate of *The Prophet*'s circulation exists. Nevertheless, in nineteenth-century America circulation was only one measure of a newspaper's effectiveness. While selling a large number of copies of a newspaper was vital to attracting advertisers who kept the printing operation solvent, a vast network of newspaper exchanges facilitated the wide transmission of a newspaper's content to a regional or even a national audience. The postal service permitted the mailing of newspapers without paid postage. Accordingly, American newspaper editors freely exchanged issues of their respective publications. At this time, a typical issue of any American newspaper would contain multiple articles reprinted from other papers.[62]

For an upstart publication such as *The Prophet*, the newspaper exchange network was essential to its mission. While the number of men and women who subscribed to the paper or paid three cents per issue may initially have been low, this would not have prevented the paper's campaign content from getting in front of American readers. The New York City Mormons who founded *The Prophet* almost certainly considered the newspaper exchange as a vital piece of their publishing strategy. After all, printing a campaign newspaper in the largest city in the United States represented an improvement on the time it took Nauvoo newspapers to reach the east coast through the postal service.

Beyond the benefits of communicating Smith's political views to a wider public and circulating tales of the repeated injuries he and his followers had sustained, *The Prophet* appears to have been an effort to add legitimacy to the efforts of the electioneering missionaries in and around New York City. Ultimately, *The Prophet* was the only campaign newspaper the Mormons established outside of Illinois. Still, the establishment of *The*

Prophet in the months after Smith announced his candidacy demonstrates the zeal and efficiency with which his supporters worked.

Indeed, while to the casual observer the initial electioneering of Smith's army of missionaries may have seemed haphazard, there was order in the chaos. The missionaries would drum up as much support as they could ahead of a nominating convention in each of the states. At those conventions, electors would be designated and delegates chosen to travel to Baltimore to participate in the Mormons' national nominating convention. Though they were running a campaign from outside the established two-party system, the Mormons were following the method of organization and mobilization that had served the Whigs and the Democrats well over the previous decade.

In late April, church leaders in Nauvoo had determined that "the State convention" for selecting electors and delegates from Illinois, "be held in the City of Nauvoo" the following month.[63] It was certain to be the largest of all the state conventions, and possibly the largest gathering of supports of Smith's presidential ambitions ahead of the July meeting in Baltimore. But there were pressing matters to attend to first if these conventions were to succeed. Most notably, Smith and his fellow church leaders needed to select a running mate.

10

······

VICE PRESIDENTS AND
PROTEST CANDIDATES

JUST DAYS BEFORE THE FORMATION OF THE Council of Fifty in March 1844, Smith and his fellow church leaders had turned their attention to selecting a vice-presidential candidate. While the Whigs and the Democrats used their national nominating conventions to make such selections, Smith and company determined that they would need to select a willing candidate prior to their summer meeting in Baltimore.[1]

A lot seemed to ride on the vice-presidential selection. The right choice could add instant legitimacy to the campaign. However, like other candidates who ran outside the established two-party system, Smith would discover that convincing someone to run on an independent ticket was a difficult task. Smith was accustomed to dealing with prejudice against religious minority groups. Now he was set to encounter the prejudice many in the American electorate held against third-party candidates.

"A WILD GOOSE CHASE"

By early March, Smith had determined to invite James Arlington Bennet to join him on the Mormon ticket.[2] Born and raised in New York, Bennet was an attorney, publisher, and educator. A veteran of the War of 1812, in 1824 he published *The American System of Practical Book-Keeping*, the country's most popular reference book on accounting for businessmen and other individuals. In 1832 he became the owner and printer of the *Brooklyn Advocate and Nassau Gazette*, but even as that paper folded in 1836, thousands of Americans continued to purchase copies of his book. By 1844, it was in its twenty-second edition. Eventually, Bennet opened an educational institution on Long Island.[3]

James Arlington Bennet's formal connection to the Mormons had started with John C. Bennett (different spelling and hence no relation). In an effort to bolster the reputation of Smith and the church, John C. Bennett had written to respectable men in the eastern United States who had written or published favorable things about the Mormons in the country's newspapers, or who he believed would look favorably upon the church. This group included James Arlington Bennet. Perhaps to thank them for their support and likely to secure more of it in the future, John C. Bennett offered several of these men officer positions in the Nauvoo Legion. In practice, these commissions were mostly honorary, but they were gestures of goodwill. So, having never set foot in Nauvoo and having never met Joseph Smith, in 1842 James Arlington Bennet became the inspector general of the city's militia.[4]

Following John C. Bennett's fall from power in Nauvoo, James Arlington Bennet remained a supporter of Smith and company, albeit from the other side of the country. Amid the various attempts to extradite Smith to Missouri in 1842, the two men corresponded.[5] In 1843, Brigham Young baptized Bennet near his home on Long Island, but Bennet never actively participated in the church.[6]

Bennet's sympathy for Smith and the Latter-day Saints appears to have been genuine, but his affiliation with the group seems to have been more strategic than faith driven—guided by a desire to advance his own public station. Following his baptism, Bennet had written to Smith, inquiring about the possibility of moving to Illinois with the goal of using the Mormons' political support to become the state's governor.[7] However, Smith saw something grander in Bennet's political future. He wanted the man who was respected in New York society and unafraid to publicly defend the Mormons to join him in his quest for the American presidency.[8]

Smith's clerk, Willard Richards, had spent time with Bennet in New York in 1842, and the two men had maintained a friendly correspondence ever since.[9] Accordingly, Smith assigned Richards to write to Bennet. In a March 4 letter, Richards explained the events that had brought about Smith's candidacy and that church leaders were "astonished at the flood of Influence, that is roling through the western states in his favor and in many instances who we might have least expected it." Richards then extended the invitation. "Gen. Smith says if he must be president Jas [James] Arlington Bennet must be vice President," he wrote. "You will receive our undivided support, and we expect the same in return for Gen. Smith for the presidency." Richards urged Bennet to "get up an electoral ticket [in] New York, New Jersey, Pennsylvania, and any other state within your reach. Open your mouth wide, and God shall fill it. Cut your quill & the ink shall flow freely."[10]

Bennet was respectful, but blunt, in his reply. "If you can by any Supernatural means Elect Brother Joseph President of these [United] States," he wrote to Richards, "I have not a doubt that he would govern the people and administer the laws in good faith, and with righteous intentions, but I can see no Natural means by which he has the slightest chance of receiving the votes of even one state." Considering the other possible reasons for the campaign beyond winning the presidency, Bennet continued: "If the object of [Smith's] friends be to aid the Cause of Mormonism in foreign lands, or in this Country among a certain class of persons . . . then I think they are somewhat in the right track, but if they are aiming in reality at that high office then I must say that at present they, in my opinion, are on a wild goose chase."[11] From Bennet's vantage point, the campaign could be good for the Mormons' public relations, but electoral success would require divine intervention.

Richards certainly recognized that Smith's presidential campaign could, indeed, produce better public relations, but he would not dismiss the possibility of electoral success. "Your views about the nomination of Gen. Smith for the presidency are correct," Richards replied. "We will gain popularity and extend influence, but this is not all, we mean to elect him, and nothing shall be wanting on our part to accomplish it."[12] Richards's insistence that "nothing would be wanting" on the Mormons' part to elect Smith suggests that although they were mounting a national electoral effort, a victory of the Mormon prophet might require help from an outside—even a divine—source. Yet, whereas Bennet referenced divine assistance as a way of trying to dissuade Smith from pursuing the presidency, Richards implied such supernatural intervention as a part of Smith's electoral strategy.

"WE MEAN TO ELECT HIM"

James Arlington Bennet's response to the invitation to run on Smith's ticket raises some fundamental questions about Smith's campaign. Was he serious about his presidential ambitions, or was he merely a protest candidate running to raise awareness of the Mormons' plight? Did Smith and his fellow Church leaders believe that he could actually win the election? If they did, how confident were they that the campaign strategy they had devised would carry Smith into the White House?[13]

The minutes of the Council of the Fifty reveal that Smith was more than a protest candidate—that is, he and other Mormon leaders viewed an electoral triumph as possible, even if unlikely. This belief is most apparent in the council's insistence that they hold conventions in every state to select electors. Indeed, various men and women have campaigned for the presidency without any expectation of winning—or even desire to win—but, rather, to raise awareness for the issues that mattered most to them and their followers. In Smith's case, his presidential ambitions could bring the plight of the Mormons—first in Missouri and then in Illinois—to the attention of the American public, as well as to savvy politicians who recognized the potential electoral boost they might receive as a result of supporting the Mormons' petitioning efforts with state and federal governments. However, if the Church was promoting Smith's candidacy simply to raise public awareness for the plight of its members, then electors were superfluous.

While it was common in the earliest American presidential elections for the legislatures of many states—and not the people—to select the men who eventually cast their votes in the Electoral College, by the 1840s only South Carolina still used this method to select its electors. The rest of the states had moved to a system in which the winner of the state's popular vote received the support of all of the electors allotted to it.[14] This meant that the selection of electors was a technical aspect in a strategy to actually elect someone president, an aspect that had little significance in a campaign focused solely on building public support for a cause. By designating a slate of electors in each state, Church leaders created an electoral infrastructure designed to convert popular support into the votes that could actually carry a person to the presidency. Of course, without popular support, that infrastructure would be useless.

The Council of Fifty's emphasis on securing electors in each state illuminates the way the council viewed the presidential campaign. To council members, Smith was not merely a protest candidate. They apparently thought that he could win but seemed to have believed that such a victory would require divine intervention. They made the necessary technical arrangements to facilitate his election should large numbers of Americans in each state cast their votes for him. After all, no amount of popular votes could make Smith president without the requisite number of electoral votes.

That Mormon leaders believed Smith *could* win the presidency did not necessarily mean that they believed he *would* win. It was merely one possible avenue through which they believed divine providence could work to restore the United States to its privileged place in God's grand plan for the world and to help the Saints reclaim their promised land of Zion. Despite Richards's insistence to James Arlington Bennet that the reason Church leaders were promoting Smith's candidacy for president was "because we are satisfied . . . that this is the best or only method of saving our free institutions from total overthrow," the Council of Fifty was simultaneously exploring several avenues that might eventually lead them to the peace and prosperity they sought.[15] Each was an unlikely solution, but if Congress made Smith a general in the United States Army, or if it granted Nauvoo territorial status, or if it designated a large tract of land in the western territories for Mormon settlement, then Smith's presidential campaign would become superfluous. Indeed, Smith's election or any of these other plans would have provided substantial relief to the Mormons amid the growing hostility they felt from their fellow citizens in Illinois.

Joseph Smith was not merely a protest candidate campaigning for the sole purpose of raising awareness of the poor treatment of the Mormons in a country that claimed to value religious freedom. The intent of the Council of Fifty was to "leave nothing wanting" on its part where the election was concerned, even as council members simultaneously planned for other contingencies, working out an array of potential paths to the building up of the kingdom of God on earth, a kingdom that they believed they were destined to lead.

"VOTE AS YOU PRAY"

Joseph Smith was not the only third-party candidate in the presidential race. James G. Birney of the Liberty Party had also thrown his hat into the ring. After a poor showing in the presidential election of 1840, Birney, like Smith, was eager to shed the label of protest candidate and elicit more serious attention from the American public.

Birney was born and raised in Danville, Kentucky. Ambitious for wealth and prestige, it is unsurprising that he became close friends with and political ally to his fellow Kentuckian, Henry Clay. Birney had supported Clay's campaign for the United States Congress in 1810 before successfully seeking a seat for himself in the Kentucky House of Representatives. Still, Birney's quest for increased wealth forced him to look beyond the borders of the Bluegrass State. In 1818 he moved further south and established a cotton plantation in Alabama. Within a year, he was elected to his new state's House of Representatives.[16]

The cotton industry was not kind to Birney, and he compounded his problems by squandering much of his fortune betting on horse races. To avoid financial ruin, he sold his plantation—and all its slaves—in 1823 and moved to Huntsville, Alabama, to set up shop as a lawyer. During this period of professional transition, he became a devout Presbyterian. His newfound faith not only helped him drop his gambling habits but also convinced him of the immorality of slavery.[17]

In 1829 Birney joined the American Colonization Society (ACS). Founded in 1816, the ACS was controversial. Members of the ACS opposed slavery but did not support racial equality. The society maintained that free blacks were unfit for white American society, that they were "unfavorable" to its "industry and morals." Accordingly, the society worked for the gradual emancipation of slaves and their recolonization in Africa. In 1821 the ACS established Liberia on the west coast of Africa, a colony eventually governed entirely by former American slaves. Of course, after centuries of race-based slavery in North America, most of the country's slaves had never set foot on the African continent. The United States was their home—the only land they had ever known. Nevertheless, members of the ACS saw their work as benevolent and designed for the benefit of the entire country.[18]

With a convert's zeal, Birney set off on a tour of the South in 1832 as an agent of the ACS. His goal was to help convince his fellow Southerners to emancipate their slaves and to promote colonization as a way to maintain the hegemony of white Americans in the aftermath. Some listened attentively to Birney's message, but most did not. Deflated and discouraged, he returned to Alabama doubting the viability of colonization as a vehicle for the abolition of slavery.[19]

By 1834 Birney had abandoned his faith in the ACS and its goal of gradual emancipation and replaced it with the more radical politics of immediate emancipation. In 1835 he moved to Cincinnati and commenced work as the editor of a weekly abolitionist newspaper he titled *The Philanthropist*. Through his newspaper, Birney honed his voice as an abolitionist and gained national attention for his efforts. In 1837 he moved with his family to New York, where he assumed a position as an officer in the American Anti-Slavery Society.[20]

Despite the growth in the number of Americans who supported abolition during the first half of the nineteenth century, it was not a cohesive movement. Members of the ACS, including its president from 1836 to 1849, Henry Clay, continued to argue that the best approach to the problem of slavery was gradual emancipation and colonization. Others, such as Birney and famed abolitionist William Lloyd Garrison, were adamant that immediate abolition was the only way to rid the country of slavery. Yet, even the immediate abolitionists were a fractured lot. They disagreed on whether their movement for the liberation of Black slaves should expand to include the advocacy for equal rights for women. They also disagreed on the arenas best suited for their fight against the slave power: whether they should focus their efforts on winning over public sentiment and petitioning state governments or electing devoted abolitionists to national office.[21]

In 1840, one faction of immediate abolitionists established the Liberty Party. A single-issue party, its slogan urged Americans to "vote as you pray."[22] With only the barest of party structures, it nominated Birney as its candidate for president in that year's election and attempted to rally as many abolitionists as it could to support the ticket.[23]

Birney epitomized the presidential protest candidate in 1840. He accepted the party's nomination but paid little attention to the campaign. Instead, he spent most of the summer in England, where he attended the World Anti-Slavery Convention. When the ballots were tallied that fall, Birney and the Liberty Party finished with 6,797 votes, a meager 0.28% of the popular vote. Perhaps the campaign had raised awareness of abolition throughout the United States, but it had virtually no impact on the election itself.[24]

When the Liberty Party selected Birney as its presidential candidate again in 1844, Birney approached the election with considerably more purpose. Through his own writings and the electioneering of his campaign surrogates, he aimed to disrupt the campaigns of the Whigs and Democrats. Slavery was a polarizing topic in each party, one that would eventually divide the partisan system along sectional lines. More than just raising awareness of slavery and getting devoted abolitionists elected in state and local elections, Birney and the Liberty Party would try to force either party to take a firmer stance by threatening to draw away enough of their abolitionist members to sway the election. Birney did not expect victory in 1844 any more than he had in 1840. But this second presidential run was about more than raising national awareness of the abolitionist movement. If he demonstrated enough electoral clout, he could force his abolitionist policies into the platform of a major party. As historian Reinhard O. Johnson explains, "Between 1840 and 1844, the Liberty Party made the transition from protest group to a genuine political party.[25]

For as much as the Liberty Party was focused on abolition, Birney expressed a desire that his candidacy promote the fair treatment of an assortment of other minority groups in the United States. He acknowledged that the country's democratic system was imperfect and left several groups vulnerable to mob violence, including Native Americans, free people of color, and Mormons. Through electoral means, he hoped to empower the federal government to correct the flaws in its political system to protect such groups.[26]

Despite Joseph Smith's earlier quest to find a presidential candidate who would pledge federal protection for the Mormons and their rights, there is no indication that he took much—if any—notice of Birney and his campaign. Perhaps Smith was unaware of Birney's anti-mobbing comments and his recognition of the injustice done to Mormons. Maybe he knew about those comments but was too turned off by the extreme abolitionist positions of the Liberty Party to get on board with its candidate. Or, Smith might have recognized that as an independent candidate for president, he needed to focus his attention on the positions and candidates of the two major political parties. Whatever the reason, Smith and Birney ran virtually parallel campaigns. Each supported the abolition of slavery—albeit with very different approaches—as well as the federal protection of minority groups against mobbing. Yet, each ran with virtually no recognition of the other, as if he were the obvious and only antiestablishment choice.

Still, Birney's campaign caused more consternation among the established political parties than Smith's did. Abolitionists belonged to both the Whig and Democratic parties, but the majority of those who broke away and joined the Liberty Party were Northern Whigs. Accordingly, critics of Birney and company argued that the third-party campaign would fail in its objective and, even worse, harm the larger cause of antislavery should the Democrats rally around a proslavery candidate from the South. To this end, the editors of one New York abolitionist newspaper wrote: "Let it be understood, that every abolitionist who, by refusing to vote as a Whig . . . does, in effect, vote for the maintenance of slavery."[27]

Such criticism of Birney and the Liberty Party showcases the continuing struggle of third-party candidates in American politics. Supporters of such candidates claim a certain moral superiority over those in the electoral mainstream, celebrating their uncompromising devotion to a set of values. Yet, many of their countrymen are quick to point out that the statistical improbability of a third-party candidate winning the presidency only weakens the party that, while willing to compromise on that set of values, is the best chance to stop the party that opposes those values outright. From the perspective of early third-party candidates Joseph Smith and James G. Birney, the systemic injustice of American democracy was upheld in part by the hegemony of a two-party electoral system.

"THE GREAT GLOBE ITSELF"

Amid the search for a vice-presidential running mate came the most significant attention that any newspaper paid to Smith's campaign. It arrived in the form of a caustic editorial titled "A New Advocate for a National Bank" from Washington's *The Daily Globe*. The paper's editor, Francis Blair, wielded considerable influence in political circles and could be ruthless in his published commentary. "We have cast our eyes hastily over General Smith's (Mormon Joe) 'Views of the Powers and Policy of the Government of the United States, Nauvoo, 1844,'" Blair wrote and, after quoting the passage from Smith's pamphlet that favored the reinstitution of a national bank, stated that "The prophet seems to be thoroughly imbued with the whig financial doctrines." In discussing the banking policy that Smith set forth in his pamphlet, they observed that "he sticks to the specie basis, dollar for dollar" and paired the position with Smith's plan for criminal justice reform—that each state "pardon every convict in their several penitentiaries"—in order to bring up the alleged corruption of the officers of the Second Bank of the United States. "We fear that [Smith's] humane recommendation be adopted, the 'specie basis' would soon disappear from Joe's mother bank and branches," the editors declared. "Perhaps, however, we are unnecessarily apprehensive of the small thieves, who fall into the clutches of the law, since the great thieves, who robbed millions from the late whig bank and its satellites, are permitted to roam at large with perfect impunity."[28]

The tone of the editorial grew even more biting in its concluding paragraphs. "Joseph is unquestionably a great scholar as well as financier," the editors wrote, "Cannot Mr. Clay persuade *the General* to accompany him on his electioneering tour?" Ultimately, the paper's satirical proposal to its readers was "that Joe Smith . . . be made president, and George Poindexter cashier, of the new whig national bank that is not to be; that the mother bank be established at Nauvoo, with branches over all creation."[29] One of the most extensive and high-profile considerations of the campaign positions set forth in *General Smith's Views*, the editorial in *The Daily Globe* was also one of the most mocking.

Smith rarely wrote to newspaper editors who criticized him. However, for Blair and *The Globe* he made an exception. He did not respond to Blair's mockery of his proposal for a new national bank with an explanation of its technical financial merits. Instead, he portrayed the decades-long bank controversy as a solely partisan contest, a battle fought by the country's elite as political "sport . . . to boost a few hungry, crafty hypocritical demagogues into office to gamble for the 'loaves and fishes'—no matter whether the game is played 'upon the tables of the living or the coffins of the dead.'" Smith was implying that a national bank was necessary for millions of average Americans suffering from the instability of the economy, but only if it was run with the relief of such people—rather than the calculated ambitions of politicians—in mind.[30]

Smith next defended his call for prison reform. "Heaven, Earth, and Hell know that the penitentiaries of the several States are a disgrace to the United States, and a stink in the nostrils of the Almighty," he wrote, adding that "the County and City Prisons are still worse." Smith was equally adamant that the justice system that condemned men and women to prison in the first place also needed an overhaul. "In ninety and nine cases out of a hundred," Smith declared, "the prisoners are treated meaner than dogs; half starved to put money into the pockets of speculators; fed upon unwholesome provisions; whipt without mercy, and even murdered with impunity." He cited examples from prisons in Auburn, New York, Alton, Illinois, and New Orleans, Louisiana, before alluding to his own mistreatment while incarcerated in Missouri. "The voice of reason," Smith pled, "now cries from the vast number of prisons and the multiplying number of Prisoners in the United States, for relief."[31]

In closing his letter, Smith repeated his familiar refrain that the United States was failing to live up to its boasts as a "Land of 'Liberty,'" dedicated to preserving the unalienable rights of its citizens. He wanted Blair and *The Globe*'s readers to consider how the oppression of minority groups appeared on the international stage. "O, Queen Victoria, and ye Lords and Commons of Great Britain," Smith asked rhetorically, "what think ye of a Republican Government?" Smith answered for them: "Your coffers are robbed with impunity; your Citizens are mobbed, and driven like chaff from the threshing floor, and the government, controlled by a set of money gambling, chicken hearted, public fed cowards, cannot redress you." He posed the same rhetorical question to "the reigning sovereigns of Europe, Africa and Asia." Again, Smith provided the answer. The world leaders would "laugh . . . and taunt the United States, by exclaiming . . . If there is any power in Republican Government, in a real case of necessity, you have failed to find just men to exercise it."[32]

All this rhetoric directed readers to the heart of Smith's campaign platform. The United States was not living up to its promise of liberty and justice. Nauvoo, like the metaphorical "city on a hill," pointed the way forward. Smith promised to return virtue and righteousness to American democracy. He would right the ship in a way that even "the 'great Globe' itself" would eventually celebrate.[33]

Smith published his response to *The Globe* in the April 15 issue of the *Times and Seasons*. However, in the days immediately following its publication he determined to send it directly to Blair, as well. Accordingly, he sent a copy of the response to John J. Hardin, who was in Washington representing Illinois in the House of Representatives. Smith asked Hardin "to solicit the Globe" to publish his reply, with the instructions that if

Blair refused, he should "try the National Intelligencer." Hardin obliged the first request, but to no avail.[34]

For Smith and the Mormons is Nauvoo, the scant and often negative news coverage continued to be disappointing, but it did not dampen their electoral hopes.

"THE NATION COULD NOT BE VEXED WORSE"

Bennet had not formally declined the vice-presidential slot on Joseph Smith's ticket. Even though the doubt he cast on the entire electoral enterprise signaled his lack of interest, it was church leaders who ultimately withdrew the invitation. In researching Bennet, they had arrived at the mistaken conclusion that he was foreign born and therefore ineligible for the office of vice president. As Bennet later explained, he had promoted false rumors of his Irish birth years earlier to help him secure a British copyright for his accounting book. He was, in fact, born in the United States. Nevertheless, by March 21, Smith and the Council of Fifty had started to look elsewhere.[35]

Solomon Copeland was the next man they tapped for the position. The forty-five-year-old from Henry County, Tennessee, was hardly a household name in his home state, let alone in the rest of the country. In 1843 he concluded his first and only term in the Tennessee General Assembly. The appeal of Copeland seems to originate with the kindness he had exhibited to Mormon missionaries in Tennessee during the 1830s and his subsequent friendship with Mormon apostle and Council of Fifty member Wilford Woodruff. Copeland's wife, Sarah, had even joined the church.

Still, Copeland was an odd choice. Perhaps the fact that he hailed from a Southern state was attractive to Smith as he worked to build national support—and to secure votes from the South.[36] Yet, the Copelands owned slaves, two of whom had joined the church about the same time as Sarah Copeland.[37] Certainly, Smith's call for the end of slavery and the inclusion of a slaveholder on his presidential ticket would have presented voters with a glaring contradiction. If Smith recognized this, it is entirely unclear how he reconciled the invitation of Copeland with his political position.

Writing on March 19, 1844, Woodruff recounted to Copeland his fond memories of their time together in Tennessee, during which the latter had proven himself "a gentleman, friend & republican" when Woodruff had been "a stranger in a strange land." After describing to his friend the ongoing persecution experienced by the Mormons, Woodruff summarized the religious community's new electoral strategy. "We deem it no longer necessary," he wrote, "to put to use our influence in promoting men to the highest office of this government who will not act for the good of the people but for their own aggrandizement & party purposes." Consequently, Woodruff explained, "We as a people have come to the conclusion to run a candidate for president of the United States in the next Election And that candidate is <u>General Joseph Smith</u>."[38]

Then came the invitation. "The request I wish to make of you is to know if you are willing to permit us to use <u>your name</u> as a <u>candidate for vice president</u> at the next Election." Woodruff also hoped that Copeland would favor him "with a visit at Nauvoo." He enclosed a copy of *General Smith's Views* for Copeland to read as he contemplated the choice before him. Woodruff read the letter to Smith the next day before mailing it.[39]

There was plenty to occupy Smith and Woodruff as they waited for Copeland's reply. However, that reply never came. Whatever thoughts and opinions Copeland may have had upon receiving the Mormons' unexpected invitation, he did not commit them to writing. Perhaps he was flattered by the invitation. Perhaps the letter confused him. He had been kind to the Mormons because he believed in protecting their rights. Still, he must have doubted the Mormons' opinion that he would make a good vice-presidential candidate.

When nearly two months passed without word from Copeland—and the Illinois state nominating convention just eleven days away—Smith could wait no longer. At a May 6 meeting of the Council of Fifty, Smith announced that he wanted his counselor in the First Presidency, Sidney Rigdon, "to go to Pennsylvania and run for vice President." Though Rigdon resided in Nauvoo, Smith instructed him to "become a resident of Pennsylvania," his native state, for the sake of the election. The move was a way of circumventing the provision in the Constitution that prohibits electors from voting for a president and vice president from the same state.[40]

Smith had known Rigdon for over a decade. Rigdon had been a Baptist minister before he converted to Mormonism. He had been influential in the church from that point on, becoming one of Smith's counselors in the church's First Presidency. But amid the John C. Bennett scandal in

1842, their relationship soured. Smith had allegedly (and unsuccessfully) proposed a plural marriage to Rigdon's daughter, Nancy. Furthermore, Smith suspected Rigdon of being in cahoots with Bennett during the latter's anti-Mormon lecture tour and accused Rigdon of working against him inside Nauvoo as the city's postmaster. There were moments of public reconciliation in the ensuing months, but some degree of distrust appears to have remained.[41]

The two men's hard feelings for one another apparently set aside, at least for this moment, Rigdon accepted Smith's invitation and asked that "after Joseph had been President [four] years, that he should be president the next term." Council member Lyman Wight recalled the revelation in which "the Lord promised to vex the nations" and seemed to joke that from the perspective of the church's enemies in the United States, "the nation could not be vexed worse than for Joseph to be president and brother Rigdon vice president."[42]

The Mormons finally had a presidential ticket, with just two weeks to spare before they held their Illinois state nominating convention in Nauvoo. Within a week the news was publicized to the country, starting with the newspapers in Nauvoo.[43]

11

· · · · · ·

CONVENTION SEASON

WHILE JOSEPH SMITH AND THE COUNCIL OF Fifty were on the verge of finalizing their vice-presidential nomination, the Whig party descended on Baltimore for its nominating convention. The city of more than 100,000 people was filled to the brim as the 275 Whig delegates were joined by throngs of other interested individuals in the scramble to secure lodging.[1] The city—and the rest of the country—waited eagerly for the convention to attend to its business. The first major party nomination would signal that the months of political speculation were finally becoming a full-fledged presidential race.

"VOCIFERATIONS IN FAVOR OF THE NOMINATION OF HENRY CLAY"

The 1844 Whig nominating convention carried little suspense. Ever since the expulsion of President Tyler from the party in September 1841, Henry Clay had been the party's presumptive nominee. American newspapers of the time commonly printed their preference for presidency on the first or second page of each issue during the months preceding an election.

Many Whig newspapers had started promoting Clay's candidacy as early as January 1842.[2]

The near certainty of Clay's nomination filled the air in the Calvert Street Universalist Church on the morning of May 1, as the delegates from the various states poured into the cramped space. The delegates waited impatiently as routine business was conducted before they came to the reason they were there. A delegate from Virginia finally took the floor and stated that the formal process for selecting the party's nominee by delegate ballots was excessive. He moved "that the convention do unanimously nominate and recommend to the People of the United States, HENRY CLAY, of Kentucky for the next President of the United States."[3]

Springing to their feet, the delegates cheered wildly. They tossed their hats into the air and waved their handkerchiefs above their heads in an animated sign of approval. Order was eventually restored to the convention, just long enough for a voice vote nominating Clay by acclamation. The convention once again erupted in cheers.[4]

Clay was not present at the convention. Instead, he was in Washington, D.C., maintaining the facade of the disinterested candidate, who would serve out of a sense of duty to the public that called upon him to do so.

The convention then turned its attention to the adoption of a party platform. In a short, 100-word paragraph, the delegates set forth a list of their legislative priorities that was entirely in line with the party's long-standing positions. They wanted a stable and well-regulated national currency, a tariff to protect American industry and to fund federal public works initiatives, a weaker executive branch (including a limit of one term for the president), and "the distribution of the proceeds of the sales of the public lands." Noticeably absent from the formal platform were the issues almost certain to divide the party on regional and ideological lines: the annexation of Texas and the abolition of slavery.[5]

Clay had been careful on the Texas question. For months he avoided the topic altogether. Then, in April 1844, Clay wrote a letter from Raleigh, North Carolina, in which he presented a convoluted position on Texas. He was open to the annexation of Texas, but only if it could be accomplished "without the loss of national character, without the hazard of foreign war, with the general concurrence of the nation, without any danger to the integrity of the Union, and without giving any unreasonable price for Texas. It appears to have been a purely political move. To Whigs in favor of annexation, he demonstrated that he was willing to consider the action. To the abolitionist wing of the Whig Party, the letter listed so many conditions unlikely to be met that they could rest assured that the annexation of Texas—and the expansion of slavery—would remain a remote possibility under a Clay presidency. The letter was published in the *National Intelligencer* on April 27. The middling position seemed enough for Clay—and for the party that nominated him, too.[6]

Whereas there was no suspense in Clay's nomination, the vote for the party's vice-presidential nominee was not predetermined. The clear frontrunner was Theodore Frelinghuysen of New Jersey, but there was enough support for Millard Fillmore of New York, John Davis of Massachusetts, and John Sergeant of Pennsylvania to keep the contest somewhat interesting. Frelinghuysen carried the day on the third ballot, and the Whig presidential ticket was set.[7]

Frelinghuysen was an advantageous choice for a number of reasons. He was a former United States senator from one of New Jersey's most prominent political families. A descendant of famed colonial revivalist preacher Theodorus Frelinghuysen, he was known as a devoutly religious man whose Protestant beliefs drove him to champion several reform movements; he was active in the American Bible Society, the American Temperance Union, and on the American Board of Commissioners for Foreign Missions.[8] These organizational ties bolstered his religious credentials in a party that Clay had built, in part, by co-opting evangelical Protestants who opposed certain policies of Andrew Jackson on religious grounds. To the vocal evangelical wing of the Whig party, Frelinghuysen was a boon to the ticket, and a reason to enthusiastically support the party in the months leading up to the November election. As one Whig editorial stated in celebration, "the name THEODORE signified 'THE GIFT OF GOD!' "[9]

Yet, Frelinghuysen's religious and organizational affiliations were also a political liability, although the Whigs do not appear to have acknowledged this fact at the time of the convention. A number of the reform organizations to which Frelinghuysen belonged were deeply Protestant and to varying degrees anti-Catholic, and there were now more Catholic voters than ever before. Particularly in the Northern states where a majority of recent Irish immigrants were settling, these newly minted Americans were acutely aware of the suspicion with which they were viewed by many of their new Protestant neighbors. The prospect of a government that shared these views suggested a systemization of the prejudice and discrimination that they would experience in their new country.

It is unclear whether Frelinghuysen himself shared these views, but his association with organizations that did was enough to generate concern. As writer John Bicknell observes, "Even if they accepted that Frelinghuysen was not personally bigoted, his close ties to some who were—and his participation in organizations that were honey-combed with anti-Catholic sentiment—made him an easy target, one the Democrats would make full use of in the fall campaign."[10]

If any of the devout Protestants in the Whig party recognized Frelinghuysen's proximity to anti-Catholicism, they may have even viewed it as desirable as the country experienced a major demographic shift. Starting in 1829, amid a rapid influx of Catholics from Ireland and the corresponding opposition that arose from nativists, Martin Van Buren found himself as the linchpin of several conspiracy theories. In his capacity as Secretary of State, he had written to Vatican City to assure church officials that Catholics were free to worship in the United States. In the years that followed, and particularly during the election of 1836, the Whigs seized on this letter to accuse Van Buren of being complicit in a Roman Catholic conspiracy to overthrow American democracy.[11]

This was an old trope descended from the political discourse of post-Reformation England. Even the Enlightenment philosopher John Locke, who was quite radical for his time in his calls to expand the scope of religious toleration in England, insisted that such tolerance should not extend to Catholics because they "pass into the allegiance and service of another prince."[12] In essence, Locke believed that the participation of Catholics in government and political processes was dangerous because their loyalty to the Pope prohibited them from ever being entirely loyal to the state. This simplistic depiction of Catholics' religious devotion was incorporated into the so-called civil religion of the United States, providing a ready-made justification for those who wished to exclude Catholics from American politics. Simply put, according to such logic, Catholics were a threat to democracy.

Indeed, even the persecuted supporters of Joseph Smith were not immune to anti-Catholicism. Despite the fact the Smith had enshrined universal religious freedom at the heart of his campaign platform, at least one of his supporters either rejected Smith's stance or ignorantly partook of the Whigs' talking points. In a letter to the editor of the *Nauvoo Neighbor*, this unique supporter wrote that "Van Buren had associated himself with Catholic usurpers, that he might gain their votes." Implying that this was an unforgivable sin in America's worship of democratic principles, the writer added: "I therefore declare, that I consider him an 'apostate, [who] has denied the faith.' "[13]

The anti-Catholicism of many Protestant Whigs—and the evangelicals within that group, in particular—illuminates an important pattern in the religious history of the United States. While conversations about religious intolerance in the present-day United States have long been framed as secular versus religious, the country's history reveals systems of religious discrimination designed, installed, and maintained by members of religious majorities. In the cases of the Catholics—and the Mormons—in nineteenth-century America, the discrimination and violent persecution they experienced was often condoned, and at other times instigated, by Christians who deemed the groups too different from mainline Protestantism—too fanatical—to deserve their constitutionally protected rights of conscience. To many Americans in this religious majority, defending religious freedom meant defending their own rights to worship—freedom for certain types of Protestants, but certainly not for all Americans.

Nevertheless, the potential problems of Frelinghuysen's religious affiliations remained unstated in Baltimore as the Whig delegates completed the work of their convention in a single day. As the jubilant delegates spilled out of the Universalist Church and returned to their respective states, they radiated optimism that they would regain control of an executive branch that John Tyler had stolen from them.

The news of Clay's nomination reached Nauvoo by May 22. "The Whig leaders are loud in their vociferations in favor of the nomination of Henry Clay and are urging the rank and file of the party to come up to the scratch or all will be lost," the *Nauvoo Neighbor* editorialized in reporting the news. The paper's editors dismissed the dire claims of the Whigs, asserting that "with Jeffersonian Democracy free trade and sailors rights, protection of person and property inscribed on his banner Gen. Smith will thoroughly cleanse the land of whiggery in November next."[14]

But the Mormons, like any other group intent on opposing the election of Clay, did not wait for his official nomination to begin campaigning against the Whig from Kentucky. In the weeks surrounding the Whig convention in Baltimore, editorials and letters to the editor in the newspapers of Nauvoo and other western Illinois cities served as preemptive strikes against the presumed nominees, Clay and Martin Van Buren.

"I DETEST THE SHRINKAGE OF CANDIDATES FOR OFFICE"

In an era when presidential candidates avoided the appearance of campaigning directly, publishing private letters was a particularly effective way to circumvent such etiquette. In such instances, a candidate would write a letter to a friend or acquaintance in which he spelled out the specifics of his policy positions. Then the friend—or the candidate himself—would give the letter to a newspaper to publish in its entirety. This way, Americans could read the letter as if it were written directly to them and candidates could maintain the appearance of disinterest.[15] Smith's January letter to John C. Calhoun had served this purpose. After all, Calhoun and Lewis Cass had offered essentially the same justification for declining to promise assistance to the Mormons if either of them was elected. But Smith appears to have only responded to Calhoun—and made sure that the letter was published. It was as much an open letter to the American people as it was a letter to the Secretary of State.

Smith took the same approach toward Henry Clay. However, his timing in responding to Clay was more strategic. Clay had responded to Smith's initial query on November 15, 1843—just two weeks after Smith had written. This was the letter in which Clay had assured Smith that while he had "sympathised in their sufferings under injustice," he insisted on going into the presidency "free and unfettered, with no guarantees but such as are to be drawn from my whole life, character and conduct."[16] Yet, Smith did not have his clerks compose his response to the Kentuckian until mid-May. Clearly, he was waiting for the Whig national nominating convention to conclude. He wanted to time his letter to Clay—and by extension to the American people—to strike in the weeks immediately following his nomination.

In January 1844, a Nauvoo resident named John Cowan visited Clay in New Orleans of his own accord. "I had a long conversation with Mr Clay," Cowan reported to Smith, "He told me he had received a letter from you, in regard to his views of the Mormons. There is one thing very certain; that he is a very good friend of yours and speaks highly in favor of your church." Cowan had left the meeting optimistic that Clay would help the Latter-day Saints if he were elected president. "Mr Clay is sure to be elected if he lives so be cautious how you vote," he cautioned, suggesting to Smith that he should "put up some of [his] boys to start a 'Clay Club' in Nauvoo." In essence, Cowan was communicating Clay's support for the Mormons, support that Clay was unwilling to express publicly. Rather than kindle hope in Smith, the news fueled indignation.[17]

Between May 13 and 15, and with the help of William W. Phelps, Smith composed a harsh rebuke to Clay. "Your answer to my inquiry . . . has been under consideration since last November," Smith explained, "in the fond expectation, that you would give . . . to the country, a manifesto of your views of the best method and means which would secure to the people, *the whole people*, the most freedom, the most happiness, the most union, the most wealth, the most fame, the most glory at home, and the most honor abroad, at the least expense; but I have waited in vain." Smith claimed that Clay had demonstrated "that peculiar tact of modern politicians" in which they avoided guaranteeing their actions following election to public office. Clay's answer "so much resembles a lottery vender's sign" that Smith could not "help exclaiming; O frail man; what have you done that will exalt you?"[18]

Smith proceeded to critique Clay's decades of public service. He depicted Clay as lacking principles and acting purely on political expediency. Such maneuvering made him unpredictable and ultimately unreliable. "Your shrinkage is truly wonderful!" he scolded the Senator. Smith wanted firm promises, not mere expressions of sympathy. But to him, Clay's political record made his assurances meaningless. "If words were not wind, and imagination not a vapor, such 'views' *'with a lively interest'* might coax out a few Mormon votes," Smith fumed. "Such 'sympathy' for their suffering under injustice, might heal some of the sick, yet lingering amongst them; raise some of the dead, and recover some of their property, from Missouri; and finally if thought was not a phantom, we might, in common with other religious communities, *'you think,' enjoy* the *security* and *protection of the constitution and laws!"*[19] Thoughts and prayers were not enough for the Mormons. They wanted action.

Smith had returned to the heart of his grievance with Clay. "When fifteen thousand free citizens of the high blooded Republic of North America, are robbed and driven from one state to another without redress or redemption," Smith averred, "it is not only time for a candidate for the presidency to *pledge* himself to execute judgment and justice in righteouness, law or no law, but it is his bounden duty, as a man, for the honor of a disgraced country and for the salvation of a once virtuous people, to call for a union of all honest men, and appease the wrath of God, by acts of wisdom, holiness and virtue!"[20] Whether a candidate refused to commit to help an oppressed people as Clay had, or cited "law" that prevented them from taking action as had Cass and Calhoun, Smith was adamant that both were fueling the country's systemic religious inequality.

In concluding his scathing missive to Clay, Smith was most likely addressing the American public, positioning himself as the outsider candidate who could rid the federal government of the politicians who had precipitated the nation's decline. "I mourn for the depravity of the world; I despise the hypocrisy of christendom; I hate the imbecility of American statesmen; I detest the shrinkage of candidates for office, from pledges and responsibility," Smith lamented. "I long for a day of right- eousness . . . and I pray God, who hath given our fathers a promise of a perfect government in the last days, to purify the hearts of the people and hasten the welcome day." Then, keeping with the conventions of corre- spondence in polite society, he closed the letter, "I have the honor to be, your ob't s'v't, Joseph Smith."[21]

Smith's response was the most prominent Mormon rebuke of Clay and his political positions, but it was not the only attack on the Whig nom- inee to appear in Nauvoo's newspapers. In one particularly harsh editorial that first appeared as a letter to the editor of the *Times and Seasons*, a writer identified only as "A. Young" filled seven columns of the paper with a carefully reasoned argument that both Clay and Van Buren were unsuit- able candidates, not only for the Mormons in their dire situation, but for the country at large. Concerning Clay, he wrote, "It seems that he persist- ently refuses to make his principles of politics public, and I think Whigs should learn a useful lesson from the experience of 1840 in electing John Tyler." Then, apparently referring to some vague estimate of the popula- tion of at-risk religious minorities in the country that possibly included the Mormons, the writer averred that his "greatest objection" to Clay was that "if he is elected, some three to five thousand free born American citi- zens, must drag out a miserable existence under persecution and tyranny; or pull up stakes and go to Oregon, and there set up a government of their own, by his Majesty's royal permission."[22]

As early as 1842, editorials written by Mormons had lashed out at those government leaders who, rather than act to protect the citizenship rights of the Mormons already living in the United States, had suggested that they should relocate to the Oregon Territory. This letter lumped Clay into this group of men unwilling to fully commit to protecting the Mormons against persecution and implied that under his presidency it would be merely a matter of time before other religious minority groups were forced to do the same. It concluded by drawing a definitive line between Smith and the presumptive nominees of the Whigs and Democrats: "To elect Van Buren is to sanction the Sub-treasury and standing army. To elect Clay would be for America to humble herself. But to elect Gen. Smith would be to re-establish union, extend our commerce and again become a happy people."[23]

Where the political sentiment in the upcoming presidential election was concerned, for the Mormons in Nauvoo it was Joseph Smith or bust. Nevertheless, Clay's supporters in Illinois knew the power of the Mormon voting bloc in that state and understood that securing their support for Clay would go a long way toward earning the "Harry of the West" the support he needed to secure the state's nine electoral votes.

Accordingly, William Goforth, the aforementioned Illinois Whig who had recently become a friend of the Mormons, set out for Nauvoo by steamboat. He was to attend the Mormons' state convention scheduled for May 17.

12

· · · · · ·

AMERICAN ROYALTY

IN MAY 1844, NAUVOO'S GROWTH CONTINUED UNABATED, but it had yet to meet the standard set forth in Smith's ambitious prophecy three years earlier. Neither king nor queen had "come unto Zion" to "pay respects to the leaders" of the Mormon people. But, just before midnight on May 14, a pair of men from two of the most illustrious families in the United States disembarked from a steamboat and set foot on the city's darkened streets.

"THE SINGULAR POLITICAL SYSTEM WHICH HAD BEEN FASTENED UPON CHRISTIANITY"

Both Charles Francis Adams and Josiah Quincy IV were from Massachusetts. The thirty-seven-year-old Adams was a lawyer, best known at this time as the grandson of revolutionary-turned-president John Adams and the son of former president John Quincy Adams. In the coming years he would have his own successful political career, including a term in the United States House of Representatives and a stint as the American ambassador to Great Britain.[1]

Quincy had no former United States presidents in his family, but, like the Adamses, the Quincys had been one of the preeminent families of Massachusetts for generations. Quincy's father had been the mayor of Boston and a United States congressman and at that time was the president of Harvard. Three years older than the thirty-eight-year-old mayor of Nauvoo, Quincy would join Smith in the ranks of American mayors just two years later when Boston elected him to that position.[2]

But in May 1844, as Adams and Quincy undertook a grand tour of the western United States, most of those accomplishments still lay in the future. On May 13, they boarded the steamboat *Amaranth* in St. Louis and traveled north on the "clear sparkling waters of the Upper Mississippi." They had not planned to stop in Nauvoo, but once aboard the "little steamboat," they met Dr. William Goforth of nearby Belleville, Illinois. Goforth was on his way to the city as a delegate to the Mormons' Illinois nominating convention—though he seems to have hoped that he might persuade Smith and company to support Henry Clay.[3]

Goforth knew that he had his work cut out for him. Yet, he exuded optimism as he told Adams and Quincy "much that was good and interesting about this strange people," and, according to Quincy, "urged us to see for ourselves the result of the singular political system which had been fastened upon Christianity, and to make the acquaintance of his friend, General Smith, the religious and civil autocrat of the community."[4] The gaunt forty-nine-year-old Goforth—described by Adams as "a living skeleton of a man"—persisted until the two men agreed to the spontaneous detour.[5] When their steamer stopped at the Nauvoo landing, the three men unloaded their luggage in the dark of night so that in the morning they might see "the promised land of the Mormons."[6]

The three men spent the night in cheap accommodations near the landing and awoke in "the gray light of the morning, to find the rain descending in torrents and the roads knee-deep in mud." Fortunately, Goforth had gone ahead to inform Smith that Adams and Quincy desired to meet him. Soon a carriage arrived to carry the visitors to Smith's home.[7]

Arriving at their destination, Adams and Quincy stepped out of the carriage and beheld Smith's home, which doubled as an inn. They strode through an opening in the white picket fence and toward the two-story frame building. A group of rough-looking men, Smith among them, stood outside the entrance speaking casually to one another.

The famed Mormon leader was "clad in the costume of a journeyman carpenter when about his work," garb that included "striped pantaloons" and "a linen jacket," neither of which, according to Quincy, had "lately seen a washtub." Yet, they looked beyond his rough exterior and quickly discovered "a man of commanding appearance," hearty and athletic, "with blue eyes standing out upon his light complexion, a long nose, and a retreating forehead."[8]

Goforth introduced the men, emphasizing Adams's recent ancestry. "God bless you, to begin with," Smith exclaimed as he familiarly clasped both of his hands on Adams's shoulders. "And now come, both of you, into the house," he continued, gesturing for his guests to cross over the threshold.[9]

The inn was crowded and finding a vacant room proved futile. Eventually, they settled for a room on the second floor in which someone was sleeping. Anxious to talk, Smith pulled the bed sheets over the head of the slumbering guest without breaking the man's repose.[10]

Both Adams and Quincy were Unitarians and as such were not inclined to accept the notions of modern-day miracles and continuing revelation that Smith preached. However, they were eager to hear about "Mormonism as a secular institution." To their delight, Smith commenced the interview with the history of his people, their persecution in Missouri, and the way their circumstances as religious refugees informed the design of their city. The story of the Missouri persecutions resonated with the visitors. Adams recorded in his journal that the Mormons' expulsion from the state "is one of the most disgraceful chapters in the dark history of slavery in the United States, and shows that the spirit of intolerance, religious and political, can find a shelter even in the fairest professions of liberty."[11]

Their discussion was interrupted by a call for breakfast. Adams and Quincy joined Smith and approximately thirty others on the main floor for the meal. While the visitors lingered at the breakfast table in conversation with some of their new acquaintances, Smith slipped away to shave and to change into a broadcloth suit, something more presentable for the occasion. The men reconvened in the same upper room where they had spoken before, its occupant having left his bed. This time Smith was joined by his brother Hyrum and about a half-dozen other church leaders. Quincy recalled that the additional guests "constituted a sort of silent chorus," letting Smith do most of the talking while fixing "a searching, yet furtive gaze upon Mr. Adams and myself, as if eager to discover how we were impressed by what we heard."[12]

If the Mormon leaders were, indeed, looking for signs that Adams and Quincy were impressed, they were disappointed. Smith explained his religious views and described his ecclesiastical role as prophet. Quincy later described it as "wild talk." He thought Smith "well versed in the letter of the scriptures, though he had little comprehension of their spirit." Perhaps it soon became clear to Smith that the two Unitarians before him were not taken with his spiritual beliefs, but before he took the men on a tour of the city, he guided them to his mother's quarters within the house to see four ancient Egyptian mummies and a corresponding set of papyrus that he had purchased years before in Ohio. Visitors to Nauvoo were typically charged twenty-five cents by Smith's mother to view these ancient artifacts. Smith implied that the men's tour was free, but they paid Mrs. Smith nonetheless.[13]

When the party "emerged from the chamber of curiosities," they found the clouds parted and the sun already hard at work drying the muddy streets. They loaded into a carriage and drove through the city. Adams and Quincy were impressed by what they saw. "Bounded on three sides by the Mississippi," Quincy wrote years later, "the curve of the river enclosed a position lovely enough to furnish a site for the Utopian communities of Plato or Sir Thomas More; and here was an orderly city, magnificently laid out, and teeming with activity and enterprise."[14]

The party ascended the hill to the temple construction site. Adams and Quincy noted the dignified respect nearly all of the city's residents paid to Smith as they passed by. "If the blasphemous assumptions of Smith seemed like the ravings of a lunatic," Quincy concluded, "he had at least brought them to a market where 'all people were as mad as he.' "[15]

The carriage returned the men to Smith's home for lunch, after which Goforth encouraged Smith to preach for his guest. Smith obliged, and a crowd of men and women passing by soon gathered to listen in front of his home. Quincy, himself a celebrated orator back in Boston, recalled that Smith delivered the discourse "with the fluency and fervor of a camp-meeting orator." As the crowd that had assembled to hear the sermon dispersed, Smith, his special guests, and a few others climbed back into the carriage to tour the farms on the prairies east of the city. There was some talk of religion as they drove, but most of the conversation centered on national politics. If Smith couldn't win the men over to his religious views, perhaps he could gain their political support.[16]

Smith spoke strongly against slavery, calling it "a curse and iniquity" of the United States, but said that he opposed the methods of the abolitionists. He described his plan to abolish slavery as spelled out in *General Smith's Views*, and "denounced the Missouri Compromise as an unjustifiable concession for the benefit of slavery." This was a perfect segue to talk about the presidential candidacy of the architect of that compromise, Henry Clay. Goforth almost certainly perked up at the mention of his candidate's name, but Smith lambasted Clay as a man who had failed to live up to his lofty rhetoric of American liberties, most notably to Smith in his unwillingness to protect the Mormons and their rights as American citizens.[17] Goforth must have realized then that Clay could not count on many votes from the country's Mormon population.

Even as they discussed such serious matters, Smith demonstrated a keen sense of humor, often directed at himself. As the carriage rolled by the vast farmlands of the western Illinois prairie, Quincy remarked to Smith, "It seems to me, General, that you have too much power to be safely trusted to one man." Without hesitation, Smith quipped, "In your hands or that of any other person, so much power would, no doubt, be dangerous. I am the only man in the world whom it would be safe to trust with." In a comical tone, he explained, "Remember, I am a prophet." Quincy playfully put the last statement to the test, asking Smith to use his powers to predict the winner of the upcoming presidential election. "Well, I will prophesy that John Tyler will not be the next president," Smith replied, "for some things are possible and some things are probable; but Tyler's election is neither the one nor the other."[18]

The carriage had returned to the city streets of Nauvoo. As the men drove back to Smith's home with the sun setting behind the river, Smith went on to describe other points in his political platform, including a decrease in the number of members admitted to the United States House of Representatives and an increase in the powers of the president to put down rebellions in a state without waiting for a request from that state's governor. Quincy acknowledged the wisdom of several of Smith's positions but saw other parts of his platform as too idealistic, naïve, or untenable. "The man mingled Utopian fallacies with his shrewd suggestions," he observed. "He talked as from a strong mind utterly unenlightened by the teachings of history."[19]

As Smith expounded on what he would do were he elected president in the fall, he leveled with Adams and Quincy about his chances. He recognized that he would not hold the nomination of a major political party, since he had not sought one. But he observed that the political polarization of the country could open a window of opportunity, perhaps a situation in which neither party's candidate won a majority of electoral votes. In such an instance, he might hold the balance between the parties. He was not prophesying victory for himself, but he was suggesting to his well-connected guests that a scenario in which he was elected president was not as unlikely as they might have thought.[20]

"THIS MOST EXTRAORDINARY MAN"

It had been a memorable day for Adams and Quincy. They spent the night in Nauvoo and the next morning boarded a steamer to continue their journey northward on the Mississippi River. As they peered at the wooded shoreline from the ship, they tried to make sense of what they had experienced the day before. "We passed the whole day in his society," Quincy wrote to his family at home, "& had one of the most extraordinary conversations I ever participated in . . . I have neither the time nor space to describe the faith or works of this most extraordinary man but reserve them for a future occasion."[21]

Indeed, coming to a clear and concise opinion of Smith and his place in American society presented a real challenge for the two travelers who were themselves well acquainted with many of the political powerbrokers in the east. "There is a mixture of shrewdness and extravagant self-conceit," Adams wrote in his journal, "of knowledge and ignorance, of wisdom and folly in this whole system of this man."[22]

Quincy was no closer to categorizing Smith when he included an account of his visit to Nauvoo in a memoir nearly forty years later. He could not accept Smith's prophetic claims, but he also could not dismiss his obviously growing impact on the country. "Fanatic, imposter, charlatan, he may have been," Quincy wrote, "but these hard names furnish no solution to the problem he presents to us. Fanatics and imposters are living and dying every day, and their memory is buried with them; but the wonderful influence which this founder of a religion exerted and still exerts throws him into relief before us, not as a rogue to be criminated, but as a phenomenon to be explained."[23]

To Quincy, there was something about Smith that seemed to encapsulate the radical social changes that the United States was undergoing in the nineteenth century. Amid these changes, an increasing number of Americans were attracted to new institutions and new authorities. Men such as Smith and the church that he founded seemed perfectly suited to fill this role. In this vein of thinking, Quincy saw in Smith a "rugged power," but also a "kingly faculty which directs, as by intrinsic right, the feeble or confused souls who are looking for guidance."[24] Yet, there seemed to be a magnetic draw to Smith that extended beyond those whom Quincy deemed "feeble" and "confused." Quincy himself had noted that Smith "was accepted by a class of men which would seem to be intellectually superior to so miserable a delusion."[25]

Social and cultural shifts in nineteenth-century America had created an environment conducive to the rise of a new type of religious leader. The democratization of American society had granted white men more control over their lives than they had previously experienced. Greater social and geographic mobility meant that common men were less beholden to society's elite. Those dissatisfied with their traditional religious choices sought or created new movements that better met their spiritual needs. As historian Nathan O. Hatch described the religious landscape in the United States during the early 1800s, "Increasingly assertive common people wanted their leaders unpretentious, their doctrines self-evident and down-to-earth, their music lively and singable, and their churches in local hands."[26]

Even as educated men raised as part of the country's elite, Quincy and Adams were enthralled by Smith. They did not agree with his religious principles—and they were certainly willing to mock some of his actions in their written accounts of their stop in Nauvoo—but their curiosity about Smith remained unabated. "The prophet's hold upon you seemed to come from the balance and harmony of temperament which reposes upon a large physical basis," Quincy explained, adding that "none had so won human hearts and shaped human lives as this Joseph."[27]

Smith may not have won the votes of his two most illustrious visitors to date, but he had captured their attention. Adams and Quincy departed Nauvoo unconvinced by Smith's religious teachings and his political platform, but certain that, in some way yet undetermined, his influence would be felt in the ongoing development of the United States.

13

······

MORE CONVENTIONS

WHILE ADAMS AND QUINCY CONTINUED THEIR SIGHTSEEING excursion through the American West, the Mormons readied Nauvoo to host Illinois's Mormon nominating convention. On May 17, the day appointed for the meeting, delegates from nine Illinois counties had arrived in the city. It was fewer than church leaders had hoped, but "the very heavy rains for the few preceeding days" had rendered "the roads entirely impassable." Still, their spirits were buoyed by the presence of delegates from the twenty-five other states in the Union. This was not the national convention—that was still scheduled for July 13 in Baltimore. But political supporters of Smith from around the county had apparently deemed the event worth the trip.[1]

"THE PEOPLE BURNED A BARREL OF TAR"

Once the convention was called to order and its leadership selected, several of the delegates rose to speak. They included William Goforth and John Reid, an attorney from New York who had successfully defended Smith in a trial in 1826. As the *Nauvoo Neighbor* reported, they "unfolded in glowing colors the unhappy state of our country, the party feuds, the political intrigues, the corrupt cliques, and the manner in which our liberties were bartered away to gratify the ambition and line the pockets of a few political aspirants." They spoke of Smith's character and compared his policy positions to those of the other candidates. "The souls of the gentlemen who addressed the meeting," the *Nauvoo Neighbor* continued, "breathed the sentiments of their hearts, and they spake in words that burned."[2]

Convention leaders read letters of support for Smith's candidacy, as well as a letter requesting his opinion on labor issues. Yet, the highlight of this publicly read correspondence was the November 1843 letter from Henry Clay and the rejoinder Smith had approved just days earlier. This was the first time the public had heard Smith's scathing rebuke of the Whig nominee. When the letter was read, the audience applauded it "by three cheers."[3]

Eventually the convention arrived at its principal item of business. It was "moved seconded and carried by acclamation that General Smith, of Illinois be the Choice of this Convention, for President of the United States." The same sequence occurred in nominating Sidney Rigdon for vice president. Smith and Rigdon each took their turn at the podium and "were cheered in the most enthusiastic manner."[4]

The convention also passed nine resolutions, most of which repeated or echoed political statements Smith had previously made. They included the convention's resolve that "the permanency and continuance of our political institutions depend on the correction of abuses." The delegates also resolved "that to redress all wrongs the government of the United States with the president at its head, is as powerful in its sphere as Jehovah is in his," and that Smith was the American best suited "to carry out the principles of liberty and equal rights, Jeffersonian Democracy, free trade and Sailors rights and the protection of person and property."[5]

The speeches went on well into the evening and were followed by toasts and celebrations. Smith excused himself for part of the convention to care for his wife, Emma, who was pregnant and feeling unwell. But as the convention drew to a close, "the people burned a barrel of Tar," hoisted Smith and Rigdon upon their shoulders, and circled the fire twice before carrying their nominees back to Smith's home.[6]

This was the most jubilant moment in the campaign to date. Praising the convention's atmosphere, the *Nauvoo Neighbor* wrote superlatively that "A greater display of patriotism, eloquence, and talent we never witnessed on any similar occasion."[7] Yet, its participants must have imagined an even greater celebration on July 13 when the scene was replayed at a national level in Baltimore.

"EVERY THING IS IN DOUBT"

In the days following the convention in Nauvoo—and more than a month before the Mormons' national convention—Baltimore was once again abuzz. This time, it was the Democrats who were holding their national convention. "This city is swarming with politicians of all classes," one of the city's newspapers reported, "and lucky is the man who can procure a bed whereon to rest his weary limbs."[8] The meeting would convene in the Odd Fellows Hall, which boasted the largest meeting room in the city.[9] The Whig convention in the same city a few weeks earlier had been more coronation than contest. But the Democratic meeting was poised to be far more fractious. "There is so many rumors, so much excitement, that it seems impossible to come to any correct conclusions for the future," wrote Tennessean Cave Johnson, "Every thing is in doubt."[10]

Mormon leaders had dispatched four electioneering missionaries to attend the Baltimore conventions of both major parties—not as delegates, but as spectators.[11] They did not arrive in time for the Whig convention. One of the missionaries, David Hollister, arrived two days after Clay had secured his party's nomination and decided to remain in Baltimore until the Democrats convened later that month.[12]

What Hollister and company planned to do in Baltimore is unclear. "I shall do what is in my power for the promotion of the good cause and endeavour to be well accoutered for the occasion," Hollister wrote to Smith regarding the impending convention.[13] Was he hoping to commit a candidate to publicly support redress and future protection for American Mormons? Or, did he hope to convince Democrats whose candidates lost the nomination to swing their support to Smith? In either case, Hollister was presumably present in the Odd Fellows Hall when the action commenced. In a letter to Smith, Hollister echoed the assessments of other political commenters. "It is quite doubtful what the Democrats will do," he wrote, "but if I judge correctly they will not nominate Van Buren."[14]

When the convention opened on the afternoon of May 27, a majority of the 266 delegates were, in fact, ready and willing to cast their votes for Martin Van Buren, who had won twelve of the state nominating conventions. Yet, the former president's front runner status did not portend an easy path to the nomination. There was a sizable anti–Van Buren faction in the party, comprised of men troubled by Van Buren's unwillingness to come out strongly in favor of annexing Texas. In fact, a letter Van Buren wrote in which he wavered on the annexation of Texas because of the unjust war it would inevitably bring with Mexico had drawn the ire of party figurehead Andrew Jackson when it appeared in newspapers a month earlier. Van Buren's long-standing relationship with Jackson was not enough to preserve Old Hickory's support. The anti–Van Buren faction was aided further by the machinations of other ambitious Democrats anxious for the architect of their party to step aside so that they might make their respective runs for the White House.[15]

Much of the anti–Van Buren faction rallied around Lewis Cass, but they were too few in number to block Van Buren from reaching a simple majority of delegates, in this case, 133. Accordingly, all their hope rested on the rules debate at the convention's outset. The Cass contingent made an all-out push for a rule that required a candidate to receive a two-thirds majority (178 or more) in order to win the nomination.[16]

The Van Buren camp recognized the strategy. They knew that they would struggle to reach a two-thirds majority. Furthermore, they feared that if the convention adopted such a rule, it was possible that the party would fail to nominate a presidential candidate altogether. Van Buren's lieutenants at the convention imagined that in such a scenario the Democrats would enter the general election as a party divided, essentially handing the victory to Clay and the Whigs.[17]

The stakes were high and well understood by both sides. A raucous debate raged well into the night and erupted again when the delegates reconvened in the morning. When the dust settled and the votes on the proposed rule were tallied, the supporters of the two-thirds majority prevailed, 148–116.[18] This was a major blow to Van Buren's electoral prospects. The stage was now set for a truly contested nomination, and it was anyone's guess who would emerge victorious.

"TYLER AND TEXAS"

Whereas some Democrats worried that the divisiveness of a prolonged nominating convention would guarantee a Whig victory in the fall, there were several candidates who saw the cracks as openings through which they could climb back into the race. Indeed, Joseph Smith's comments to Josiah Quincy and Charles Francis Adams suggested that a disruption among the country's two entrenched political parties could leave him holding the balance of power in a national contest.

Such a scenario seemed to underlie one Baltimore newspaper's report that Senator Daniel Webster was considering entering the race. A Whig Senator from Massachusetts, Webster had long been a polarizing figure in national politics. William Henry Harrison had appointed him Secretary of State in 1840, and he had remained in the post when Tyler assumed the office in 1841. His continued service to Tyler had driven a wedge between Webster and many in the Whig Party, but he was still a powerful force in New England. Webster himself never publicly commented on his intention to run for president in 1844. Even though he had publicly expressed his support for Clay following the latter's nomination, Webster's ambitious desire for the office remained well known—he had unsuccessfully sought the Whig nomination in both 1836 and 1840. He seemed to recognize—and if not, the country's newspapers brought it to his attention—that his path would not be through a straight party nomination, but one in which the party split along regional lines, turning the contest into a regional rather than a partisan one. In such a scenario, Webster could rise to the top.[19]

Election season had already produced political casualties. Richard M. Johnson's presidential hopes never gained traction. Calhoun had already recognized that Van Buren was too strong for him to overcome and exited the race in January, eventually finding solace in accepting the position of Secretary of State for the remainder of the Tyler administration.[20] Whether or not Webster was contemplating a late entry into the race, the *New York Herald* reasoned that in a free-for-all regional contest, the timing would be right for someone such as Webster to carry the banner of the states in New England.[21]

While Smith and Webster were watching the Democratic convention from afar to see how its outcome would impact their respective hopes for the presidency, one candidate's supporters were already at work in

Baltimore to stoke the dying flames of his presidential ambitions. Just a few blocks away from the Odd Fellows Hall, supporters of President John Tyler set up their own convention. The president-without-a-party had not yet abandoned hope of re-election, but he knew his chances were shrinking. So, he kept his campaign running, waiting for the right time to retake the spotlight.

According to the newspapers covering the Tyler convention, the majority of the men supporting Tyler were officeholders the president had appointed and office seekers who hoped that a public display of support for the president would bolster their prospects. Several of the city's papers reported that there were thousands of people in attendance but clarified that the majority were merely spectators—and the convention proved to be quite the spectacle.[22]

Tyler's plan to ingratiate himself with the Democrats rested on one issue: the annexation of Texas. The hall was accordingly adorned with banners, one proclaiming "Tyler and Texas," and another "Re-annex Texas." A third banner insisted that, with regard to the proposed annexation, "Postponement is Rejection." Once the meeting opened for business, a fist fight nearly broke out on the convention floor when one delegate suggested that they wait to see the outcome of the Democratic convention a few blocks away before taken any definitive action of their own. He was quickly shouted down and in the resulting commotion was escorted from the building. Order restored, the convention proceeded to nominate Tyler by acclamation. The main business of the meeting complete in a matter of hours, the delegates then turned their attention to the task of selecting committees to relay the information to the President and to undertake a variety of other mundane matters.[23]

"POLK—POLK—WHO THE DEVIL IS POLK?"

Meanwhile, in the Odd Fellows Hall, the Democrats' nominating process was moving much more slowly. Following the raucous rules debate, the convention adjourned for lunch. At three thirty in the afternoon, the delegates returned to the hall, refreshed and ready for the main event: selecting a presidential candidate.[24]

The first ballot reflected the sharp division within the party. Van Buren received 146 votes—32 short of the 178 he needed to win the nomination.

Cass was second with 83 votes and Richard M. Johnson a distant third with 29. A few stray votes were scattered about for John C. Calhoun, James Buchanan, and others. This would prove to be the high-water mark for Van Buren. With each of the next six ballots his totals declined. On the fifth ballot Cass surpassed Van Buren, but the former governor of Michigan Territory peaked at 123 votes. While still far from reaching a resolution after seven ballots, the voting was clearly trending toward Cass.[25]

For Van Buren's staunchest supporters, the nomination of Cass was a worst-case scenario. Van Buren was fading. The situation called for desperate measures. The Van Buren delegates moved to adjourn the convention in order to buy more time to regroup. When that motion was denied, one of the delegates from Ohio motioned that the convention abandon the two-thirds rule and nominate Van Buren outright. This was likely a ploy, as the resulting uproar granted the Van Buren camp the time they needed. They used the time to consider alternative scenarios and candidates.[26]

When the delegates reconvened the next day, a change was in the air and the name of a new candidate was buzzing on the convention floor. The eighth ballot resulted in 114 votes for Cass, 104 for Van Buren, and 44 for the former Tennessee congressman, James K. Polk.[27]

Things moved quickly from there. Van Buren's convention manager, Benjamin Butler, withdrew Van Buren's name from consideration. All but two of the former president's delegates switched their support to Polk. When all the votes were counted, Polk had 233—a resounding majority.[28]

The emergence of Polk as the Democratic nominee surprised everyone—with the exception of the delegates from Tennessee. They had arrived at the convention intent on securing Polk the vice-presidential nomination. Still, some among them knew that the convention's sharp division between the Van Buren and Cass camps could create a window of opportunity for their fellow Tennessean. A Nashville newspaper had even included Polk on a list of potential Democratic presidential nominees should Van Buren falter at the convention.[29] Even Andrew Jackson had urged Polk to consider and prepare for such a possibility.[30] When that fortuitous window had appeared, Polk's men pounced.

Historians point to Polk as the epitome of a dark horse presidential candidate. When the convention opened for business, Polk was not even in the conversation for the presidential nomination. His name did not even appear on a ballot prior to the eighth and he was the clear winner on the ninth.[31] In the history of American nominating conventions, Polk's sudden entrance into a prolonged debate and subsequent meteoric rise has not been matched: Polk is as dark a horse as there has ever been.

But Polk did not emerge entirely out of thin air. He had long been a force in Tennessee politics. He was elected to the Tennessee House of Representatives in 1823. Polk then hitched his wagon to the rising star of Andrew Jackson and won a seat in the United States House of Representatives. He had been a dependable congressional ally of Jackson during the Bank War and rose to become Speaker of the House in 1834. Polk was so tightly allied with Jackson that he gained the nickname "Young Hickory." In 1839 Polk returned to Tennessee after the state elected him Governor. Yet, with his eye on the vice presidency in 1840, he hoped he would not be there for long.[32]

The Democratic national convention denied Polk the vice-presidential nomination in 1840, the first of several political hits. He lost re-election as governor in 1841 and was defeated again in 1843 when he sought to re-claim his seat.[33] When the Tennessee delegation to the 1844 Democratic convention arrived in Baltimore, Polk's star appeared to be fading. Beyond Jackson and a handful of other Tennessee Democrats, nobody considered Polk a viable candidate for the presidency.

Polk was a compromise candidate. Paired with George M. Dallas of Pennsylvania as his running mate, Polk would have to unify the splintered Democrats if he was to stand any chance of defeating Henry Clay and the immensely more unified Whig party. Indeed, despite the agreement of the Democratic delegates in the Odd Fellows Hall, one newspaper reported that when word of Polk's selection spread throughout the streets of Baltimore, the crowd "called out 'Polk—Polk—who the devil is Polk?' "[34]

In a series of electronic dots and dashes on recently installed telegraph wires, the news of Polk's nomination was transmitted from Baltimore to Washington, D.C. The rest of the country, still without Samuel Morse's invention, had to wait for the news to spread the old-fashioned ways— through letters, in newspapers, and by word of mouth.

Whig newspapers poked fun at the Democratic nominee. The *Nashville Republican Banner*—a longtime opponent of Polk in his home state of Tennessee—coined the phrase: "Who is James K. Polk?"[35] The slogan stuck. Underlying the mockery of Polk's compromise status was a false sense of confidence among the Whigs. They rejoiced in their rivals' divisions and viewed Polk and Dallas as political weaklings whom Clay and Frelinghuysen could readily vanquish. More sensible Whigs, however, knew that it was only May and that a lot could happen before November.[36]

Despite the initial surprise of Polk's nomination, Democrats had a lot to be excited about in their party's choice. If nothing else, they knew that Polk was devoted to the annexation of Texas. Indeed, President Tyler's unwavering commitment to annexation had been one of the beleaguered president's few remaining selling points to Democrats, particularly to those in the South. Polk held a strong position on Texas and now had the Democratic Party machinery behind him. Although it would take a few months before Tyler officially withdrew from the race, Polk's nomination had sealed his fate and considerably narrowed the contest.[37]

The news of Polk's nomination was slow on its way to Nauvoo, which was on the far western edge of American settlement. By June 5, the news had still not arrived, as the editor of the *Nauvoo Neighbor* wrote that "All parties are looking for the result of the National Convention, to see who is to be the nominee . . . The Convention only can decide." The Mormon publication seemed to take extra joy in reporting the pre-convention rumors of a movement within the Democratic Party to block the nomination of Van Buren. "The waters of Van Burenism are beginning to be troubled," the editorial stated, "and the great wave of public opinion, sweeping from one extremity of the Union to the other, threatens to wreck the magician's bark."[38] Indeed, the intra-party strife of the Democrats seemed to bode well for candidates on the fringe of the two parties as well as those, like Smith, who were running from without.

Eventually, the news of the convention's result did reach Nauvoo. But by then, space in Nauvoo's newspapers—as well as Smith's attention—had been almost entirely occupied with problems within the community. Internal dissent threatened to cause the gathering storm of anti-Mormon sentiment in Illinois to rain violence down on Nauvoo, the city that Smith had designed to protect himself and his people.

14

. . . . . .

ASSASSINATION

ANTI-MORMON HOSTILITY IN WESTERN ILLINOIS—AND IN HANCOCK
County in particular—had risen to a fever pitch in December 1843.
However, the tension soon abated enough to pull the Mormons and their
neighbors back from the precipice of violence. Editorials in the *Nauvoo
Neighbor* in early 1844 emphasized that "All is peace at Nauvoo."[1] But
there were still Illinoisans determined to rid the state of Smith and his
followers. These anti-Mormons planned and waited for the ideal moment
to strike.

As enemies lurked outside Nauvoo, dissent among church members
threatened Smith from within the city. The sources of this growing unrest varied. Some Nauvoo residents resented Smith for the power he
wielded over civic affairs. Others operating stores and inns in Nauvoo,
as Smith did, saw him as an economic rival whose civic and ecclesiastical
positions gave him an unfair advantage. Plural marriage was also among
the causes of dissent, a sign to many that Smith and the church had lost
their way.

These concerns eventually spurred some dissenters in Nauvoo to seek
violent solutions. In March 1844, rumors spread of a plot in the city

to "destroy all the Smith family."[2] Then, in April, a disgruntled church member pulled a pistol on Smith, but others intervened to save the prophet.[3] Even though these plots and attempts at violence in the spring of 1844 were ultimately foiled, they cemented pockets of dissent within the city that enemies elsewhere could co-opt in their plans to drive the Mormon community from the state.

In late April 1844, several prominent dissenters organized a new church that they called the True Church of Jesus Christ of Latter-day Saints. The president of the new church was William Law, who had been a counselor to Smith in the First Presidency until they had a falling out earlier that year.[4] Law was accompanied by his brother, Wilson, who had been the Major General of the Nauvoo Legion prior to a court martial that resulted in his removal.[5] The new church also included Robert D. Foster, who had traveled with Smith to Washington, D.C., in 1839, and his brother, Charles.[6] Other prominent dissenters similarly had ties to that monumental trip to the capital, namely, the Higbee brothers, Francis and Chauncy, the sons of the late Elias Higbee, who had represented Smith and the church before Congress.[7]

The initial goal of these dissenters was not to destroy the church, but to reform it. They revolted against the practice of plural marriage, Smith's concentration of civic and ecclesiastical power in himself, and some of his more recent religious teachings, including the belief in a plurality of gods and the potential of men and women to achieve godhood in the afterlife. Smith was not a fraud, they declared, but a fallen prophet.[8]

In addition to founding a rival church, these dissenters brought legal charges against Smith. On May 1, Francis Higbee charged Smith in court with defaming his character.[9] Three weeks later, William Law charged Smith with adultery because of one of his plural marriages.[10] In both cases Smith initially used Nauvoo's liberal habeas corpus ordinance to remain in the city a free man. However, by May 27 circumstances had forced him to Carthage, Illinois, to answer these charges. While in that city, rumors that anti-Mormons in the county were determined to kill him were confirmed.[11] And so, just days after the jubilant nominating convention in Nauvoo, Smith was forced to divert his attention from his campaign. Instead, he focused on remaining alive and protecting his people.

"TO EXPLODE THE VICIOUS PRINCIPLES OF
JOSEPH SMITH"

The absence of a key witness forced the court to postpone Smith's hearing until its next term. Aware of the danger lurking in the town, Smith and his friends left Carthage as expeditiously as possible for the safety of Nauvoo. To the Higbees and Laws, Smith had once again escaped justice. Frustrated, they returned to the city determined to bring down the man they once followed as a prophet.[12]

Their weapon of choice was the print media. In a building near the still-unfinished temple, the Laws, Fosters, and Higbees quickly collected all the materials needed to publish an anti-Mormon newspaper. Sylvester Emmons, a non-Mormon member of the Nauvoo City Council who had grown wary of the concentration of power in Smith, signed on as the newspaper's editor-in-chief. However, he would rely on the newspaper's founders for publishable material.[13]

When the first and only issue of the *Nauvoo Expositor* came off the press on June 7, it filled the city with apprehension. The issue featured the "Preamble, Resolutions and Affidavits of the Seceders from the Church at Nauvoo," in which the Laws, Fosters, and Higbees had declared that "The religion of the Latter-Day Saints as originally taught by Joseph Smith . . . is verily true," but that Smith had departed from this true religion. They made the intent of the rival church —and, by extension, the *Nauvoo Expositor*—abundantly clear: "We are earnestly seeking to explode the vicious principles of Joseph Smith."[14]

The editors of the *Nauvoo Expositor* condemned plural marriage in salacious terms, dismissing Smith's religious justifications as part of an elaborate scheme for his own sexual gratification. It deemed Smith's teaching on a plurality of Gods as blasphemous. The newspaper even waded into the presidential campaign, insinuating the unfitness for office of a candidate who "has two indictments against him," a reference to the charges recently leveled at Smith by two of the paper's founders. In multiple places throughout the newspaper's columns, Smith is referred to as "Joe," a moniker almost exclusively used in the press by his critics and sworn enemies.[15] The *Nauvoo Expositor* had come out swinging, determined to knock Smith from ecclesiastical and civic power.

While the *Nauvoo Expositor* represented a significant threat to Smith, it also threatened the tenuous peace between Nauvoo and the rest of Hancock County. Smith and his fellow church leaders recognized the potential for allegations of polygamy—particularly when sensationalized—to bring mob violence upon the city. In an emergency session on June 8, the city council weighed its options. Smith proposed that they "pass an ordinance to prevent misrepresentation & Libellous publication," arguing that it was "not safe that such things should exist—on account of the mob spirit, which they tend to produce." Ultimately, the city council agreed and determined to draft "an ordinance to suppress Libels &c in Nauvoo."[16]

On June 10, the city council met again—this time for seven hours. Council members discussed the merits of the ordinance, "investigating the Merits of the *Nauvoo Expositor*" and hearing testimony concerning the actions of the "Laws Higbees Fosters &c." The council eventually voted in favor of the ordinance, permitting Smith as mayor "to destroy the *Nauvoo Expositor* establishment as a nuisance." Smith acted expeditiously. He ordered the marshal, John P. Greene, "to destroy [the printing operation] without delay" and at the same time ordered the acting Major General of the Nauvoo Legion, Jonathan Dunham, "to assist the Marshall with the legion if calld upon so to do."[17]

Greene and Dunham formed a posse that very evening and marched to Law's printing shop. Chauncey Higbee and Charles Foster were at the shop when the posse arrived, but, after an initial protest, could do little more than look on in distress. The posse commenced its work, demolishing the press with sledgehammers, scattering type into the street below, and burning any and all printed paper discovered within the building.[18]

The posse included church members who had lived through the Missouri persecutions. Perhaps they remembered that just over a decade earlier, a mob had dismantled their own printing operations and thus attempted to differentiate their actions from those of the Missouri mob. "There was no noise or tumult," one posse member later testified. "All was done in perfect order." To this member of the posse the men's comportment—and the fact that they were following the orders of municipal leaders—mattered greatly. The destruction of the *Nauvoo Expositor* was done "as peaceably as people move on a Sunday."[19]

Of course, to the men whose property had been destroyed, the scenario looked very different. Charles Foster called the action "the work of destruction and desperation."[20] William Law deemed the posse a "mob" comprised of "Joseph's agents."[21] Whether by a lawful posse or by an unruly mob, the result was the same. The *Nauvoo Expositor* was no more.

The job complete, the posse wound through the streets of Nauvoo before gathering in front of Smith's house near the river. Smith emerged and addressed the crowd. "I gave them a short address," Smith's journal reports, "telling them they had done right" and "that they had executed my orders." He explained further that it was required of him by the city council to "never submit to have another Libellous publication" established in the city, and that he "cared not how many papers there were in the city if they would print the truth." The short speech was met with three cheers and "the posse dispersed all in good order."[22]

"A WAR OF EXTERMINATION SHOULD BE WAGED"

The destruction of the *Nauvoo Expositor* provoked outrage throughout western Illinois and even elicited comments from newspapers on the East Coast.[23] Mormon dissenter Francis Higbee had predicted that if Smith and his supporters destroyed the paper and its press, they could "date their downfall from that very hour."[24] Indeed, for Hancock County's many anti-Mormons, the act was enough to justify war. The group's de facto spokesman, Thomas Sharp, editorialized the incident in the *Warsaw Signal*. "War and extermination is inevitable!" he declared, further stoking the fire of violence. "Citizens, ARISE, ONE and ALL . . . We have no time for comment, every man will make his own. Let it be made with POWDER and BALL!!!"[25]

Smith was adamant that the destruction of the *Nauvoo Expositor* had been legal. An unsigned proclamation printed in the *Nauvoo Neighbor* made his case on the same day Sharp called for war. "In removing the *Nauvoo Expositor* as a nuisance," the proclamation read, "let it be distinctly understood that every step has been sanctioned by legal proceedings founded upon testimony had before the City Council." Continuing, it asserted that inasmuch as "Nauvoo is a corporated body, as well as any other city in the United States; [it] has 'reserved rights' as well as the State or States." As an example, the proclamation quoted a provision in the Springfield, Illinois, charter that allowed that city to identify and remove public nuisances through official proceedings. In addition, the proclamation cited William Blackstone's *Commentaries on the Laws of England*, which had been a mainstay of American legal analysis since the country's colonial era. "Blackstone holds the rule just," the proclamation explained, "'that a libelous print or paper, affecting a private individual, may be destroyed.'"[26] Finally, the proclamation acknowledged that some would see a parallel with the destruction the Mormons' printing operation in Missouri more than a decade earlier but insisted that the action in Nauvoo was an entirely different case.[27]

The Nauvoo dissenters had already taken legal action. On June 12, Francis Higbee appeared before a justice of the peace in the county seat and made a formal complaint against Smith and seventeen others. Later that day, all but one of the accused were arrested in Nauvoo, but they did not remain in custody for long. Smith appealed to Nauvoo's municipal court and was discharged on a writ of habeas corpus. The following day, Smith assumed his place as the chief justice of the court and discharged the other sixteen men.[28]

Smith's explanation of the legal justification for the destruction of the *Nauvoo Expositor* was unsatisfactory to Sharp and the country's other anti-Mormons. So was his release from custody by a Nauvoo court. When the anti-Mormons convened in Carthage on June 13, they insisted that Smith and company fully submit to the law. If they would not, the meeting determined, then "a war of extermination should be waged, to the entire destruction, if necessary for our protection, of his adherents."[29]

Trying to avoid violence while remaining adamant that he was justified in his actions, Smith and the other accused men again submitted to arrest. But once again the arresting officers were in Nauvoo, and once again Smith and company were discharged, this time by a justice of the peace.[30] The arrests and discharges only worked to confirm what many of Smith's critics had long maintained, that Nauvoo's charter and the city's liberal habeas corpus ordinance placed Smith above the law. Of course, Smith had helped design the controversial charter and ordinances in the wake of church members' expulsion from Missouri, clearly believing that they were necessary to ensure the Latter-day Saints' equal treatment under the law.

Threats of a mob attack on Nauvoo swirled throughout the county. Smith, as determined as ever to protect his city and his people, took extraordinary measures. On June 18, he donned his regal blue militia uniform. He ascended the steps to a wooden platform near his home and addressed the Nauvoo Legion and a large number of the city's residents. Smith proclaimed the city under martial law.[31]

Later that day, Smith's proclamation appeared in writing. Citing a variety of reports in print or otherwise, Smith explained, "I have good reason to fear that a mob is organizing to come upon this city and plunder and destroy said city and the lives of its citizens." Accordingly, he continued, "I do hereby declare the said city within the limits of its incorporation, under martial law." He ordered the officers of the Nauvoo Legion and the city's police force to "strictly see that no person or property pass in or out of the city without due orders."[32]

This was unprecedented. Never had a mayor of an American city proclaimed martial law. Yet, Nauvoo had repeatedly proven itself an unprecedented city. The precise parameters of martial law were unsettled, and its legality at different levels of the country's government had periodically been the subject of heated debate. For instance, during the War of 1812, Andrew Jackson had declared martial law in New Orleans, the first army general to make such a declaration. A United States district court subsequently fined Jackson $1,000. Between 1842 and 1844, decades after the war, Congress debated whether or not to refund Jackson. In the process, they revealed how ambiguous conceptions of martial law were in nineteenth-century America. About this same time, the country debated the 1841 use of martial law by Samuel Ward King, the governor of Rhode Island. King had used the action to put down the so-called Dorr Rebellion, in which a rival government formed to revise the state's constitution.

Clearly, when Smith declared martial law in Nauvoo in 1844, the country had yet to determine precisely who should be allowed to issue such declarations and under what circumstances.[33]

"THAT PROTECTION WHICH THE CONSTITUTION GUARANTEES"

Nauvoo was on lockdown when John C. Calhoun Jr. and his brother, Patrick Calhoun, arrived in the city by steamboat on June 22. The sons of South Carolina Senator John C. Calhoun, who had been the target of Smith's famous diatribe against states' rights, the brothers were touring the western United States with friends. Anxious to meet Smith, Calhoun

Jr. begged the captain of the boat to stop in Nauvoo and "to wait two or three hours" for them. The captain consented, likely because he could use the time to repair his boat after a rival captain had rammed it on the river earlier that day.[34]

There would be no leisurely rides with Smith through the city's streets and the surrounding countryside for the Calhouns as there had been for Josiah Quincy and Charles Francis Adams a month earlier. The traveling party discovered Smith's home surrounded by 300 armed guards. Once the guards determined that they were not enemies, Calhoun Jr. and company were welcomed into the drawing room for an interview with Smith.[35]

"He gave us a full description of his difficulties," Calhoun Jr. recounted in a letter to his brother, "and also an exposition of his faith, frequently calling himself the Prophet, in the course of the conversation." If Smith's contentious and public correspondence with the elder Calhoun came up, it was not recorded. Smith may have hoped that having the Secretary of State's sons witness firsthand the difficulties of the Mormons in western Illinois would help budge him from his intransigent position of federal protection for religious minority groups.[36]

Feeling that he and his community were under siege, Smith had sought relief from President John Tyler. The *Warsaw Signal* had reported that Missourians, eager to eliminate Smith and his religious movement once and for all, were traveling to Illinois to join the mob. They would be joined in this interstate conspiracy by men from Iowa Territory. Such reports must have unnerved Smith, but they also opened a window of opportunity.[37]

"I am sorry to say that the State of Missouri," Smith wrote to President Tyler on June 20, "not contented with robbing, driving, and murdering many of the Latter day Saints, are now joining the mob of this state for the purpose of the 'utter extermination' of the Mormons, as they have resolved." As Smith saw it, the transportation of men and arms across state lines to wage war upon a group of American citizens was an interstate affair. Accordingly, Smith argued that situation warranted federal intervention under Article IV, Section 4 of the Constitution. "And now, Sir," Smith implored Tyler, "as president of the united States, will you render that protection which the constitution guarantees in case of 'Insurrection and rebellion,' and save the innocent and oppressed from such horrid persecution?"[38]

With the letter, Smith enclosed a copy of *General Smith's Views*, the edition of the *Warsaw Signal* reporting on the impending arrival of armed men from Missouri and Iowa, and affidavits from Hancock County residents that detailed the interstate conspiracy. It would take weeks for the letter to arrive at the White House, and there was no guarantee that Tyler would respond with federal troops. That Smith reached out to Tyler, the man he was trying to replace as president, is telling. Smith was desperate and determined to exhaust all possible avenues for protection that were available to him. In this moment, the protection of the community he led superseded his presidential ambitions.[39]

Smith was not exaggerating the desperate state of Nauvoo. On the same day he wrote directly to the president of the United States for help, Smith even considered halting his own campaign for that office. On June 22, he wrote to Brigham Young that the twelve apostles should cease their electioneering and "come home." This letter was never mailed, but it demonstrates how the rising hostilities in and around Nauvoo had quickly become his main priority.

"I DO NOT KNOW WHERE I SHALL GO"

Amid all the commotion that followed the destruction of the *Nauvoo Expositor*, Governor Ford struggled to maintain peace and order. He worried that the western portion of his state was on the brink of civil war—and he was right. Ford had arrived in Carthage from Springfield on June 21, apparently hoping that his presence would help quell the unrest.

Smith wrote several letters to Ford to explain his reasons for ordering the *Nauvoo Expositor*'s destruction.[40] He also sent apostle John Taylor to Carthage to present the Mormons' side of the affair to the governor. However, Ford was unconvinced by Smith's arguments. He believed that the matter should have been taken up by a court and not by the city council Smith led as mayor. "I now express to you my opinion that your conduct in the destruction of the press was a very gross outrage upon the laws and liberties of the people," Ford wrote to Smith. "It may have been full of libels, but this did not authorise you to destroy it." Ford instructed Smith to submit to the law and warned of dire consequences if he did not. "If you by refusing to submit, shall make it necessary to call out the Militia," Ford explained, "I have great fears that your city will be destroyed and many of them exterminated."[41]

Smith was in an impossible situation. He did not believe he would be tried fairly in Carthage, or that he would even survive there long enough to receive a trial. Yet, if he did not surrender, he and his people risked extermination at the hands of the state. Ultimately, Smith decided to leave the city, but not for Carthage. Instead, he would go into hiding. This strategy had worked in 1842 when officials were seeking his arrest and extradition to Missouri. It had allowed him the time and freedom he needed to work through legal and political channels to defuse the situation. He had every reason to believe it would work again.

After dark on June 22, just hours after concluding his visit with the Calhoun brothers, Smith, his brother Hyrum, Willard Richards, and Porter Rockwell crossed the Mississippi River into Iowa Territory. The men rowed a leaky boat that required its passengers to constantly bail water from the hull. Adding to the danger, the river itself had recently swollen to record-breaking levels. It must have seemed symbolic of the violence threatening to engulf Smith.[42]

Upon reaching the shore in Iowa, Smith remained near the river while Rockwell returned to the city to obtain horses. He carried with him a letter from Smith to his wife, Emma. The letter exuded uncertainty but assured Emma that regardless of what happened, there were financial resources available for the support of her and their children. "If God evr opens a door that is possible for me I will see you again," he wrote. "I do not know where I shall go, or what I shall do, but shall if possible endeavor to get to the city of Washington."[43] Presumably, once in Washington, Smith would appeal to the federal government for intervention as a last resort.

However, when Rockwell returned to the Iowa side of the river, he brought news that changed those plans. People in Nauvoo were on edge and worried that Ford would order the militia to tear the city apart until they had found Smith. Rockwell also reported that Ford was determined to instigate a manhunt if Smith fled. After only a few hours on the lam, Smith determined that his absence from the city would not spare his people. So he returned home.

"I GO LIKE A LAMB TO THE SLAUGHTER"

On June 24, at six thirty in the morning, Smith mounted his horse. Alongside the other men charged with the destruction of the *Nauvoo*

Expositor and several others, the party rode out of Nauvoo. But before they arrived, they met an officer of the state militia carrying an order from Governor Ford demanding that the citizens of Nauvoo surrender their weapons. It was likely a precautionary measure by Ford to prevent an all-out war in Hancock County. However, James Dunn, a colonel in the Nauvoo Legion, worried that the order itself could provoke violence from the Mormons. Resigned to abide by Ford's decision, and hoping to prevent bloodshed in Nauvoo, Smith countersigned the order and then rode back to Nauvoo to ensure that it was fulfilled. Later that day, the group completed its trip to Carthage.[44]

During these comings and goings, Smith bade farewell to his family. He hugged and kissed his children and his wife, Emma, who was approximately four months pregnant. It was a tender moment for all, but Smith seemed to believe he was saying goodbye for the last time. "I am going like a lamb to the slaughter," he reportedly declared to friends, "but I am as calm as a summer's morning; I have a conscience void of offence towards God, and towards all men."[45] Smith spoke like a man ready to die.

The final three days of Joseph Smith's life have long fascinated scholars. Numerous articles and books have examined the events in western Illinois at the end of June 1844.[46] The flurry of events that occurred simultaneously produced a flurry and reminiscent accounts colored by later events have only made it more difficult for scholars to pin down precisely what happened. However, clear and at the center of all these events were Smith, Governor Ford, and the anti-Mormons of Hancock County.

On June 25, Smith and his fellow defendants stood before a Carthage justice of the peace to answer charges of inciting a riot. Bail was set at $500 each, an astronomically high amount for the time and disproportionate to the offense. Cash-strapped, the Mormon defendants were unable to make bail until several of their coreligionists offered their land as collateral. The justice of the peace accepted the terms.

However, Joseph and Hyrum were not permitted to return to their homes on bail as their fellow defendants were. In addition to the rioting charges, the Smith brothers had been charged earlier that morning with treason stemming from their declaration of martial law as the mayor and vice mayor of Nauvoo; with a treason charge bail was not an option. It was a unique case that would have fueled the ongoing national debate over the acceptable use of martial law. Practically, since the parameters of the law remained ambiguous, acceptance of declarations of martial law depended on what the American people were willing to tolerate.[47] Accordingly, treason was an extreme charge for the case, and the court would have to determine its aptness.

Had the charges been entered in a court in Nauvoo, a writ of habeas corpus might have set the Smiths free. But they were in Carthage now, and the legal proceedings seemed to have been designed to prevent their return to their safe haven on the Mississippi. Joseph and Hyrum Smith were subsequently incarcerated in the jail in Carthage until they could stand trial.

However, the Smiths were not alone. Several friends volunteered to join them in the jail, including John Taylor and Willard Richards, the only members of the Quorum of the Twelve Apostles who had not departed on electioneering missions. These friends were not under arrest themselves but, rather, chose to be with their prophet and his brother to provide company and protection. The friends also managed to smuggle two pistols to the prisoners, just in case.[48]

While Smith and his associates planned their legal defense, Governor Ford traveled to Nauvoo. Before Ford left, he placed a local unit of the state militia, the Carthage Greys, in charge of protecting the jail and its high-profile prisoners. This may have been a practical choice on Ford's part, one based on availability and proximity to the jail. But it was ultimately ill-advised, as the ranks of the Carthage Greys included dozens of avowed anti-Mormons.[49]

The jailer and his family treated the prisoners well. They did not insist that the Smith brothers and their friends remain confined in their cell. Instead, they allowed them to occupy the adjacent bedroom, where the jailer and his wife typically slept. It was a kind gesture, but not enough to take the prisoners' minds off the activities of their friends—and their enemies—outside the jail's walls.[50]

"THE JOB WAS DONE IN AN INSTANT"

Early in the morning of June 27, 1844, Joseph Smith awoke in the confines of his shared room in the jail at Carthage, Illinois. After eating breakfast, he composed a letter to Emma. Trying to be stoic, he insisted on his innocence. But his words betrayed his somberness and the pervasive sense that his enemies would get the better of him this time. He would soon discover that this sense was right.

If Smith's head was racing with possible scenarios by which he could regain his freedom and the company of his family, he did not reveal it in his letter home. "I am very much resigned to my lot," he confided to Emma, "knowing that I am justified and have done the best that could be done."[51] Throughout the morning and early afternoon on June 27, Joseph Smith dispatched several of his friends on errands. By evening, even the jailer and his family had left, leaving only a guard of eight men to keep watch over the prisoners. Only four Mormons remained in the jail: Joseph and Hyrum Smith, John Taylor, and Willard Richards.[52]

The men attempted to relieve the almost palpable tension in the air. They sang melodic songs, read from books, and shared a bottle of wine. But their efforts failed, as the sense of impending trouble was all but confirmed when the guard suggested that the prisoners would be safer if they moved into the jail's cell. Within minutes of that suggestion, but before the prisoners could heed it, a bustle outside the jail signaled that the once distant, but ever-ominous, threat had at last arrived. An angry mob had assembled to kill Joseph Smith.[53]

The Carthage Greys were camped a quarter mile away from the jail, too far away to respond quickly to any attack.[54] The moment the anti-Mormons of Hancock were waiting for had at long last arrived. Away from his city and without the Nauvoo Legion, Smith would never be more vulnerable. Members of the mob, their faces painted black, surrounded the jail. A contingent charged inside.

"The job was done in an instant," reported Willard Richards. Their "guard was forced on" by a band of more than 100 armed men. The mob fired several shots into the air before spilling through the jail's door and ascending the narrow wooden staircase to the second-floor room in which the guards were keeping the prisoners. Hearing the commotion, Smith scrambled across the room and grabbed a revolver he had hidden in his coat. The four prisoners rushed to the brown walnut door in a futile effort to secure it against their approaching assailants. While piling up the stairs, the vanguard of the mob opened fire on the four-paneled door, the only thing standing between them and their target. A lead ball pierced this wooden barrier and struck Hyrum in the face. He collapsed to the floor, clasped his face, and exclaimed, "I am a dead man!"[55]

At this point Smith returned fire until he had emptied the chambers of his revolver. More balls whizzed into the room and struck the fourth prisoner, John Taylor, in his thigh, knee, wrist, and side. Seeing no chance for survival if he remained in the jail, Smith rushed to the open window only to discover gunmen taking aim from below. He exclaimed, "O Lord my God" as several shots tore into his body and he tumbled from the windowsill. Once the mob dispersed, and the smoke cleared, Smith lay dead on the ground outside the jail.[56]

Not long after the smoke had cleared, and he had attended to the wounded Taylor, Richards took up his pen. His was a heart-wrenching task. He needed to tell the people of Nauvoo what had transpired. He needed to inform Emma Smith that she was now a widow.

Yet, time was of the essence. Flowery language of condolences would have to wait. "Joseph and Hyrum are dead," Richards scribbled. He speculated that the mob that had attacked the men had "fled toward Nauvoo," possibly to attack the city. As for Richards and Taylor, the citizens of Carthage promised to protect them, apparently on the condition that the Mormons not fall upon the city for revenge. "The citizens here are afraid of the Mormons attacking them," Richards explained, emphasizing that such an action would spell almost certain death for him and Taylor. He hastily folded the letter and addressed it to four individuals to whom the courier should deliver the message. One of the recipients was Emma Smith.[57]

The mob that killed Joseph and Hyrum Smith did not proceed to Nauvoo as Richards had feared. And the Mormons at Nauvoo did not launch a retributive attack on Carthage. Instead, the shocked Mormon community mourned.

The mob had acted on a variety of overlapping motives, driven by the animosity many Illinois residents expressed toward the Mormon community over the years. They had long mocked the Mormons' religious beliefs and some of their more radical practices, whether real or rumored: plural marriage in particular. Anti-Mormons also feared that Mormons would control the county's economy and exert undue influence on the state's government. Furthermore, they had long been apprehensive about the concentration of power in Smith's hands. For some, the destruction of the *Nauvoo Expositor* may have been the final straw, the act through which Smith forfeited any shred of sympathy that may have still existed. However, other anti-Mormons had already determined to rid the state of the Mormons at any cost. Smith's incarceration simply provided them an opportunity.

There is no evidence that Smith was assassinated because he was a presidential candidate. A Smith victory was extremely improbable and the anti-Mormons in Illinois knew it. Inasmuch as political motives were at play in the assassination, they were almost certainly state and local. Smith's campaign for the country's highest elected office may have exacerbated these concerns. Illinoisans did not fear that Smith would win the election, but his candidacy may have signaled a level of political ambition that confirmed their belief that Smith would not relent in seeking political power. He became the first assassinated presidential candidate in American history, but he was not assassinated to prevent his election.[58]

"EVERY HEART IS FILLED WITH SORROW"

Exactly one week later, on July 4, 1844, Illinois joined the other 25 states in the Union in celebrating Independence Day. Men, women, and children gleefully paraded down city streets. Speakers proudly praised their Revolutionary forebears for their courage and sacrifice on the fields of battle in securing freedom for their countrymen. At lavish banquets, toast after toast expressed the hope and confidence that through vigilance Americans might enjoy those same freedoms and preserve them for future generations. In the state capital of Springfield, just over 100 miles east of the site of Smith's murder, city residents embraced these patriotic traditions.[59]

This celebration of the rights and freedoms associated with the founding of the United States occurred in Springfield even as the city's newspaper reported on the denial of these very rights to men and women throughout the country. An article on page three reported rumors of Smith's murder but urged readers not to put too much stock in them until such rumors were confirmed. The paper's editors were themselves hesitant to believe the news, owing to the fact that Smith and company were in the custody of law enforcement at the time of the purported act. "We are incredulous in regard to the truth of this rumor," they wrote, "The rumor is too preposterous to be true."[60]

Furthermore, this celebration of Independence Day came on the heels of another case of men committing violence against religious outsiders.

On May 6, Irish families in Philadelphia had come into the crosshairs of a growing political movement that blamed recent immigrants—and the Catholicism that many of them espoused—for what its members perceived as the country's decline. Using this simplistic and intolerant explanation of complex social and economic disruption to justify abuse of these families who worshiped differently than they did, these nativists ransacked the houses of dozens of Irish immigrants before setting the buildings ablaze.

News of these so-called Bible Riots reached Springfield in the days immediately preceding Smith's death. Local members of the Whig Party— including a young Abraham Lincoln—publicly decried such religious intolerance.[61] This violence against Catholic immigrants was neither the first nor the last instance of intense religious persecution in the history of the United States. Yet, it is particularly relevant where the assassination of Joseph Smith is concerned because it demonstrates how, in the weeks surrounding his murder, Americans in general—and Illinoisans in particular—were witnessing a stark contrast between celebrations of liberty and violent actions of against religious minority groups.

Whereas the citizens of Springfield were reluctant to believe that a mob had killed Joseph and Hyrum Smith, the people of Nauvoo were in shock. Joseph and Hyrum's bodies had arrived in Nauvoo on June 28. A veil of somberness covered Nauvoo and the people who came out to witness the return of their lifeless prophet and his beloved brother. "Every heart is filled with sorrow, and the very streets of Nauvoo seam to morn," Vilate Kimball wrote of the occasion.[62] Almira Mack Covey, a cousin of the Smith brothers, reported "that a dry eye I did not behold that day among that large assembly of people." She blamed the Nauvoo dissenters for instigating the events that culminated in the murders. "It was enough to rend the heart of a stone to behold two Prophets of the Lord laid prostrate by those who were once their friends."[63] Smith's mother, Lucy, reportedly trembled and sobbed, asking aloud, "How could they kill my poor boys O how could they kill them when they were so precious?"[64] On June 30, the public filed through Joseph Smith's home to view the bodies a final time before their burial.[65]

Accompanying the Mormons' grief was a profound sense of uncertainty. Richards and Taylor had promised the citizens of Carthage that they would not retaliate against the city that had fostered many of the anti-Mormons who had murdered their prophet, but threats of further violence against the community continued. How should the Mormons protect themselves? Who would lead now that the prophet was dead?

In order to answer these questions, Willard Richards determined that his fellow apostles needed to return to Nauvoo as soon as possible. Accordingly, on June 30, he penned a four-page letter to Brigham Young, explaining what had transpired and urging him and the other members of the Quorum of the Twelve Apostles to "return immediately." He added that he and Taylor "consider it best for all the travelling elders to stop preaching politics."[66]

15

......

AFTERMATH

THERE IS NO GOOD TIME TO MEET a violent death. But, practically speaking, it is hard to imagine a worse time for this to happen to the leader of the Latter-day Saints. Hundreds of church's members—including ten of the twelve members of the Quorum of the Twelve Apostles—were scattered throughout the United States campaigning. The church needed to regroup, and regrouping required notifying the electioneering missionaries what had occurred in the jail in Carthage.

However, before the courier carrying Willard Richards's letter could reach them, the apostles and most of the other electioneering missionaries heard of their prophet's death in the country's newspapers or by private correspondence. Some of the missionaries heard the news of Smith's murder but continued to campaign while they waited for verification. On July 8, the *Cleveland Herald* reported that "Mormon preaching took place in the grove yesterday, and the meetings were conducted with decorum. No allusion was made by the speakers on Saturday or Sunday to the murder of the two Smiths."[1]

Wilford Woodruff learned of the murder from a Boston newspaper on July 15 and received confirmation of the news the next morning in two letters from Nauvoo. However, Woodruff's emotional response to the death of his friend and religious leader was delayed. On July 17, he wrote in his journal: "I have never shed a tear since I heard of the prophets until this morning." Brigham Young had arrived in the city and the two men sat together. Covering his face with his hands, Woodruff "gave vent to [his] grief and mourning." He was "bathed by a flood of tears," but soon "felt composed." Young departed for Nauvoo that day; Woodruff followed a week later. When he boarded a canal barge in Albany, New York, he discovered several other apostles and electioneering missionaries on board, similarly journeying home.[2]

Several Mormons convened in Baltimore on July 13 for what was supposed to be their national nominating convention. As one newspaper reported, the attendees "assembled in a gloomy spirit, the delegates having just received intelligence of the murder of the man they all contemplated to have named as their candidate for the presidency."[3] Those assembled mourned together and then dispersed, ending another odd first in American political history: a nominating convention for a dead candidate.[4]

Whereas Mormons throughout the country mourned the death of the Smith brothers, the responses of American Protestant Christians to the gruesome assassination varied. Some unequivocally sympathized with the Mormons. Some believed that the Mormons had brought these problems on themselves, but still lamented the violence.[5] A smaller group of Protestants reveled in Smith's demise. Famed Protestant reformer Alexander Campbell, a long-time critic of the Mormons, wrote that "Joseph Smith and his brother Hiram have been cut off in the midst of their diabolical career. They were most lawlessly and mobocratically put to death." Campbell insisted that such mob violence and murder, though illegal, did not constitute persecution. Instead, he blamed the victims and claimed that their treatment was justified. "Religion or religious opinions had nothing to do with it. It was neither more or less than the assassination of one whose career was in open rebellion against God and heaven."[6]

Campbell's callous response typified a major obstacle to universal religious freedom in nineteenth-century America: bigotry among the Protestant clergy. Led by their clergymen, nineteenth-century American Protestants often operated on the belief that religious freedom was a right reserved for Protestants. They would deem "fanatical" those whose beliefs were too different from their own. It was a skewed, but pervasive, view of religious freedom. It was a view that justified the discrimination and violent persecution of religious minorities because it protected the privileged place of Protestant denominations in American society. Such a perspective maintained that their denominations deserved such a privileged place and that religious freedom meant protecting it through legal mechanisms from secular and "fanatical" forces alike. When those mechanisms failed, they could resort to extra-legal mob violence to put down threats.[7] To these Protestants, violence against religious minorities was not bigotry because they did not accept the beliefs of those groups as "religion."

News of Smith's assassination was often accompanied by rumors of open warfare in Illinois. It was hard for many of the electioneering missionaries to distinguish fact from fiction. By July 18, missionary Henry G. Boyle recalled that in Virginia, "News of Joseph Smith's murder had reached us, accompanied with tales of horror of the burning of the city of Nauvoo, that the Mormons was Slaying the people of Illinois by hundreds and that the towns of Carthage, and Warsaw had been laid in ashes and their inhabitants had fled to Quincy, and Many other things." The newspapers were so "full of news of this kind," Boyle recorded, that "I felt depressed in my feeling. I had to meet all this flood of lies and false reports, and all the prejudices that is generally excited against us on such occasions."[8]

By August 6, most of the apostles had returned to Nauvoo, as had many of the other electioneering missionaries.[9] Together they mourned and discussed a path forward. There was near universal resolve among the Saints to continue in their faith, but questions of whether to remain in Nauvoo—and who should lead them—threatened to fracture the community.

The succession question initially centered on Sidney Rigdon and the Quorum of the Twelve Apostles. In a meeting of the church on the morning of August 8, Rigdon spoke for two hours, explaining why he, as the sole surviving member of the First Presidency, should lead the church. He insisted that as the church's president, he would serve less as Smith's replacement than as his "spokesman" and the church's guardian. Young addressed the congregation in the afternoon and claimed that the apostles should lead because it was upon that group that Smith had bestowed "all the keys and powers" of the priesthood. The majority of church members in Nauvoo were persuaded by Young and he eventually assumed the leadership of the church.[10] But others followed Rigdon, who stayed in Nauvoo for another month before the church excommunicated him on charges that he was setting up a rival church and performing unauthorized ordinations and rituals. On September 10 he departed for Pittsburgh, Pennsylvania, where he and some of the Mormons who followed him established a new church.[11]

"THE STRONGEST NATIONAL VOTE EVER GIVEN"

The Mormons were still reeling from the fallout of the contest between Young and Rigdon when November arrived, and Election Day with it. Prior to Smith's death, they must have pictured this moment in triumphant color, fixated on the joy of voting for their prophet. Instead, Election Day in Nauvoo was somber. In an August 1844 letter to the church, Young advised that, "As rulers and people have taken counsel together against the Lord, and against his anointed, and have murdered him who would have reformed and saved the nation, it is not wisdom for the saints to have anything to do with politics, voting, or president-making at present." Instead, Young suggested that the Mormons "stand aloof . . . and wait, at least, till a man is found, who, if elected, will carry out the enlarged principles, universal freedom, and equal rights and protection expressed in the views of our beloved Prophet and martyr, General Joseph Smith."[12]

Accordingly, on Election Day many Mormons in Nauvoo stayed home. Those who did vote shuffled to the city's polls, cast their votes, and went back to their daily work. Most of them voted for James K. Polk.[13]

The rest of the country followed suit. With 170 electoral votes, Polk was elected president. "Little Hickory," the man who was not even on Smith's radar when he first wrote to presidential candidates in November 1843, a man whose political career was perceived, prior to the Democratic convention, as waning everywhere except for Tennessee, had reached the pinnacle of elected office in the United States.

Of course, the Democrats reveled in the electoral results. Within a year, the annexation of Texas was complete. Then, in December 1845, Texas entered the Union as a slave state. Just as many opponents of annexation had warned, the move expanded slavery and increased the severity of the sectional crisis.

As for Clay, he had lost again. With Theodore Frelinghuysen and the rest of the Whig Party, Clay searched for an explanation of their defeat. They readily cast blame on James G. Birney and the Liberty Party. Birney had won more than 62,000 votes for 2.3% percent of the popular vote. He did not come close to winning any state's electoral votes, but he had drawn enough support away from the Whigs in New York that it cost Clay victory in that state and the entire election as a result. Frelinghuysen was blunt in his criticism of the third-party candidate and lumped him in with the Catholic voters who had supported Polk. "The alliance of the foreign vote, & that most impracticable of all organizations, the abolitionists," he fumed, "has defeated the strongest national vote ever given, to a Presidential candidate." To Frelinghuysen, Birney and his supporters were "invincibly obstinate."[14] In blocking a Whig victory, the party dedicated to the immediate abolition of slavery had paved the way for a Southern Democrat devoted to its expansion.[15]

"As for myself, it would be folly to deny that I feel the severity of the blow most intensely," Clay wrote to his friend, William Seward, on a fourth failed presidential bid. "I feel it for myself, but, unless my heart deceives me, I feel it still more for my country and my friends."[16] Many Whigs saw the defeat as a sign that Clay's career in public service was at an end. "Now, I hope to spend the remainder of my days in peace and quiet," he told a newspaper shortly after the election.[17] But his ambition for the presidency and his dissatisfaction with the men who sought to replace him as the Whigs' figurehead would not let him retire just yet. Clay would try for the presidency again in 1848 but fail to secure his party's nomination.[18] Still, Clay continued to serve in the Senate and died in office in 1852.[19]

Birney's health declined dramatically during the year that followed the election. He suffered a serious stroke in the immediate aftermath of a horse-riding accident in the summer of 1845. As a result, he experienced several bouts of paralysis. By the time of his death in 1857, his communication had long been restricted to writing and hand gestures. The abolitionist movement continued to gain supporters in the North in the years after Birney's forced retirement from public life. But he became increasingly convinced that slavery's demise would not come about through peaceful means. It would take a war.[20]

Indeed, Polk, Clay, and Birney—the three presidential candidates who survived through the election—watched from their respective vantage points as the Union grew more and more fractured over the issue of slavery. They, like many of their countrymen, were justified in wondering whether the country could find a way to survive.

"I DO NOT INTEND TO STAY IN SUCH A HELL OF A HOLE"

In late 1844 many Mormons had already given up on the United States— and that number only rose in the months that followed. The country had failed the Mormons multiple times. Now, more earnestly than ever before, the Mormons considered whether to stay in the United States or seek a fresh start beyond its borders.

Their disenchantment with the myth of American religious freedom was only heightened by the trial of Smith's accused murderers. In October 1844, a Hancock County grand jury received a list of sixty men suspected of participating in the mob that had stormed the jail four months earlier. The grand jury proceeded to whittle the list down to nine, each of whom was indicted. The list included prominent anti-Mormons, including the editor of the *Warsaw Signal*, Thomas Sharp. However, because the state circuit court only came to the county twice a year, the trial would have to wait for six months.[21] Four of the indicted suspects used the delay to flee the county. Three of them had been wounded during the mob's attack when Smith had fired back; their scars would almost certainly have condemned them.[22]

The trial's preliminary proceedings commenced on May 19 in Carthage. Presiding was Richard M. Young of the Illinois Supreme Court, who had, coincidentally, financed Smith's 1839 trip to Washington, D.C., and introduced the church's memorial on the floor of United States Senate. The courtroom overflowed with spectators. The jury was initially a mix of Mormon and non-Mormon residents of Hancock County, but after an unusual motion by the defense on May 21, Judge Young ruled that a new jury should be selected. The new jury was comprised entirely of non-Mormons and, after several days of testimony, it acquitted the five accused murderers.[23]

Once again, Mormons had been victims of violence, and their assailants had experienced no consequences. The verdict stung many church members and must have strengthened their resolve to leave the country altogether. Brigham Young directed other church leaders to write to the governors of 24 states, excepting Missouri and Illinois, to see if they would promise the Mormon community safety within their borders.[24] But he must have known that none of them would make such a commitment.

The annexation of Texas and its subsequent admission into the Union in 1845 was a move that for many Mormons removed the Nueces Strip from serious consideration of places to relocate. This was especially the case for Young. He and many of his followers had come to the realization that without significant reform, the United States was incapable of protecting him and his people. Increasingly, they looked westward, beyond the boundaries of the United States and into the unorganized and ungoverned northern reaches of Mexico.[25] They intended their departure to be permanent. "I never intend to winter in the United States except on a visit," Young declared to the Nauvoo Legion on September 26, 1845. "We do not owe this country a single Sermon . . . I do not intend to Stay in such a Hell of a Hole."[26]

Eventually, tensions between the Mormons and their fellow citizens of Illinois ballooned to the point that the two sides seemed destined for armed conflict. In September 1845 Young signed an agreement that he and the Mormons would leave the state by the following May.[27] Young and his fellow church leaders spent months preparing their people for the arduous trek west. They finally finished the temple.[28]

Spring was too far off for some Illinois anti-Mormons. They brought up old charges that the Mormons were running a counterfeiting operation in Nauvoo and then spread rumors that federal officials were headed to Nauvoo to arrest Mormon leaders. On February 4, 1846, the first company of Mormons loaded their wagons, crossed the frozen Mississippi River, and started west to their new home.[29]

Not all Mormons followed Young. Smith's wife, Emma, and their children remained in Nauvoo. Some went to Wisconsin with a man named James Strang, a church member who in 1845 produced a letter in which Smith had declared him his successor. The letter was forged, but many believed it was real and followed Strang.[30] Others followed Lyman Wight, a member of the Council of Fifty who had not given up the dream of a Mormon kingdom in Texas. Hundreds went south with Wight, but their settlement never matched the vision of its leader.[31] There would be more challenges to Young's leadership and additional splinter groups would form. But the largest body of Latter-day Saints followed Young into the west.[32]

As desperate as their situation was, Young and company believed that they would soon be out of the United States and living in a self-governed society in the unorganized territory of Mexico. Perhaps in one of the greatest ironies of the Mormon experience, by the time they settled in the valley of the Great Salt Lake, that territory had become part of the United States as a result of the Mexican-American War, a war that Polk had started under disingenuous circumstances. The United States, and the persecution of religious minorities enabled by its system of governance, had followed the Mormons to their new home.

CONCLUSION

Systemic Religious Inequality

UNTIL RELATIVELY RECENTLY, THE REVEALING HISTORY OF Smith and the Mormons in American politics has been largely unknown to the general public. Few have recognized just how well Smith and the Mormons represent a microcosm of the major developments that characterized the United States in the nineteenth century, particularly the effects of the Second Great Awakening, westward migration, an increase in social mobility, and the formation of utopian societies. As revealed in the preceding pages, Smith's history fits into this historical interpretation.[1]

However, elevating the Mormon past to a more accurate place in United States history does not mean elevating Smith's presidential candidacy to the point that we depict him as a serious contender in 1844. From the outset, Smith's presidential prospects were bleak; there was virtually no chance that he would beat his Democratic and Whig rivals. Indeed, Smith and other church leaders were hesitant to put all their eggs in the presidential basket. The presidency was always just one potential solution to the Mormons' problems.

But long-shot presidential campaigns remain vital to the history of the United States, though their significance is less about the stories of elections than it is about stories of American discontent. Presidential bids launched outside the two-party system often illuminate the opinions of marginalized Americans, of men and women who feel left behind or damaged by the political and social status quo. Such campaigns can showcase the desperation felt by such citizens.

Even though the campaign seemed doomed from the beginning, Americans in particular should examine Joseph Smith's presidential campaign and its tragic end because his plight encapsulates the failure of nineteenth-century Americans to establish universal religious freedom—and it foreshadows the same struggles in the present. In many cases, laws facilitating the free exercise of religion have long been in place in state and federal constitutions. But the failure—and in some cases, unwillingness—of the governments created by such constitutions to enforce these laws allowed for the widespread persecution of American Catholics, Jews, and several other religious minority groups during the 1800s. Where Smith and the Mormons are concerned, this failure of the American political system allowed the destruction and confiscation of Mormon property, the rape of Mormon women, the murder of Mormon men, and the expulsion of the entire Mormon community from the boundaries of a state under the threat of state-sanctioned extermination. The perpetrators of such acts ultimately faced no legal consequences.

Mormons, along with other minority religious groups, were also hindered in their quest for legal equality by contemporary political rifts, particularly the divide between proponents of states' rights and those of a strong federal government. Before the Civil War, the Bill of Rights did not apply to the individual states. And even after the Civil War, federal courts did not readily enforce the First Amendment's free exercise of religion clause. As one prominent historian of American religion and politics explains, "Because most disputes about religious liberty occurred on the state or local level, and because the federal government had limited power until the New Deal, the First Amendment had almost no effect on the protection of religious belief or non-belief until the 1920s, when the federal courts began expanding the protections of the Bill of Rights to include all levels of government."[2]

Accordingly, religious bigotry and persecution continued to thrive, and white Protestant men continued to exercise dangerous levels of authority over religious minorities. In many cases, they justified this discrimination by deeming certain religious groups too "fanatical" and "superstitious," and therefore undeserving of total religious freedom. They maintained that extending full legal protection and citizenship rights to members of such groups would bring about a tragic and disastrous end to the American democratic experiment.[3]

Smith's presidential campaign showcases an aspect of American religious inequality that, until now, has not been fully explored, namely, that the inability of Americans to fully realize universal religious freedom in the nineteenth century goes beyond issues of doctrine and ritual. Prejudice against Mormon beliefs and practices was certainly a major factor in the Mormons' persecution in Missouri and their expulsion from that state under the governor's threat of "extermination." But other factors that—on the surface, at least—appeared entirely secular were more significant for the federal government's refusal to protect them. There is little evidence to support claims that the federal government denied the Mormons' petitions because they objected to their religious beliefs. There is, however, ample evidence that the president and Congress refused to support the Mormons because doing so would affect re-election bids or the political philosophy some had designed, among other things, to maintain the institution of race-based slavery.

Historians have overwhelmingly demonstrated that for many antebellum Americans, states' rights was more of a political strategy than a philosophy of governance; it was championed by men who sought to hold other humans as property in order to maintain a carefully constructed—and deeply unjust—economic and social hierarchy.[4] Yet, the strategy imposed and protected inequality in other areas of American society. When viewed through the lens of Smith's appeals to the federal government, we see that the states' rights strategy was as effective at impeding efforts to establish the full citizenship rights of religious minorities as it was at blocking efforts to establish the personhood of men and women of African descent enslaved in the American South. Electoral politics and the states' rights strategy, then, were among the most formidable obstacles preventing the federal government from protecting the rights of religious minorities to life, liberty, and property—obstacles that made the federal government complicit in fostering a culture of religious intolerance throughout the country.[5]

Smith recognized this political obstacle. When he ran for president, his first and foremost goal was to obtain religious freedom, not just for himself and his coreligionists, but for all religious minorities, including non-Christians. "If the General Government has no power to reinstate expelled citizens to their rights," Smith wrote to ardent states' rights proponent John C. Calhoun, "there is a monstrous hypocrite fed and fostered from the hard earnings of the people." Smith added emphatically that "Congress, with the President as Executor, should be as almighty in its sphere as Jehovah is in His."[6]

Smith was clear that if elected president he would work to grant the federal government the authority it needed to protect religious minority groups from persecution when individual states failed to do so. While the experience of his own followers was at the forefront of his mind, Smith intended this expansion of federal power to benefit all religious minorities. "If it has been demonstrated that I have been willing to die for a Mormon," Smith explained in a sermon, "I am bold to declare before heaven that I am just as ready to die in defending the rights of a Presbyterian, a Baptist or a good man of any other denomination; for the same principle which would trample upon the rights of the Latter day Saints would trample upon the rights of the Roman Catholics or of any other denomination who may be unpopular or too weak to defend themselves."[7]

Smith seemed to understand that the issue of religious freedom for all Americans was not compelling enough by itself to earn the votes of men comfortably situated within the denominations of mainstream Protestant Christianity. Accordingly, he wrapped his quest to eradicate the political protections of religious bigotry and persecution in a radical reform platform. Each issue made Smith's presidential campaign relevant to nineteenth-century Americans, whether or not his countrymen engaged with his ideas. But Smith was not a one-issue candidate, nor was the rest of his platform merely filler. The radical reforms proposed in his campaign were designed to remedy social ills that had little to do with religion but that had plagued him and thousands of other men and women throughout the country since its inception. Indeed, Smith's campaign remains relevant to twenty-first-century Americans for a host of reasons, but none more than the lens the campaign provides for viewing the political obstacles to religious freedom.

Joseph Smith's failed presidential campaign is more than a relic of the Mormon past, and more than a piece of historical trivia. It is a vital, but too often overlooked, moment in the turbulent history of American democracy. His attempt to obtain the country's highest elective office and the context in which it occurred illuminate a part of the country's history that speaks to several pressing political and cultural questions in the present. Who deserves the rights of full American citizenship? When a group of Americans combine violence with judicial and political coercion to deny some of their countrymen their "self-evident" rights "to life, liberty, and the pursuit of happiness," should the federal government intervene? How can religious minorities effectively combat the discriminatory effects of ostensibly secular laws, policies, and political philosophies? Inasmuch as these questions suffuse twenty-first-century political discourse in the United States, Americans should be concerned with Joseph Smith's run for the presidency.

WAS JOSEPH SMITH CORRECT WHEN HE WROTE to John C. Calhoun that "the states' rights doctrines are what feed mobs"?[8] The Mormon experience in Missouri and Illinois in the 1830s and 1840s demonstrates that he was. When federal officials refused to intervene on behalf of the Mormons after the governor of a state ordered their expulsion under the threat of extermination, Smith and company were left with few options. Consequently, they built a city-state on the Mississippi River to guard against the recurrence of the Missouri persecutions. But that act of self-preservation only fueled violent backlash. Smith had long advocated for increased federal power to protect religious minorities. In the end, he lost his life to the very type of mob violence he had pleaded with the federal government to end.

In 1854, ten years after Smith's death, Missouri was once again dealing with a minority group that was drawing the ire of the state's residents. However, this time it was a political minority. In the heightening tension of the sectional crisis over slavery, more and more abolitionists moved to the western United States intent on curtailing the expansion of slavery and destroying it in the states where it already existed. A large number of them moved to Kansas or Nebraska, with others spilling over those states' borders into Missouri. As a slave state, Missouri officials viewed the abolitionists as a threat to their power, just as they had the Mormons. Something had to be done.[9]

The Missouri state militia prepared to act against the abolitionists. On September 24, 1854, Senator David Atchison of Missouri wrote to the

United States Secretary of War, Jefferson Davis. Atchison had been one of the militia officers involved in the expulsion of the Mormons more than a decade earlier and applied that experience to the trouble on his state's border with Kansas. "We will before six months rolls around, have the Devil to pay in Kansas and this State" he wrote, but he assured Davis that Missouri was "organizing to meet their organization." Atchison did not warn of violence. Instead, he was counting on it. "We will be compelled to shoot, burn and hang but the thing will soon be over. We intend to 'Mormonize' the Abolitionists."[10]

Missouri officials—including a sitting United States Senator—had turned the word "Mormon" into a verb. They had used a mixture of militia and mob violence to drive out the Mormons—and they got away with it. Knowing that the federal government would not intervene emboldened the state and allowed their expulsion of the Mormons to serve as a blueprint for the treatment of other unwanted groups. They would simply "Mormonize" them. In this instance, "the states' rights doctrines" really had fed mobs.

WAS JOSEPH SMITH RIGHT IN HIS BELIEF that a stronger federal government—and easier access to federal intervention—would be required if the Mormons and other religious minority groups were to enjoy all of their rights as American citizens? After all, his political engagement—from his meeting with President Martin Van Buren in the White House in 1839 to the abrupt and violent end of his presidential campaign in 1844—was dedicated to empowering the federal government to protect religious minorities. Once the Mormons settled in Utah Territory, they were squarely in federal jurisdiction; there was no longer a need to find a way around the states' rights philosophy.

However, the Mormons did not find greater protection in their new home. Brigham Young served as the first governor of the territory. But some of the theocratic principles Young brought to his governorship alarmed federal officials. So, too, did plural marriage, which was practiced only by a minority of Mormons, but much more publicly in Utah than it had been in Illinois. Accordingly, Young and the Mormons often clashed with non-Mormons appointed by the president to fill positions in the territorial government. The tension grew until 1857, when President James Buchanan determined to remove Young as governor and dispatched 2,500 troops from the United States Army to the territory to install and defend his replacement, Alfred Cumming. The bloodless Utah War that followed succeeded in removing Young from his governorship. But it also helped convince the Mormons that territorial status had merely replaced the set of obstacles they faced in Nauvoo with an entirely new set. They determined that self-government through statehood was the only solution.[11]

The Mormons in Utah had applied for statehood in 1849 and 1856. In the wake of the Utah War, they applied again in 1862, 1867, 1872, and 1882. Ultimately, they had to wait until 1896. The intervening years were difficult for the Mormons in large part because of continuing discrimination from the highest levels of government. The federal government instituted an immigration ban in 1879, denying Mormons from Europe entry into the United States. Furthermore, two acts in Congress and a Supreme Court decision aimed to eradicate the practice of plural marriage in the territory, forcing Mormon men engaged in the practice to choose between their religious beliefs and prison.[12] Indeed, the federal government proved just as willing to discriminate against Mormon citizens as state governments had.

This does not necessarily mean that Joseph Smith was wrong about the need for federal protection of religious minorities. Rather, it demonstrates that the states' rights doctrine was not the only obstacle the Mormons faced in securing their citizenship rights. Without a federal government committed to equality for all men and women regardless of their religious beliefs, the unequal and often violent treatment of religious minority groups would continue throughout the country. The experience of Mormons in nineteenth- and early-twentieth-century Utah demonstrates that, for many men in power, the states' rights doctrine had actually been a convenient excuse for inaction.

SYSTEMIC RELIGIOUS INEQUALITY IN AMERICAN SOCIETY IS born of prejudice and bigotry. But such oppressive systems are often maintained by dogmatic or disingenuous devotion to political philosophies that are not inherently connected to religion. In many cases, such systems are more concerned with maintaining power.

In the nineteenth century, many Americans championed states' rights as a way to maintain race-based slavery in the Southern states. Very few acknowledged that in its implementation, the philosophy also disadvantaged religious minority groups. Those who tried to raise such awareness among their fellow citizens were themselves usually part of such religious minorities. This group included Joseph Smith in Illinois, the Shakers in New York, and Catholic priest Bernard Permoli in Louisiana. By their trying circumstances alone, they found themselves on the vanguard of those calling for a change. It would take a civil war and the passage of the Fourteenth Amendment in 1868 for the constitutional mechanism for such change to come into being. And it would take several more decades for the federal government to consistently apply the free exercise of religion clause to individual states.[13]

So, when we talk about the political obstacles to universal religious freedom in nineteenth-century America—as well as in the present—we are not merely talking about a list of overtly discriminatory laws or public policies or philosophies of governance. We are also talking about the way Americans use seemingly neutral policies to enact and maintain discrimination against minority groups. Some do so out of ignorance, unaware of the way their political devotion is abridging the rights of some of their fellow citizens. Some may do so to defend inaction, as a way of claiming that their hands are tied. Still others may use these laws as a thin veil covering their prejudice against one religious minority group or another.

Joseph Smith ran for president because he recognized this problem. He fought religious bigotry, but he knew that the fight was against more than just religious bigots. The fight was also against the systems of governance that empowered and ultimately protected such bigotry. Through his candidacy Smith promoted the idea that, as important as rooting out prejudice and misunderstanding was to his cause, Americans would never experience true universal religious freedom until they could also address the flaws in their laws and government that maintained such systemic inequality.

NOTES

. . . .

INTRODUCTION

1. "Minutes of a Convention," *Nauvoo Neighbor*, 22 May 1844; "State Convention," *Nauvoo Neighbor*, 22 May 1844.
2. Joseph Smith, Journal, 17 May 1844, in *JSP-J*, 3:253.
3. Lilburn W. Boggs to John Clark, 27 October 1838, The Missouri Mormon War Collection, Missouri State Archives, Jefferson City, Missouri.
4. Letter to Presidential Candidates, 4 November 1843, draft, Joseph Smith Collection, CHL; Henry Clay to Joseph Smith, 15 November 1843, Joseph Smith Collection, CHL; John C. Calhoun to Joseph Smith, 2 December 1843, Joseph Smith Collection, CHL; Lewis Cass, 2 December 1843, Joseph Smith Collection, CHL.
5. Joseph Smith, Journal, 29 January 1844, in *JSP-J*, 3:169–170.
6. Thomas Gregg, *History of Hancock County, Illinois* (Chicago: C.C. Chapman, 1880), 106; John Lee Allaman, "Uniforms and Equipment of the Black Hawk War and Mormon War," *Western Illinois Regional Studies* 13, no. 1 (Spring 1990): 5; and Glen M. Leonard, *Nauvoo: A Place of Peace, a People of Promise* (Salt Lake City: Deseret Book, 2002), 112–119.
7. Joseph Smith, *General Smith's Views of the Power and Policy of the Government of the United States* (Nauvoo, IL: John Taylor, 1844).
8. For an overview of the discrimination and persecution experienced by Jews in the United States, as well as attempts to establish belonging in the country, see Peter Gottschalk, *American Heretics: Catholics, Jews, Muslims, and the History of Religious Intolerance* (New York: St. Martin's Press, 2013); and Howard Rock, *Haven of Liberty: New York Jews in the New World* (New York: New York University Press, 2012).

9. For an overview of anti-Catholicism in United States history, see Maura Jane Farrelly, *Anti-Catholicism in America, 1620–1860* (New York: Cambridge University Press, 2017). Notable examples of anti-Catholic riots include a mob that burned the Ursuline Convent in Charlestown, Massachusetts, in 1834, and a series of anti-Catholic riots in Philadelphia in 1844 known as the Bible Riots. See Nancy Lusignan Schultz, *Fire and Roses: The Burning of the Charlestown Convent* (New York: The Free Press, 2000); Michael Feldberg, *The Philadelphia Riots of 1844: A Study of Ethnic Conflict* (Westport, CT: Greenwood Press, 1975); and Amanda Beyer-Purvis, "The Philadelphia Bible Riots of 1844: Contest over the Rights of Citizens," *Pennsylvania History* 83 (Summer 2016): 366–393.

10. For an overview of the discrimination and persecution of Shakers in the United States, see Stephen J. Stein, *The Shaker Experience in America* (New Haven: Yale University Press, 1992). Also see Jennifer Hull Dorsey, "Conscription, Charity, and Citizenship in the Early Republic: The Shaker Campaign for Alternative Service," *Church History* 85, no. 1 (March 2016): 140–149.

11. For an overview of the enduring myth that the American Revolution brought about universal religious liberty in the United States of America, see David Sehat, *The Myth of American Religious Freedom* (New York: Oxford University Press, 2011).

12. Nancy Isenberg, *White Trash: The 400-Year Untold History of Class in America* (New York: Viking, 2016), 1.

CHAPTER 1

1. Letter to Hyrum Smith and Nauvoo High Council, 5 December 1839, in *JSP-D*, 7:58. There are several accounts of the meeting between Smith, Higbee, and Van Buren written over the ensuing decades. For examples, see Discourse, 1 March 1840, in *JSP-D*, 7:172–174; Discourse, 7 April 1840, in *JSP-D*, 7:223–225; John Reynolds, *My Own Times, Embracing Also, the History of My Life* ([Belleville], Illinois: 1855), 575; Lucy Mack Smith, *History*, 1845, 274–275, CHL; Letter from Robert D. Foster to Joseph Smith III, 14 February 1874, in the *Saints Herald*, 14 April 1888, 226; Joseph Smith, journal, 5 April 1843, in *JSP-J*, 3:333; and *General Joseph Smith's Appeal to the Green Mountain Boys* (Nauvoo, IL: Taylor and Woodruff, 1843), 3.

2. For a contemporary Mormon summary of the religious community's difficulties with their fellow Missourians, see "A History, of the Persecution of the Church of Jesus Christ, of Latter Day Saints in Missouri," in *JSP-H*, 2:204–286. For the executive order to expel or exterminate the Mormons

from Missouri, see Lilburn W. Boggs to John Clark, 27 October 1838, The Missouri Mormon War Collection, Missouri State Archives, Jefferson City, Missouri.

3. Appeals to the Missouri Judiciary by Smith and other church leaders include documents associated with several court cases. For instance, see Edward Partridge v. Samuel D. Lucas and others, Jackson County Records Center, Independence, MO; William W. Phelps and Oliver Granger v. Richard Simpson and others, Jackson County Records Center, Independence, MO; Charles Allen v. Joseph C. David and others, Jackson County Records Center, Independence, MO; and Petition to George Thompkins, 15 March 1839, in *JSP-D*, 6:340–352. In 1834, several church members marched to Jackson County under the guard of the militia in order to testify before a grand jury but were informed by the Attorney General that the prejudice against the church was too strong in that county for them to receive a fair trial. See Letter from William W. Phelps, 27 February 1834, in *JSP-D*, 3:468–472.

4. Discourse, 1 March 1839, in *JSP-D*, 7:174.

5. Reynolds, *My Own Times*, 174.

6. Reynolds, *My Own Times*, 174. Van Buren's earliest exposure to Mormonism may have been on an 1831 "listening tour" he undertook as New York's secretary of state with newspaper editor James Gordon Bennett. Bennett interviewed several residents near Palmyra, New York, and recorded their mostly negative opinions of Smith and his religious followers in an editorial. See "Mormonism—Religious Fanaticism Church and State," *Morning Courier and Enquirer* [New York City], 15 August 1831; "Mormon Religion—Clerical Ambition—Western New York—The Mormonites Gone to Ohio," *Morning Courier and Enquirer*, 1 September 1831.

7. Joseph Smith, History, 1832, in *JSP-H*, 1:11. For more on Smith's childhood, see Bushman, *RSR*, 17–29.

8. Bushman, *RSR*, 30–38.

9. Joseph Smith, History, 1832, in *JSP-H*, 1:11.

10. Joseph Smith, History, 1838, in *JSP-H*, 1:208–211.

11. Steven C. Harper, *Joseph Smith's First Vision: A Guide to the Historical Accounts* (Salt Lake City: Deseret Book, 2012). On efforts to discover and establish the "primitive church" in nineteenth-century America, see Richard T. Hughes, *The American Quest for the Primitive Church* (Urbana and Chicago: University of Illinois Press, 1988).

12. The Book of Mormon (Palmyra, NY: 1830), 1. On the process of translating and publishing the Book of Mormon, see Bushman, *RSR*, 58–83; Michael Hubbard Mackay and Gerrit J. Dirkmaat, *From Darkness unto Light: Joseph Smith's Translation and Publication of the Book of Mormon* (Salt Lake City

and Provo, UT: Deseret Book and BYU Religious Studies Center, 2015); Volume Introduction to *JSP-R*, 3:xvii–xxviii.

13. Joseph Smith, History, 1838, in *JSP-H*, 1:218.

14. Bushman, *RSR*, 128–143, 251–260, 277–278.

15. Bushman, *RSR*, 109–112; Jan Shipps, *Mormonism: The Story of a New Religious Tradition* (Urbana and Chicago: University of Illinois Press, 1985), 28–38. Despite their preference for the names "Latter-day Saints" or "Saints," Smith and other church members occasionally used the name "Mormons" to describe themselves and "Mormonism" to describe their religious movement. For example, see Letter to James Arlington Bennet, 8 September 1842, in *JSP-D*, 11:76.

16. Bushman, *RSR*, 122–126.

17. On Smith's move to Ohio, see Revelation, 30 December 1830, *JSP-D*, 1:226–227; Revelation, 2 January 1831, in *JSP-D*, 1:226–227; Revelation, 4 February 1831, in *JSP-D*, 1:241–245; and Bushman, *RSR*, 144–146.

18. On the significance of the millennialism in the early Mormon worldview, see Grant Underwood, *The Millenarian World of Early Mormonism* (Urbana and Chicago: University of Illinois Press, 1993).

19. Revelation, 20 July 1831 [Doctrine & Covenants 57], in *JSP-D*, 2:7–8.

20. Alexander L. Baugh, *A Call to Arms: The 1838 Mormon Defense of Northern Missouri* (Provo, UT: BYU Studies, 2000), 6–7. For much of the surviving correspondence between church leaders in Kirtland, Ohio, and Jackson County, Missouri, see *JSP-D*, vols. 2 and 3. Also see Bushman, *RSR*, 164–168, 219–222.

21. Ronald W. Walker, "Seeking the 'Remnant': The Native American during the Joseph Smith Period," *Journal of Mormon History* 19, no. 1 (1993): 1–33.

22. Volume Introduction, *JSP-D*, 3:xxvii–xxix; and Bushman, *RSR*, 222–223.

23. William Phelps, "Free People of Color," *The Evening and the Morning Star* [Independence, Missouri], July 1833. Also see Letter from John Whitmer, 29 July 1833, in *JSP-D*, 3:186–194.

24. William Phelps, "To His Excellency, Daniel Dunklin," *The Evening and the Morning Star*, December 1833.

25. Letter from John Whitmer, 29 July 1833, in *JSP-D*, 3:186–194.

26. Letter from John Whitmer, 29 July 1833, in *JSP-D*, 3:194–195; and Memorial to the United States Senate and House of Representatives, circa 30 October 1839–27 January 1840, in *JSP-D*, 7:122–124; and Baugh, *A Call to Arms*, 7–24.

27. Letter to Church Leaders in Jackson County, Missouri, 18 August 1833, in *JSP-D*, 3:268.

28. Letter, 30 October 1833, in *JSP-D*, 3:331–336; and Bushman, *RSR*, 227–230.

29. Letter, 30 October 1833, in *JSP-D*, 3:331–336; Letter from William W. Phelps, 6–7 November 1833, in *JSP-D*, 3:336–341; Letter from Edward Partridge, between 14 and 19 November 1833, in *JSP-D*, 3:344–351; Letter from John Corrill, 17 November 1833, in *JSP-D*, 3:351–354; Memorial to the United States Senate and House of Representatives, circa 30 October 1839–27 January 1840, in *JSP-D*, 7:125–127; and Bushman, *RSR*, 227–230.

30. On the designation of Caldwell County, Missouri, as a place for the Mormons to settle, and their movement to that place, see Letter to John Thornton and Others, 25 July 1836, in *JSP-D*, 5:258–267; Letter to William W. Phelps and Others, 25 July 1836, in *JSP-D*, 5:268–270; and Letter from William W. Phelps, 7 July 1837, in *JSP-D*, 6:401–403; Baugh, *A Call to Arms*, 12–14; and LeSueur, *The 1838 Mormon War in Missouri* (Columbia: University of Missouri Press, 1987), 17–27.

31. On Joseph Smith and thousands of church members relocating to Missouri from Ohio, see Revelation, 12 January 1838-C, in *JSP-D*, 5:500–502; and Bushman, *RSR*, 338–341.

32. Memorial to the United States Senate and House of Representatives, circa 30 October 1839–27 January 1840, in *JSP-D*, 7:131; and Affidavit, 5 September 1838, in *JSP-D*, 6:219–225.

33. Affidavit, 5 September 1838, in *JSP-D*, 6:219–225; Baugh, *A Call to Arms*, 47–48; and LeSueur, *The 1838 Mormon War in Missouri*, 58–64. On Election Day brawls in the United States during the 1830s, see Amy S. Greenberg, *Lady First. The World of First Lady Sarah Polk* (New York, Knopf, 2019), vii

34. Volume Introduction, in *JSP-D*, 6:xxiv–xxv; Baugh, *A Call to Arms*, 56–59; and LeSueur, *The 1838 Mormon War in Missouri*, 90–111.

35. Thomas B. Marsh and Orson Hyde, Affidavit, 24 October 1838, The Missouri Mormon War Collection, Missouri State Archives, Jefferson City, Missouri; William Peniston to Lilburn W. Boggs, 21 October 1838, The Missouri Mormon War Collection, Missouri State Archives, Jefferson City, Missouri; Bill of Damages, 4 June 1839, in *JSP-D*, 6:500; Bushman, *RSR*, 366–367; Baugh, *A Call to Arms*, 36–46, 87–89, 91–92; and LeSueur, *The 1838 Mormon War in Missouri*, 67–76, 117–128

36. Lilburn W. Boggs to John Clark, 27 October 1838, The Missouri Mormon War Collection, Missouri State Archives, Jefferson City, Missouri.

37. Volume Introduction, in *JSP-D*, 6:xxv–xxvii; Letter to Emma Smith, 4 November 1838, in *JSP-D*, 6:279–282; and LeSueur, *The 1838 Mormon War in Missouri*, 175–179, 204–205, 241–242.

38. Part 3 Introduction, in *JSP-D*, 6:269; Memorial to the United States Senate and House of Representatives, circa 30 October 1839–27 January 1840, in *JSP-D*, 7:144–145; Baugh, *A Call to Arms*, 118–123; and LeSueur, *The 1838 Mormon War in Missouri*, 162–168.

39. Robert Bruce Flanders, *Nauvoo: Kingdom on the Mississippi* (Urbana and Chicago: University of Illinois Press, 1965), 56; and Dallin H. Oaks and Marvin S. Hill, *Carthage Conspiracy: The Trial of the Accused Assassins of Joseph Smith* (Champaign: University of Illinois Press, 1975), 11.

40. Sidney Rigdon to Joseph Smith, 10 April 1839, in *JSP-D*, 6:406–409; Historical Introduction to Letter to Hyrum Smith and Nauvoo High Council, 5 December 1839, in *JSP-D*, 7:56–57; and Memorial to the United States Senate and House of Representatives, circa 30 October 1839–27 January 1840, in *JSP-D*, 7:147–148.

41. Letter to Emma Smith, 9 November 1839, in *JSP-D*, 7:48.

42. Historical Introduction to Letter to Hyrum Smith and Nauvoo High Council, 5 December 1839, in *JSP-D*, 7:56–57.

43. Letter to Hyrum Smith and Nauvoo High Council, 5 December 1839, in *JSP-D*, 7:58.

44. McBride, "When Joseph Smith Met Martin Van Buren: Mormonism and the Politics of Religious Liberty in Nineteenth-Century America," *Church History* 85, no. 1 (March 2016): 156–158.

45. Letter to Hyrum Smith and Nauvoo High Council, 5 December 1839, in *JSP-D*, 7:59.

46. Harry L. Watson, *Liberty and Power: The Politics of Jacksonian America* (New York: Hill & Wang, 1990), 226.

47. On several occasions, Smith expressed concern that anti-Mormon prejudice would doom his petitioning efforts. For examples, see Letter from James Adams, 4 January 1840, in *JSP-D*, 7:90–92; and Letter from John B. Weber, 6 January 1840, in *JSP-D*, 7:92–93. Also see McBride, "When Joseph Smith Met Martin Van Buren," 150–158.

48. *The Sun* [New York], 28 July 1840.

49. Discourse, 1 March 1840, in *JSP-D*, 7:174.

CHAPTER 2

1. Letter to Hyrum Smith and Nauvoo High Council, in *JSP-D*, 7:70–71.

2. For Clay's reaction, see Robert D. Foster, "A Testimony of the Past," *The True Latter Day Saints' Herald*, 15 April 1875; Historical Introduction to Memorial to the United States Senate and House of Representatives, circa 30 October 1839–27 January 1840, in *JSP-D*, 7:142. Calhoun's reaction to Smith's lobbying efforts in 1840 is found in a letter from Calhoun several years later. See John C. Calhoun to Joseph Smith, 2 December 1843, in Joseph Smith Collection, CHL.

3. Letter to Hyrum Smith and Nauvoo High Council, 5 December 1839, in *JSP-D*, 7:70n108; and Letter to Seymour Brunson and Nauvoo High Council, 7 December 1839, in *JSP-D*, 7:77–81.
4. Letter from James Adams, in *JSP-D*, 7:105–107; Letter from John B. Weber, in *JSP-D*, 7:107–109.
5. Reynolds, *My Own Times*, 575.
6. Reynolds, *My Own Times*, 574. Also see Graham A. Peck, "Was There a Second Party System?: Illinois as a Case Study in Antebellum Politics," in Daniel Peart and Adam Smith, eds., *Practicing Democracy: Popular Politics in the United States from the Constitution to the Civil War* (Charlottesville: University of Virginia Press, 2015), 145–169.
7. Letter to Hyrum Smith and Nauvoo High Council, 5 December 1839, in *JSP-D*, 7:71. The book was likely Sidney Rigdon's *An Appeal to the American People*, but it is not clear that the Mormon delegation used money borrowed from Young to publish the book. See Sidney Rigdon, *An Appeal to the American People: Being an Account of the Persecutions of the Church of Latter Day Saints; and of the Barbarities Inflicted on Them by the Inhabitants of the State of Missouri* (Cincinnati: Glezen and Shepard, 1840).
8. Historical Introduction to Memorial to the United States Senate and House of Representatives, circa 30 October 1839–27 January 1840, in *JSP-D*, 7:138–143.
9. Memorial to the United States Senate and House of Representatives, circa 30 October 1839–27 January 1840, in *JSP-D*, 7:144.
10. Memorial to the United States Senate and House of Representatives, circa 30 October 1839–27 January 1840, in *JSP-D*, 7:170.
11. Memorial to the United States Senate and House of Representatives, circa 30 October 1839–27 January 1840, in *JSP-D*, 7:172–174.
12. Historical Introduction to Memorial to the United States Senate and House of Representatives, circa 30 October 1839–27 January 1840, in *JSP-D*, 7:138–143.
13. Alexander Johnson, "Broad Seal War," in John J. Lalor, ed., *Cyclopaedia of Political Science, Political Economy, and of the Political History of the United States, by the Best American and European Writers* (Chicago: Melbert B. Carey, 1883), 3 vols., 1:309; and Letter to Hyrum Smith and Nauvoo High Council, 5 December 1839, in *JSP-D*, 7:72.
14. Letter to Hyrum Smith and Nauvoo High Council, 5 December 1839, in *JSP-D*, 7:72; and Letter to Seymour Brunson and Nauvoo High Council, 7 December 1839, in *JSP-D*, 7:81.
15. Letter to Hyrum Smith and Nauvoo High Council, 5 December 1839, in *JSP-D*, 7:72.

16. Anne Royall, *Letters from Alabama on Various Subjects* (Washington, DC: 1830), 191. Also see Elizabeth J. Clapp, *A Notorious Woman: Anne Royall in Jacksonian America* (Charlottesville: University of Virginia Press, 2016).

17. Letter to Hyrum Smith and Nauvoo High Council, 5 December 1839, in *JSP-D*, 7:70.

18. Letter to the Editor, 22 January 1840, in *JSP-D*, 7:130.

19. Parley P. Pratt, *History of the Late Persecution Inflicted by the State of Missouri upon the Mormons* (Detroit: Dawson and Bates, 1839), iv.

20. Rigdon, *An Appeal to the American People*, 4.

21. Robert D. Foster, "A Testimony of the Past," *The True Latter Day Saints' Herald*, 15 April 1875.

22. Davis was perhaps best known in Washington circles as a political ally and the principal biographer of Aaron Burr. See Historical Introduction to Discourse, 5 February 1840, in *JSP-D*, 7:175–177.

23. Matthew Livingston Davis to Mary Davis, 6 February 1840, CHL; and Discourse, 5 February 1840, in *JSP-D*, 7:175–179.

24. Letter to Hyrum Smith and Nauvoo High Council, 5 December 1839, in *JSP-D*, 7:73.

25. J. Spencer Fluhman, *"A Peculiar People": Anti-Mormonism and the Making of Religion in the Nineteenth-Century* (Chapel Hill: University of North Carolina Press, 2012), 9–20; Maura Jane Farrelly, *Anti-Catholicism in America, 1620–1860* (New York: Cambridge University Press, 2017); Peter Gottschalk, *American Heretics: Catholics, Jews, Muslims, and the History of Religious Intolerance* (New York: St. Martin's Press, 2013); and McBride, "When Joseph Smith Met Martin Van Buren," 150–158.

26. *Debates & Proceedings of the Congress of the United States,* 13th Congress, 1398. Also see Adam Jortner, "'Some Little Necromancy': Politics, Religion, and the Mormons, 1829–1838," in McBride, Rogers, and Erekson, eds., *Contingent Citizens: Shifting Perceptions of Latter-day Saints in American Political Culture* (Ithaca: Cornell University Press, 2020), 17–28.

27. "Twenty-Sixth Congress," *Daily National Intelligencer*, 29 January 1840; and Historical Introduction to Memorial to the United States Senate and House of Representatives, circa 30 October 1839–27 January 1840, in *JSP-D*, 7:142.

28. *Congressional Globe*, 26th Congress, 1st Session, 149 (1840); and Historical Introduction to Memorial to the United States Senate and House of Representatives, circa 30 October 1839–27 January 1840, in *JSP-D*, 7:142–143.

29. Historical Introduction to Memorial to the United States Senate and House of Representatives, circa 30 October 1839–27 January 1840, in *JSP-D*, 7:142.

30. Letter from Elias Higbee, 20 February 1840–A, in *JSP-D*, 7:181.

31. Letter from Elias Higbee, 20 February 1840–A, in *JSP-D*, 7:181.
32. Letter from Elias Higbee, 20 February 1840–A, in *JSP-D*, 7:180–185.
33. Letter from Elias Higbee, 20 February 1840–A, in *JSP-D*, 7:181–183.
34. Letter from Elias Higbee, 20 February 1840–A, in *JSP-D*, 7:181–183.
35. Letter from Elias Higbee, 20 February 1840–A, in *JSP-D*, 7:184–185.
36. Letter from Elias Higbee, 20 February 1840–A, in *JSP-D*, 7:184–185.
37. Letter from Elias Higbee, 21 February 1840, in *JSP-D*, 7:189–190.
38. Letter from Elias Higbee, 21 February 1840, in *JSP-D*, 7:189–190; and Declaration on Government and Law, circa August 1835, in *JSP-D*, 4:479–484.
39. Letter from Elias Higbee, 21 February 1840, in *JSP-D*, 7:189–190.
40. Letter from Elias Higbee, 22 February 1840, in *JSP-D*, 7:194–195.
41. Letter from Elias Higbee, 26 February 1840, in *JSP-D*, 7:199–200.
42. Report of the Senate Committee on the Judiciary, 4 March 1840, in *JSP-D*, 7:543.
43. Letter from Elias Higbee, 24 March 1840, in *JSP-D*, 7:233–234.
44. Reynolds, *My Own Times*, 575–576.
45. Minutes and Discourse, 6–8 April 1840, in *JSP-D*, 7:247.
46. Minutes and Discourse, 6–8 April 1840, in *JSP-D*, 7:247–250.
47. Reynolds, *My Own Times*, 576.

CHAPTER 3

1. Minutes and Discourse, 6–8 April 1840, in *JSP-D*, 7:248–249.
2. "Correspondent of the Richmond Palladium," *Nauvoo Neighbor*, 7 May 1843.
3. Manuscript History of the Church, 11 June 1839, CHL.
4. John L. Butler, Autobiography, 33, CHL.
5. Isenberg, *White Trash*, 17–24.
6. Flanders, *Nauvoo*, 39–40, 51, 53.
7. Letter to Robert D. Foster, 11 March 1840, in *JSP-D*, 7:228–229.
8. Proclamation, 15 January 1841, in *JSP-D*, 7:500–501.
9. "The Mormons," *Ohio Democrat and Dover Advertiser* [Canal Dover, Ohio], 15 May 1840. For more on the construction of homes in Nauvoo and the rise of corresponding industries in and around the city, see Leonard, *Nauvoo*, 127–131.
10. Discourse, 19 July 1840, in *JSP-D*, 7:336, 343.
11. Discourse, 19 July 1840, in *JSP-D*, 7:342.
12. Revelation, 19 January 1841 [Doctrine & Covenants 124], in *JSP-D*, 7:517–519. Also see Benjamin E. Park, *Kingdom of Nauvoo: The Rise and Fall of a Religious Empire on the American Frontier* (New York: Liveright, 2020), 58–61.

13. Revelation, 19 January 1841 [Doctrine & Covenants 124], in *JSP-D*, 7:519–520.

14. There is no reliable record of the number of church members in the United States in 1840, but the documents that Smith, Higbee, and Rigdon submitted to the United States Senate suggest that there were approximately 15,000 church members at the time they made their appeal to the federal government. See Memorial to the United States Senate and House of Representatives, circa 30 October 1839–27 January 1840, *JSP-D*, 7:152n102.

15. Letter from Parley P. Pratt, 22 November 1839, in *JSP-D*, 7:61; Letter to Robert D. Foster, 30 December 1839, in *JSP-D*, 7:91; and Historical Introduction to Minutes and Discourse, 13 January 1840, in *JSP-D*, 7:111–113.

16. Revelation, February 1829 [Doctrine & Covenants 4], in *JSP-D*, 1:9.

17. Letter from Heber C. Kimball, 9 July 1840, in *JSP-D*, 7:326.

18. "Minutes of the General Conference," *Latter-day Saint Millennial Star*, October 1840; Letter from Heber C. Kimball, 9 July 1840, in *JSP-D*, 7:324–327; and Letter to Quorum of the Twelve, 15 December 1840, in *JSP-D*, 7:468. For an overview of the mission of the Quorum of the Twelve Apostles to England, see James B. Allen, Ronald K. Esplin, and David J. Whittaker, *Men with a Mission: The Quorum of the Twelve Apostles in the British Isles, 1837–1841* (Salt Lake City: Deseret Book, 1992).

19. Letter from John C. Bennett, 25 July 1840, in *JSP-D*, 7:349.

20. Letter to John C. Bennett, 8 August 1840, in *JSP-D*, 7:371–372.

21. Letter to the Church and Others, 23 June 1842, in *JSP-D*, 10:178–187.

22. Bennett's quotation of his phrenologist, B.A. Parnell, appeared in John C. Bennett, *The History of the Saints* (Boston: Leland and Whiting, 1842), 186. Also see Andrew F. Smith, *The Saintly Scoundrel: The Life and Times of Dr. John Cook Bennett* (Urbana: University of Illinois Press, 1997), 55.

23. Act to Incorporate the City of Nauvoo, 16 December 1840, in *JSP-D*, 7:472–488.

24. Act to Incorporate the City of Nauvoo, 16 December 1840, in *JSP-D*, 7:472–488.

25. Act to Incorporate the City of Nauvoo, 16 December 1840, in *JSP-D*, 7:481. On the function of writs of habeas corpus in the nineteenth-century American legal system, see Eric M. Freedman, *Habeas Corpus: Rethinking the Great Writ of Liberty* (New York: New York University Press, 2003).

26. Historical Introduction to Act to Incorporate the City of Nauvoo, 16 December 1840, in *JSP-D*, 7:472–476. Illinois law allowed the creation of independent militia companies, many of which were associated with cities or unincorporated communities. However, in Illinois no militia had been included in a city's incorporating act prior to Nauvoo's militia. See An Act

Organizing the Militia of This State [26 March 1819], *Laws of the State of Illinois* [1819] (*Laws Passed by the First General Assembly of the State of Illinois, at Their Second Session, Held at Kaskaskia, 1819* (Kaskaskia, IL: Blackwell and Berry, 1819)), 275–276, sec. 10. For examples in the charters of other Illinois cities, including Chicago and Alton, of provisions granting the municipal courts the power to issue writs of habeas corpus, see An Act in Relation to the Municipal Court of Chicago, and for Other Purposes [21 July 1837], *Laws of the State of Illinois* [1837] (*Laws of the State of Illinois, Passed by the Tenth General Assembly, at Their Session Commencing December 5, 1836, and Ending March 6, 1837* (Vandalia, IL: William Walters, 1837)), 15–16; and An Act to Amend an Act, titled "An Act to Incorporate the City of Alton" [2 March 1839], *Incorporation Laws of the State of Illinois* (*Incorporation Laws of the State of Illinois, Passed by the Eleventh General Assembly, Their Session Began and Held at Vandalia, the Third Day of December, One Thousand Eight Hundred and Thirty-Eight* (Vandalia, IL: William Walters, 1839)), 240, sec. 1. Also see Alex D. Smith, "Untouchable: Joseph Smith's Use of the Law as Catalyst for Assassination," *Journal of the Illinois State Historical Society* 112, no. 1 (Spring 2019): 8–42.

27. Thomas Ford, *History of Illinois, from Its Commencement as a State in 1818 to 1847* (Chicago: S.C. Griggs, 1854), 263.

28. Historical Introduction to Act to Incorporate the City of Nauvoo, 16 December 1840, in *JSP-D*, 7:474.

29. "Communications," *Times and Seasons*, 1 January 1841. Also see Historical Introduction to Act to Incorporate the City of Nauvoo, 16 December 1840, in *JSP-D*, 7:474.

30. "Communications," *Times and Seasons*, 1 January 1841.

31. "General Bennett," *Times and Seasons*, 1 January 1841.

32. Proclamation, 15 January 1841, in *JSP-D*, 7:500.

33. Proclamation, 15 January 1841, in *JSP-D*, 7:500.

34. Proclamation, 15 January 1841, in *JSP-D*, 7:506.

35. Discourse, 19 July 1840, in *JSP-D*, 7:336, 343.

36. Officers of the Nauvoo Legion, 1841, CHL.

37. Months later, in October 1842, the church's newspaper estimated Nauvoo's population as 14,000–15,000. See "Nauvoo," *Times and Seasons*, 1 October 1842. Chicago was the second largest city in Illinois at this time. By 1845 its population was only 7,580. See Bessie Louise Pierce, *A History of Chicago* (New York: Knopf, 1937), 2 vols., 1:415.

38. Leonard, *Nauvoo*, 117. Also see John Lee Allman, "Uniforms and Equipment of the Black Hawk War and the Mormon War," *Western Illinois Regional Studies* 13, no. 1 (Spring 1990): 12.

39. Ordinances, 30 January 1843, in *JSP-D*, 11:376–385.

40. Discourse, 29 October 1842, in *JSP-D*, 11:190.

41. Leonard, *Nauvoo*, 313–321, 222–226, 192–199; Jill Mulvay Derr, Carol Cornwall Madsen, et al., eds., *The First Fifty Years of Relief Society: Key Documents in Latter-day Saint Women's History* (Salt Lake City: Church Historian's Press, 2016), 3–16. For more on the Nauvoo Lyceum, see Historical Introduction to Accounts of Meeting and Discourse, 5 January 1841, in *JSP-D*, 7:490–491.

42. Leonard, *Nauvoo*, 219–220.

43. Mary S. Clark, Autobiography, 2, CHL.

44. Proclamation, 15 January 1841, in *JSP-D*, 7:508.

45. Discourse, 29 January 1843, in *JSP-D*, 11:372.

46. "An Ordinance in Relation to Religious Societies," *Times and Seasons*, 15 March 1841.

47. For examples, see Historical Introduction to Land Transaction with Jane Miller, 6 March 1840, in *JSP-D*, 7:203; Bond to Elijah Abel, 8 December 1839, in *JSP-D*, 7:81–85. Also see Paul W. Reeve, *Religion of a Different Color* (New York: Oxford University Press, 2015), 23.

48. Act to Incorporate the City of Nauvoo, 16 December 1840, in *JSP-D*, 7:479; Land Transaction with Jane Miller, 6 March 1840, in *JSP-D*, 7:203–211; and Bond to Elijah Able, 8 December 1839, in *JSP-D*, 7:81–85.

49. John 3:5, KJV; 1 Corinthians 15:29, KJV; Letter to the Quorum of the Twelve Apostles, 15 December 1840, in *JSP-J*, 7:469–470; Letter to All Saints, 1 September 1842, in *JSP-D*, 11:5–9; and Letter to the Church, 7 September 1842, in *JSP-D*, 11:56–69. Also see Erik R. Seeman, *Speaking with the Dead in Early America* (Philadelphia: University of Pennsylvania Press, 2019), 180–188.

50. Jonathan Stapley, *The Power of Godliness: Mormon Liturgy and Cosmology* (New York: Oxford University Press, 2018), 82–84; Bushman, *RSR*, 447–452; and Volume Introduction, in *JSP-J*, 3:xx–xxi.

51. Matthew 18:18, KJV. Also see Stapley, *The Power of Godliness*, 37–42; Bushman, *RSR*, 443–446; and Volume Introduction, in *JSP-J*, 3:xx–xxi.

52. Revelation, 12 July 1843, Revelations Collection, CHL; Bushman, *RSR*, 437–446; Laurel Thatcher Ulrich, *A House Full of Females: Plural Marriage and Women's Rights in Early Mormonism, 1835–1870* (New York, Knopf, 2017), 91–93; and Volume Introduction, in *JSP-J*, 3:xix–xx.

53. Bushman, *RSR*, 437–443; and *Times and Seasons*, 1 September 1842.

54. Bushman, *RSR*, 439–440; and Ulrich, *A House Full of Females*, 84–134.

55. Bushman, *RSR*, 445.

56. Ulrich, *A House Full of Females*, 67.

57. Ulrich, *A House Full of Females*, xvi–xvii.

58. Volume Introduction, in *JSP-J*, 3:xix–xx.

59. For examples, see Kathryn Danes, *More Wives than One: Transformation of the Mormon Marriage System, 1840–1910* (Urbana: University of

Illinois Press, 2001), 17–51; Ulrich, *A House Full of Females*, 57–134; Bushman, *RSR*, 437–446; Brian Hales, *Joseph Smith's Polygamy* (Salt Lake City: Greg Kofford Books, 2013) 3 vols.; Todd Compton, *In Sacred Loneliness: The Plural Wives of Joseph Smith* (Salt Lake City: Signature Books, 1997); and Gary James Bergera, "Identifying the Early Mormon Polygamists, 1841–1844," *Dialogue: A Journal of Mormon Thought* 38, no. 3 (Fall 2005): 1–74.

CHAPTER 4

1. "A Foul Deed," *Daily Missouri Republican*, 12 May 1842.
2. Joseph Smith, Journal, 14–15 May 1842, in *JSP-J*, 2:56–57.
3. "For the Wasp," *The Wasp* (Nauvoo, IL), 28 May 1842.
4. "Assassination of Ex-Governor Boggs of Missouri," *Quincy Whig*, 21 May 1842.
5. Bennett, *The History of the Saints*, 10. On the honors, titles, and authority Bennett obtained in Nauvoo, see Smith, *The Saintly Scoundrel*, 63–77.
6. Smith, *The Saintly Scoundrel*, 78–83; Bushman, *RSR*, 459–460; and Volume Introduction in *JSP-D*, 10:xxxi–xxxiii.
7. Smith, *The Saintly Scoundrel*, 78–83, 86–87; Bushman, *RSR*, 460–462; and Volume Introduction in *JSP-D*, 10:xxxi–xxxiii.
8. Joseph Smith, Journal, 11 May 1842, in *JSP-J*, 2:55n207; Joseph Smith, Journal, 30 June 1842, in *JSP-J*, 2:73; and Ulrich, *A House Full of Females*, 78–82.
9. Letter to the Church and Others, 23 June 1842, in *JSP-D*, 10:182.
10. "The History of the Saints: Or, an Expose of Joe Smith and Mormonism," *New York Tribune*, 1 November 1842.
11. Bennett, *The History of the Saints*, 293.
12. Bennett, *The History of the Saints*, 4.
13. Bennett, *The History of the Saints*, 306.
14. Discourse, 29 August 1842, in *JSP-D*, 10:449–454; and Letter to James Arlington Bennett, 8 September 1842, in *JSP-D*, 11:74–83.
15. *Wasp*, 27 July 1842; Minutes and Discourse, 29 August 1842, in *JSP-D*, 10:454–459.
16. For example, after Smith allegedly proposed marriage to Nancy Rigdon, this appears to have contributed to the strained relationship Smith had with her father and counselor in the church's First Presidency, Sidney Rigdon. Nancy's brother-in-law, George W. Robinson, commenced openly criticizing Smith following the publication of Bennett's exposé, and Smith accused Robinson of being in league with Bennett. See Letter to Nancy Rigdon, circa mid-April 1842, in *JSP-D*, 9:413–418; Letter to George

W. Robinson, 6 November 1842, in *JSP-D*, 11:196–199; and Letter from George W. Robinson, 6 November 1842, in *JSP-D*, 11:199–201.

17. John M. Bernhisel to Joseph Smith, 1 October 1842, in *JSP-D*, 11:116.

18. Patricia Cline Cohen, Timothy J. Gilfoyle, and Helen Lefkowitz Horowitz, *The Flash Press: Sporting Male Weeklies in 1840s New York* (Chicago: University of Chicago Press, 2008), 105–106, 185.

19. "Mormonism—Gen. Bennett, &c.," *Essex County Washingtonian* [Salem, MA], 15 September 1842.

20. "A Row among the Mormons," *New York Spectator*, 20 July 1842.

21. "From Nauvoo and the Mormons," *New York Herald*, 9 October 1842.

22. Hubert Howe Bancroft, *The Works of Hubert Howe Bancroft, Volume XXVI, History of Utah, 1540–1886* (San Francisco: The History Company, 1889), 150.

23. Bennett's accusation was first published in the St. Louis Paper, the *American Bulletin*. John C. Bennett, "For the Bulletin," *American Bulletin*, 14 July 1842.

24. Lilburn W. Boggs, Affidavit, 20 July 1842, in *JSP-J*, 2:379–380.

25. Bushman, *RSR*, 468.

26. Thomas Reynolds, Requisition, Jefferson City, MO, to Thomas Carlin, 22 July 1842, in *JSP-J*, 2:380–381.

27. Thomas Carlin, Writ, 2 August 1842, copy, Nauvoo, IL, Records, CHL; Joseph Smith, Journal, 8 August 1842, in *JSP-J*, 2:81n318; and Bushman, *RSR*, 468–469.

28. Joseph Smith, Journal, 8 August 1842, in *JSP-J*, 2:81; and Bushman, *RSR*, 469.

29. Joseph Smith, Journal, 12 August, in *JSP-J*, 2:85n330.

30. Joseph Smith, Journal, 11 August–28 November 1842, in *JSP-J*, 2:83–164; and Bushman, *RSR*, 468–479.

31. Joseph Smith to James Arlington Bennett, 8 September 1842, in *JSP-D*, 11:79.

32. Emma Smith to Thomas Carlin, 16 August 1842, in *JSP-J*, 2:111–114.

33. Thomas Carlin to Emma Smith, 24 August 1842, in *JSP-J*, 2:126–128. Emma Smith responded to Carlin on 27 August 1842; and Emma Smith to Thomas Carlin, 27 August 1842, in *JSP-J*, 2:128–130.

34. Letter from Wilson Law, 16 August 1842, in *JSP-D*, 10:409–412.

35. Letter from Thomas Ford, 17 December 1842, in *JSP-D*, 11:278–282.

36. Joseph Smith, Journal, 4 January 1842, in *JSP-J*, 2:216–225; Court Ruling, 5 January 1843, in *JSP-J*, 2:390–402; and Thomas Ford, Order Discharging Joseph Smith, 6 January 1843, in *JSP-J*, 2:402.

37. Jubilee Songs, between 11 and 18 January 1843, in *JSP-D*, 11:335–344.

38. Willard Richards to Levi Richards, 11 January 1843, Levi Richards Family Correspondence, 1827–1848, CHL.

CHAPTER 5

1. Letter to Justin Butterfield, 16 January 1843, in *JSP-D*, 11:326–332.
2. Historical Introduction to Promissory Note to John Brassfield, 16 April 1839, in *JSP-D*, 6:422–426. Also see the dismissals filed in August 1840 relating to the 1839 Daviess County grand jury indictments involving JS and others in Boone County, MO, Circuit Court Records, 1821–1925, vol. C, 316–317, microfilm 981,755, U.S. and Canada Record Collection, Family History Library, Salt Lake City, UT.
3. Requisition for Joseph Smith, 1 September 1840, State of Missouri v. Joseph Smith for Treason [Warren County Circuit Court 1841], Joseph Smith Extradition Records, Abraham Lincoln Presidential Library, Springfield, IL; "Letter from the Editor," *Times and Seasons*, 15 June 1841; and "The Late proceedings," *Times and Seasons*, 15 June 1841. Also see Park, *Kingdom of Nauvoo*, 78–79.
4. William Clayton, Journal, 23 June 1843, CHL. Also see Bushman, *RSR*, 504–505.
5. William Clayton, Journal, 23 June 1843, CHL. For an examination of the June 1843 attempt to arrest Smith and extradite him to Missouri, see Andrew H. Hedges, "Extradition, the Mormons, and the Election of 1843," *Journal of the Illinois State Historical Society* 109, no. 2 (Summer 2016): 127–147; and Bushman, *RSR*, 504–508.
6. Minutes and Discourse, 6–8 April 1840, in *JSP-D*, 7:251.
7. "State Gubernatorial Convention," *Times and Seasons*, 1 January 1842.
8. Discourse, 21 February 1843, in *JSP-D*, 11:466.
9. Spencer W. McBride, *Pulpit and Nation: Clergymen and the Politics of Revolutionary America* (Charlottesville: University of Virginia Press, 2016), 105–108.
10. John Locke, *A Letter Concerning Toleration* (London: 1689), reprinted in John Locke, *Second Treatise of Government and a Letter Concerning Toleration* (Oxford: Oxford University Press, 2016), 158. Also see Farrelly, *Anti-Catholicism in America, 1620–1860*.
11. Adam Jortner, *Blood from the Sky: Miracles and Politics in the Early American Republic* (Charlottesville: University of Virginia Press, 2017); and Jortner, "'Some Little Necromancy.'"
12. Andrew H. Hedges, "Thomas Ford and Joseph Smith, 1842–1844," *Journal of Mormon History* 42, no. 4 (October 2016): 98–99. Snyder died on May 14, 1842. See John Francis Snyder, *Adam W. Snyder and His Period in Illinois History, 1817–1842*, second and revised edition (Virginia, IL: E. Needham, 1906), 399.
13. Letter to Friends in Illinois, 20 December 1841, in *JSP-D*, 9:34–37.

14. "Gov. Duncan," *Alton Telegraph and Democratic Review*, 14 May 1842. The editors of Nauvoo's *Times and Seasons* reprinted the article in which Duncan's speech was reported, adding rebuttals to Duncan's claims. See "From the Alton Telegraph and Review," *Times and Seasons*, 1 June 1842.

15. Joseph Smith, Journal, 11 July 1842, in *JSP-J*, 2:74n301; and "The Election," *The Quincy Whig*, 6 August 1842.

16. "Let Him That Readeth Understand," *Sangamo Journal*, 10 June 1842.

17. Bushman, *RSR*, 508; Marvin S. Hill, *Quest for Refuge: The Mormon Flight from American Pluralism* (Salt Lake City: Signature Books, 1989), 129; Ford, *History of Illinois*, 314–319.

18. Ford, *History of Illinois*, 318; Joseph Smith, Journal, 5 August 1843, in *JSP-J*, 3:71.

19. *Chicago Democrat*, 18 August 1843. Also see Hedges, "Thomas Ford and Joseph Smith, 1842–1844," 111–112.

20. Hedges, "Thomas Ford and Joseph Smith, 1842–1844," 111–115; Bushman, *RSR*, 509. In 1842, church member J.B. Backenstos traveled to Springfield to meet with state Democratic leaders to discuss the benefit of the Mormons voting for Democrats in that year's election. Allegedly, an unidentified party leader assured Backenstos that if the Mormons voted for the Democratic candidate, then Ford would not dispatch the state militia to Nauvoo to enforce any extradition orders from Missouri. See Ford, *History of Illinois*, 317–318; and Hill, *Quest for Refuge*, 131–132.

21. "Gov. Ford and the Mormons," *Sangamo Journal*, 7 September 1843.

22. Ford, *History of Illinois*, 330. Also see Park, *Kingdom of Nauvoo*, 157–160.

23. Ford, *History of Illinois*, 319. Although Ford's *History of Illinois* was published in 1854, Ford wrote the book in 1847. See Terance A. Tanner, "Bibliographic Note," and Rodney O. Davis, "Introduction to the 1995 Edition," in Thomas Ford, *A History of Illinois: From Its Commencement as a State in 1818 to 1845* (Urbana: University of Illinois Press, 1995), xiii, xx–xxi.

24. For more information on Thomas Sharp, see Annette P. Hampshire, "Thomas Sharp and Anti-Mormon Sentiment in Illinois, 1842–1845," *Journal of the Illinois State Historical Society* 72, no. 2 (May, 1979): 82–100; and Bushman, *RSR*, 527–530.

25. "The Mormons," *Warsaw Signal*, 14 May 1841. For the Latter-day Saint response to this editorial, see "The Warsaw Signal," *Times and Seasons*, 1 June 1841.

26. "Fellow Citizens," *Warsaw Signal*, 28 July 1841.

27. "Recent Attempt to Arrest the Prophet," *Warsaw Signal*, 13 August 1842. Smith referenced this editorial in a letter to James Arlington Bennet later that month. See Letter to James Arlington Bennet, 8 September 1842, in *JSP-D*, 11:81.

28. *Warsaw Signal,* 7 July 1841, quoted in George R. Gayler, "The Mormons and Politics in Illinois: 1839–1844," *Journal of the Illinois State Historical Society* 49, no. 1 (Spring, 1956), 50.

29. "Great Meeting of Anti-Mormons," *Warsaw Message,* 13 September 1843.

30. Paul A. Gilje, *Rioting in America* (Bloomington: Indiana University Press, 1996); and David Grimstead, *American Mobbing, 1828–1861: Toward Civil War* (New York: Oxford University Press, 1998).

31. Amy S. Greenberg, "'The Way of the Transgressor Is Hard': The Black Hawk and Mormon Wars in the Construction of Illinois Political Culture," in McBride, Rogers, and Erekson, eds., *Contingent Citizens,* 75–91.

32. David Grimstead, *American Mobbing, 1826-1861: Toward Civil War* (New York: Oxford University Press, 1998), viii.

33. Ford, *A History of Illinois,* 42.

34. Joseph Smith, Journal, 15 September 1843, in *JSP-J,* 3:99.

35. Joseph Smith to Thomas Ford, 20 September 1843, Joseph Smith Collection, CHL; and Joseph Smith, Journal, 19 September 1843, in *JSP-J,* 3:101.

36. Park, *Kingdom of Nauvoo,* 279.

CHAPTER 6

1. Robert V. Remini, *Henry Clay: Statesman for the Union* (New York: W.W. Norton, 1991); and James C. Klotter, *Henry Clay: The Man Who Would Be President* (New York: Oxford University Press, 2018).

2. Maurice G. Baxter, *Henry Clay and the American System* (Lexington: University of Kentucky Press, 1995).

3. *Baltimore Sun,* 9 December 1839; and Klotter, *Henry Clay,* 257–258.

4. For example, see *Jonesborough Whig* [Jonesborough, TN], 5 January 1842.

5. Miles Smith, "'Turning Up Their Noses at the Colonel': Eastern Aristocracy, Western Democracy, and Richard Mentor Johnson," *The Register of the Kentucky Historical Society* 111, no. 4 (Autumn 2013): 525–561; and Tanisha C. Ford, "Slavery, Interracial Marriage, and the Election of 1836," *OAH Magazine of History* 23, no. 2 (April 2009): 57–61.

6. Irving H. Bartlett, *John C. Calhoun: A Biography* (New York: W.W. Norton, 1993); and John G. Grove, *John C. Calhoun's Theory of Republicanism* (Lawrence: University Press of Kansas, 2016).

7. Bartlett, *John C. Calhoun,* 130–138, 190–201.

8. Frank Bury Woodford, *Lewis Cass, the Last Jeffersonian* (New Brunswick, NJ: Rutgers University Press, 1950); and Willard Karl Klunder, *Lewis Cass and the Politics of Moderation* (Kent, OH: Kent State University Press, 1996).

9. On the generation of American statesmen represented by the field of presidential candidates in 1844, see Merrill D. Peterson, *The Great*

Triumverate: Webster, Clay, and Calhoun (New York: Oxford University Press, 1987).

10. Letter to the Church in Clay County, Missouri, 22 January 1834, in *JSP-D*, 3:407–412; and Edward Partridge et al., Petition to Andrew Jackson, 10 April 1834, copy, William W. Phelps, Collection of Missouri Documents, CHL.

11. Lewis Cass to Sidney Gilbert et al., 2 May 1834, William W. Phelps, Collection of Missouri Documents, CHL.

12. Letter from Elias Higbee, 24 March 1840, in *JSP-D*, 7:233–234; History, 1838–1856, vol. D-1, 1552, CHL.

13. Joseph Smith, Journal, 2 November 1843, in *JSP-J*, 3:124.

14. Joseph Smith, Journal, 4 November 1843, in *JSP-J*, 3:124.

15. Letter to Presidential Candidates, 4 November 1843, draft, Joseph Smith Collection, CHL.

16. Letter to Presidential Candidates, 4 November 1843, draft, Joseph Smith Collection, CHL.

17. JS, Journal, 5–30 November 1843, in *JSP-J*, 3:126–136.

18. During this time, church leaders drafted another petition to Congress for redress and reparations for their lost property in Missouri. The text of this petition was considerably shorter than in previous petitions, but this time the Mormons intended to append to the document thousands of signatures. This way they could deliver the petition to Congress in the form of a long scroll, a visual representation of the number of Americans whose rights had been abridged because of their religious beliefs. Accordingly, the petition eventually became known informally as the "scroll petition." Joseph Smith, Journal, 26–28 November, in *JSP-J*, 3:134–135; Memorial, 28 November 1843, Records of the Senate, Record Group 46, NARA. Also see Brent M. Rogers, "To the 'Honest and Patriotic Sons of Liberty': Mormon Appeals for Redress and Social Justice, 1843–44," *Journal of Mormon History* 39, no. 1 (Winter 2013): 44–45.

19. Joseph Smith, Journal, 5 November 1843, in *JSP-J*, 3:126.

20. It is possible that the vomiting was not caused by poisoning. According to Smith's biographer, Richard Bushman, Smith was susceptible to vomiting and had once vomited so violently that he had dislocated his jaw. Years later Brigham Young accused Emma Smith of attempting to poison her husband on the occasion in question, but this accusation is suspect, in part, because Young made it years later in an atmosphere in which Emma Smith had been vilified in the view of many Mormons. See Bushman, *RSR*, 498.

21. Joseph Smith, Journal, 5–6 December 1843, in *JSP-J*, 3:139–140. "Kidnapping," *Nauvoo Neighbor*, 20 December 1843; Joseph Smith to Thomas Ford, 6 December 1843, Joseph Smith Office Papers, CHL; Daniel Avery, Affidavit, 28 December 1843, Joseph Smith Office Papers, CHL.

22. Joseph Smith, Journal, 8 December 1843, in *JSP-J*, 3:142; Henry G. Sherwood to Joseph Smith, 8 December 1843, Joseph Smith Office Papers, CHL; and Joseph Smith to Wilson Law, 8 December 1843, Joseph Smith Collection, CHL.

23. Minutes, December 8 and 21, 1843,12 February 1844, Nauvoo City Council Minute Book, CHL; Hyrum Smith et al., Memorial to the United States Senate and House of Representatives, 21 December 1843, Record Group 46, Records of the U.S. Senate, National Archives, Washington, DC; and *JSP-A*, 1:127–128.

24. "An Extra Ordinance for the Extra Case of Joseph Smith and Others," 8 December 1843, Nauvoo City Council Minute Book, CHL.

25. Joseph Smith to Thomas Ford, 6 December 1843, Joseph Smith Office Papers, CHL.

26. "The Mormons and Their Prophet," *New York Tribune*, 3 February 1844.

27. "Nauvoo City Council—Gen. Joseph Smith—Special Privileges, &c.," *Quincy Whig*, 27 December 1843. The controversial ordinance was repealed on 12 February 1844. See Ordinance, 12 February 1844, Nauvoo, IL, Records, CHL.

28. Joseph Smith to Thomas Ford, 7 January 1844, Joseph Smith Collection, CHL.

29. Manuscript History of the Church, 29 November 1843, E-1, 1790, CR 100 102, CHL.

30. Joseph Smith, Journal, 21 November 1843, in *JSP-J*, 3:132.

31. Willard Sterne Randall, *Ethan Allen: His Life and Times* (New York: W.W. Norton, 2011).

32. Joseph Smith, *General Joseph Smith's Appeal to the Green Mountain Boys* (Nauvoo, IL: Taylor and Woodruff, 1843), 4–7.

33. Vermonters appear to have largely ignored Smith's pamphlet, at least publicly. Researchers have discovered a letter among the documents kept by the anti-Mormon editor of the *Warsaw Signal*, Thomas Sharp, in which a Vermonter mocks Smith's appeal and warns that Vermont will take a decidedly anti-Mormon stance. This letter was intended for publication in the *Warsaw Signal* but never appeared in print. Because the letter demonstrates a detailed awareness of anti-Mormon activity in Hancock County, Illinois, it is possible—and even likely—that the letter was actually written by an anti-Mormon in Illinois pretending to be a resident of Vermont. See Letter to "the Editor of the Warsaw Message or Warsaw Signal," Thomas C. Sharp and Allied Anti-Mormon Papers, 1844–1846, Beinecke Rare Book and Manuscript Library, Yale University, New Haven, CT.

34. Joseph Smith, Journal, 5 December 1843, in *JSP-J*, 3:139; and Rogers, "To the 'Honest and Patriotic Sons of Liberty,'" 48.

35. For examples of Mormon addresses written to the people and governments of their home states, see Parley P. Pratt, *An Appeal to the Inhabitants of the State of New York* (Nauvoo, IL: John Taylor, 1844); Benjamin Andrews, "An Appeal to the People of the State of Maine," *Nauvoo Neighbor*, 17 January 1844; Sidney Rigdon, "To the Honorable, the Senate and House of Representatives of Pennsylvania, in Legislative Capacity Assembled," *Nauvoo Neighbor*, 31 January 1844; Phineas Richards, "An Appeal to the Inhabitants of Massachusetts," manuscript, CHL; and Noah Packard, "The Following Memorial," *Nauvoo Neighbor*, 24 April 1844. Also see Rogers, "To the 'Honest and Patriotic Sons of Liberty,'" 49–61.

36. McBride, *Pulpit and Nation*, 1–3.

37. On debates over nature and scope of religious toleration and freedom in the early American republic, see Christopher Beneke, *Beyond Toleration: The Religious Origins of American Pluralism* (New York: Oxford University Press, 2006); Sehat, *The Myth of American Religious Freedom*, 13–69; McBride, *Pulpit and Nation*, 120–126; Denise A. Spellberg, *Thomas Jefferson's Qur'an: Islam and the Founders* (New York: Knopf, 2013); John A. Ragosta, *Wellspring of Liberty: How Virginia's Religious Dissenters Helped Win the American Revolution and Secured Religious Liberty* (New York: Oxford University Press, 2010); Maura Jane Farrelly, *Papist Patriots: The Making of an American Catholic Identity* (New York: Oxford University Press, 2012); Howard B. Rock, *Haven of Liberty: New York Jews in the New World, 1654–1865* (New York: New York University Press, 2012); and Eric R. Schlereth, *An Age of Infidels: The Politics of Religious Controversy in the Early United States* (Philadelphia: University of Pennsylvania Press, 2013).

38. Andrew Burstein, *America's Jubilee: A Generation Remembers the Revolution after Fifty Years of Independence* (New York: Knopf, 2001).

39. Henry Clay to Joseph Smith, 15 November 1843, Joseph Smith Collection, CHL.

40. Joseph Smith to Henry Clay, 13 May 1844, in *Nauvoo Neighbor*, 29 May 1844. For a description and examination of Smith's response to Clay, see chapter 11 herein.

41. Lewis Cass to Joseph Smith, 9 December 1843, Joseph Smith Collection, CHL.

42. John C. Calhoun to Joseph Smith, 2 December 1843, in Joseph Smith Collection, CHL.

43. John C. Calhoun to Joseph Smith, 2 December 1843, in Joseph Smith Collection, CHL.

44. Joseph Smith, Journal, 23 December 1843, in *JSP-J*, 3:152.

45. Joseph Smith, Journal, 5 January 1844, in *JSP-J*, 3:157.

46. Joseph Smith to John C. Calhoun, 2 January 1844, Joseph Smith Collection, CHL.

47. Joseph Smith to John C. Calhoun, 2 January 1844, Joseph Smith Collection, CHL.

48. Andrew Burstein and Nancy Isenberg, *Madison and Jefferson* (New York: Random House, 2010), 166–208; Jack N. Rakove, *Original Meanings: Politics and Ideas in the Making of the Constitution* (New York: Random House, 1996), 288–338.

49. Hendrik Hartog, "The Constitution of Aspiration and 'The Rights That Belong to Us All,'" *Journal of American History* 74, no. 3 (Dec. 1987), 1014.

50. The temperature on January 28, 1844, fell to negative 15 degrees Fahrenheit in Nauvoo. On January 29, Smith recorded in his journal that it was "Cold—very." See Joseph Smith, Journal, 29 January 1844, in *JSP-J*, 3:169–170.

51. Joseph Smith, Journal, 29 January 1844, in *JSP-J*, 3:169–170.

CHAPTER 7

1. Joseph Smith, Journal, 29 January 1844, in *JSP-J*, 3:171.

2. On Phelps's role as a clerk for Smith and his occasional ghostwriter, see Samuel Brown, "The Translator and the Ghostwriter: Joseph Smith and W.W. Phelps," *Journal of Mormon History* 34, no. 1 (Winter 2008): 26–62.

3. Smith, *General Smith's Views*, 7.

4. Joseph Smith, Journal, 26 January 1844, in *JSP-J*, 3:168. The compilation of the addresses and messages of American presidents that Phelps and Smith referenced was likely [Edward Walker, ed.] *The Addresses and Messages of the Presidents of the United States, from Washington to Tyler*, 4th ed. (New York: Edward Walker, 1843).

5. McBride, *Pulpit and Nation*, 165–170.

6. Andrew Burstein, *America's Jubilee*, 6.

7. Smith, *General Smith's Views*, 6. The quote from Monroe's first inaugural address appears in *The Addresses and Messages of the Presidents of the United States*, 206.

8. Smith, *General Smith's Views*, 7 8.

9. Smith, *General Smith's Views*, 8.

10. U.S. Constitution, art. I, §2.

11. Smith, *General Smith's Views*, 8–9.

12. In 1816 a congressional act had fixed the compensation for members of Congress at $1,500 per year instead of daily compensation. However, this act was short-lived, and, in 1818, another act changed congressional pay to $8 per day plus 40¢ compensation for each mile traveled. See Jonathan Chace, "Inadequate Congressional Salaries," *The North American Review* 148, no. 389 (April 1889): 504.

13. Smith, *General Smith's Views*, 9.

14. Smith, *General Smith's Views*, 8, 11.

15. Smith, *General Smith's Views*, 10.

16. Amy S. Greenberg, *Manifest Manhood and the Antebellum American Empire* (New York: Cambridge University Press, 2005), 14, 22.

17. Ralph Waldo Emerson, "The Young American," *Essays and Lectures* (London: John Chapman, 1844). Also see Daniel Walker Howe, *What Hath God Wrought: The Transformation of America, 1815–1848* (New York: Oxford University Press, 2007), 96–97, 112–116.

18. Howe, *What Hath God Wrought*, 658–682.

19. Michael A. Morrison, *Slavery and the American West: The Eclipse of Manifest Destiny and the Coming of the Civil War* (Chapel Hill: University of North Carolina Press, 1997), 26–36; Patricia Nelson Limerick, *Legacy of Conquest: The Unbroken Past of the American West* (New York: W.W. Norton, 1987), 259–266.

20. Amy S. Greenberg, *A Wicked War: Polk, Clay, and the 1846 Invasion of Mexico* (New York: Knopf, 2012), 15.

21. Joseph Smith would repeat these rumors of British meddling in Texas in a March 1844 political speech. See Wilford Woodruff, Journal, 7 March 1844, CHL.

22. Sam W. Haynes, *Unfinished Revolution: The Early American Republic in a British World* (Charlottesville: University of Virginia Press, 2010), 230–250; Lelia M. Roeckell, "Bonds over Bondage: British Opposition to the Annexation of Texas," *Journal of the Early Republic* 19, no. 2 (Summer 1999): 257–278; and Howe, *What Hath God Wrought*, 672.

23. Henry Clay to Peter Porter, 26 January 1838, in Hopkins et al., *The Papers of Henry Clay*, 9:135. Also see Klotter, *Henry Clay*, 294.

24. On Clay and the Texas question as it pertained to his 1844 presidential campaign, see Klotter, *Henry Clay*, 294–299.

25. Silas Wright to Martin Van Buren, 6 April 1844, [Collection]. Also see Donald B. Cole, *Martin Van Buren and the American System* (Princeton: Princeton University Press, 1984), 391–392.

26. Willard Carl Klunder, *Lewis Cass and the Politics of Moderation*, 98, 136–138. Later in 1844, James Pinckney Henderson wrote to Texas President Sam Houston and informed him that if Cass won the nomination of the Democratic Party he would beat Clay in the general election and thus ensure the annexation of Texas. See James Pinckney Henderson to Sam Houston, 20 May 1844, Andrew Jackson Houston Papers #3473, Archives and Information Services Division, Texas State Library and Archives Commission.

27. *Niles' Weekly Register*, 22 July 1843. Also see Miles Smith, "'Turning Up Their Noses at the Colonel': Eastern Aristocracy, Western Democracy, and

Richard Mentor Johnson," *The Register of the Kentucky Historical Society* 111, no. 4 (Autumn 2013), 558.

28. Howe, *What Hath God Wrought*, 675–682.

29. Smith, *General Smith's Views*, 10.

30. On the divisions within the antislavery movement in the United States and abroad, see Minsha Sinha, *The Slave's Cause: A History of Abolition* (New Haven: Yale University Press, 2017); Eric Burin, *Slavery and the Peculiar Solution: A History of the American Colonization Society* (Gainesville: University of Florida Press, 2005).

31. Letter to Oliver Cowdery, circa 9 April 1836, in *JSP-D*, 5:238.

32. Joseph Smith, Journal, 2 January 1843, in *JSP-J*, 2:212. For an overview of Smith's evolving views on race, see W. Paul Reeve, *Religion of a Different Color: Race and the Mormon Struggle for Whiteness* (New York: Oxford University Press, 2015), 122–128.

33. Reeve, *Religion of a Different Color*, 106; Historical Introduction to Bond to Elijah Abel, 8 December 1839, in *JSP-D*, 7:81–85. In the 1850s, under the leadership of Brigham Young, the church would restrict priesthood ordination for men of black ancestry. Reeve, *Religion of a Different Color*, 153–157, 160.

34. "General Assembly," *Latter Day Saints' Messenger and Advocate* (Kirtland, OH), August 1835.

35. Park, *Kingdom of Nauvoo*, 140–141.

36. For example, see Selections from *Times and Seasons*, 1 October 1842, in *JSP-D*, 11:130. Also see Reeve, *Religion of a Different Color*, 122–128.

37. Historical Introduction to Bond to Elijah Abel, 8 December 1839, in *JSP-D*, 7:81–85.

38. Smith, *General Smith's Views*, 3.

39. Smith, *General Smith's Views*, 9.

40. Smith, *General Smith's Views*, 9. Joseph Addison, *Cato* Act II, scene i, lines 99–100.

41. In *General Smith's Views*, Joseph Smith does not explicitly state what would become of the slaves after they were freed. While he never appears to have settled on a definite plan, in a March 1844 speech Smith suggested relocating freed slaves to Mexico. See Wilford Woodruff, Journal, 7 March 1844, CHL.

42. Gordon S. Wood, *Empire of Liberty: A History of the Early Republic, 1789–1815* (New York: Oxford University Press, 2009), 98–99, 143–145, 293–296, 673; and Sharon Ann Murphy, *Other People's Money: How Banking Worked in the Early American Republic* (Baltimore: Johns Hopkins University Press, 2017), 34–39.

43. Howe, *What Hath God Wrought*, 373–386; Murphy, *Other People's Money*, 80–82, 95–99.

44. Smith, *General Smith's Views*, 9. Joseph Smith and the Latter-day Saints had experienced the failure of a financial institution of their own in 1837. See "Volume Introduction," *JSP-D*, 5:xxvii–xxxii.

45. Smith, *General Smith's Views*, 10.

46. Murphy, *Other People's Money*, 106–127.

47. Murphy, *Other People's Money*, 106–127.

48. Murphy, *Other People's Money*, 114–116. On the hardship the banking crisis caused in western Illinois and the city of Nauvoo in particular, see Historical Introduction to Discourse, 25 February 1842, in *JSP-D*, 11:474–477. On the shortage of specie during the 1830s and 1840s, see Jessica M. Lepler, *The Many Panics of 1837: People, Politics, and the Creation of a Transatlantic Financial Crisis* (Cambridge: Cambridge University Press, 2013), 132–136.

49. Joseph Smith, Journal, 5 February 1844, in *JSP-J*, 3:173.

50. *JSP-D*, 6:274–278.

51. On the vision for and function of penitentiaries in the United States during the nineteenth century, see Edward L. Ayers, *Vengeance and Justice: Crime and Punishment in the Nineteenth-Century South* (New York: Oxford University Press, 1984); and Jen Manion, *Liberty's Prisoners: Carceral Culture in Early America* (Philadelphia: University of Pennsylvania Press, 2015).

52. For examples of the reports on conditions in American prisons, see *Reports of the Prison Discipline Society, Boston, 1836–1845* (Boston: T.R. Marvin, 1855). Social activist Dorothea Dix published her landmark essay on American prison reform in 1845, the year after Smith published his campaign pamphlet. Dix's essay describes conditions in American prisons— including penitentiaries—and sets forth detailed measures for reform. See Dorothea Dix, *Remarks on Prisons and Prison Discipline in the United States* (Boston: Munroe and Francis, 1845). Starting in the 1820s, some reform groups began advocating specifically for reform related to the treatment of female prisoners. See Marie Gottschalk, *The Prison and the Gallows: The Politics of Mass Incarceration in America* (New York: Cambridge University Press, 2006), 116–117.

53. Alexis de Tocqueville, *Democracy in America*, trans. Henry Reeve, 4th ed. (New York: J. and H. G. Langley, 1841), 2 vols., 1:44.

54. Manion, *Liberty's Prisoners*, 14.

55. Smith, *General Smith's Views*, 9.

56. Smith, *General Smith's Views*, 9.

57. On debtor prisons in the United States and their role in impeding the social mobility of lower classes, see Bruce H. Mann, *Republic of Debtors: Bankruptcy in the Age of American Independence* (Cambridge: Harvard University Press, 2003), 78–108.

58. Lucy Mack Smith, History, 1844–1845, 2–4, CHL.

59. Letter from Jacob W. Jenks, 31 December 1839, in *JSP-D* 7:95.

60. Edward J. Balleisen, *Navigating Failure: Bankruptcy and Commercial Society in Antebellum America* (Chapel Hill: University of North Carolina Press, 2001), 12–15, 81.
61. Act to Establish a Uniform System of Bankruptcy, 27th Congress, 1841. Also see Balleisen, *Navigating Failure*. Smith had applied for bankruptcy under the 1841 act (before Congress repealed it in 1843), but his proceedings did not conclude during his lifetime. See Bushman, *RSR*, 433–434.
62. Joseph Smith, Journal, 5 February 1844, in *JSP-J*, 3:173. The manuscript draft of General Smith's *Views* that Smith signed is in the handwriting of clerk Thomas Bullock. See Joseph Smith, General Smith's Views on the Powers and Policy of Government of the United States, draft, Joseph Smith Collection, CHL.
63. Wilford Woodruff, Journal, 8 February 1844, CHL.
64. Wilford Woodruff, Journal, 8 February 1844, CHL.
65. Wilford Woodruff, Journal, 8 February 1844, CHL.
66. Wilford Woodruff, Journal, 8 February 1844, CHL.
67. Joseph Smith, Journal, 24 February 1944, in *JSP-J*, 3:183.
68. Joseph Smith, Journal, 24–25 February 1944, in *JSP-J*, 3:183.
69. Smith mailed approximately 200 copies of *General Smith's Views* on February 27, 1844. See Joseph Smith, Journal, 27 February 1844, in *JSP-J*, 3:184.

CHAPTER 8

1. For a thorough examination of the development of Smith's political ideology concerning the United States and its government during the 1830s, see Mark Roscoe Ashurst-McGee, "Zion Rising: Joseph Smith's Early Social and Political Thought" (Ph.D. dissertation, Arizona State University, 2008).
2. Council of Fifty, Minutes, 10 March 1844, in *JSP-A*, 1:20. Clayton used his personal journal to reconstruct the first several entries in the council's minute books months after those meetings occurred. See *JSP-A*, 1:20.
3. Council of Fifty, Minutes, 10 March 1844, in *JSP-A*, 1:39.
4. Council of Fifty, Minutes, 10 March 1844, in *JSP-A*, 1:21–37.
5. Council of Fifty, Minutes, 10 March 1844, in *JSP-A*, 1:39.
6. Council of Fifty, Minutes, 10 March 1844, in *JSP-A*, 1:39.
7. Council of Fifty, Minutes, 11 March 1844, in *JSP-A*, 1:41–42, underlining in original.
8. William Clayton recorded the minutes of the Council of Fifty for its first several meetings retroactively and based on entries in his personal journal. Accordingly, it is in the minutes entry for March 19, 1844, that Clayton records the resolution to draft a constitution passed on March 11, 1844. See

Council of Fifty, Minutes, 19 March 1844, in *JSP-A*, 1:54. Also see editorial note in *JSP-A*, 1:40.

9. Council of Fifty, Minutes, 11 April 1844, in *JSP-A*, 1:101.

10. Council of Fifty, Minutes, 14 March 1844, in *JSP-A*, 1:49.

11. Daniel 2:35, 44, KJV.

12. J.F.C. Harrison, *The Second Coming: Popular Millenarianism, 1780–1850* (New Brunswick, NJ: Rutgers University Press, 1979).

13. *The Testimony of Christ's Second Appearing*, 2nd ed. (Albany, NY: E. and E. Hosford, 1810); and *A Summary View of the Millennial Church, or United Society of Believers, Commonly Called Shakers* (Albany, NY: Packard and Van Benthuysen, 1823). Also see Stephen J. Stein, *The Shaker Experience in America* (New Haven: Yale University Press, 1992), 29–30, 76–81.

14. For an overview of Miller's millennial predictions, see David L. Rowe, *God's Strange Work: William Miller and the End of the World* (Grand Rapids, MI: Eerdmans, 2008).

15. Joseph Smith, Journal, 12 February 1843, in *JSP-J*, 3:262–263.

16. Noah Packard, *Political and Religious Detector: In Which Millerism Is Exposed, False Principles Detected, and Truth Brought to Life* (Medina, OH: Michael Hayes, 1843).

17. Packard, *Political and Religious Detector*, 23–29; and Joseph Smith, Journal, 7 April 1843, in *JSP-J*, 2:341–342.

18. Joseph Smith, Journal, 3 April 1843, in *JSP-J*, 2:326.

19. Council of Fifty, Minutes, 11 March 1844, in *JSP-A*, 1:40.

20. Council of Fifty, Minutes, 5 April and 11 April 1844, in *JSP-A*, 1:84, 93–95. Ancient Israel had long served as a legitimizing model for American organizations and political movements. Examples include the Continental Army during the American Revolution, the Federalists during the debates over the ratification of the United States Constitution, and both proslavery and antislavery advocates in debates over the abolition of slavery. See Charles Royster, *A Revolutionary People at War: The Continental Army and American Character, 1775–1783* (Chapel Hill: University of North Carolina Press, 1979), 54–126; Eran Shalev, *American Zion: The Old Testament as a Political Text from the Revolution to the Civil War* (New Haven: Yale University Press, 2013), 50–83, 179–184; McBride, *Pulpit and Nation*, 40–45, 109–113; and Mark A. Noll, *The Civil War as a Theological Crisis* (Chapel Hill: University of North Carolina Press, 2006), 51–74.

21. Council of Fifty, Minutes, 18 April 1844, in *JSP-A*, 1:120.

22. Council of Fifty, Minutes, 5 April 1844, in *JSP-A*, 1:82.

23. On Young's authoritarian tactics in Utah Territory, see Brent M. Rogers, *Unpopular Sovereignty: Mormons and the Federal Management of Early Utah Territory* (Lincoln: University of Nebraska Press, 2017), 10–11.

24. Council of Fifty, Minutes, 11 April 1844, in *JSP-A*, 1:95–96.

25. Historians Office, General Church Minutes, 8 April 1844, CHL. For more analysis of the anointing of Smith as a prophet, priest, and king, as well as the action's connection to Mormon religious beliefs, see Park, "The Council of Fifty and the Perils of Democratic Governance," Matthew J. Grow and R. Eric Smith, *The Council of Fifty: What the Records Reveal about Mormon History*, 48–49; and Volume Introduction, in *JSP-A*, 1:xxxviii.

26. Council of Fifty, Minutes, 18 April 1844, in *JSP-A*, 1:128.

27. "The Globe," *Times and Seasons*, 15 April 1844. Smith is listed as the author of this editorial but apparently relied on the ghostwriting services of William W. Phelps. See Patrick Q. Mason, "God and the People: Thedemocracy in Nineteenth-Century Mormonism," *Journal of Church and State* 53, no. 3 (Summer 2011), 357; and Brown, "The Translator and the Ghostwriter: Joseph Smith and W.W. Phelps," 50.

28. Council of Fifty, Minutes, 11 April 1844, in *JSP-A*, 1:92.

29. Council of Fifty, Minutes, 11 April 1844, in *JSP-A*, 1:97–100.

30. Council of Fifty, Minutes, 18 April 1844, in *JSP-A*, 1:110–114.

31. Council of Fifty, Minutes, 25 April 1844, in *JSP-A*, 1:135–137.

32. Council of Fifty, Minutes, 11 April 1844, in *JSP-A*, 1:120.

33. Joseph Smith, Journal, 14 March 1844, in *JSP-J*, 3:204.

34. Michael Scott Van Wagenen, *The Texas Republic and the Mormon Kingdom of God* (College Station: Texas A&M University Press, 2002), 40–41.

35. Council of Fifty, Minutes, 11 April 1844, in *JSP-A*, 1:88.

36. Council of Fifty, Minutes, 19 and 21 March 1844, in *JSP-A*, 1:52–57.

37. Council of Fifty, Minutes, 19 and 21 March 1844, in *JSP-A*, 1:52–57.

38. For example, see Smith, *General Smith's Views*, 10.

39. Samuel J. Watson, *Peacekeepers and Conquerors: The Army Officer Corps on the American Frontier, 1821–1846* (Lawrence: University Press of Kansas, 2013), 186. During the 1840s the United States Army would only begin to approach 100,000 members during wartime. The combined number of regulars and volunteers who served in the army during the Mexican-American War between 1846 and 1848 is estimated at approximately 86,000. See Greenberg, *A Wicked War*, 130.

40. Lyman Wight and Heber C. Kimball, petition, June 7, 1844, Records of the United States Senate, 28th Congress, Petitions and Memorials, Committee on Public Lands [SEN 28A-G17.1, Box no. 111], NARA.

41. Joseph Smith to Henry Clay, 13 May 1844, in *Times and Seasons*, 29 May 1844.

42. Orson Hyde to Sidney Rigdon, 26 April 1844, Joseph Smith Collection, CHL.

43. Council of Fifty, Minutes, 11 April 1844, in *JSP-A*, 1:90.

44. Paul A. Gilje, *Free Trade and Sailors' Rights in the War of 1812* (New York: Cambridge University Press, 2013), chapters 16–17 and 23. Also see Council of Fifty, Minutes, 11 April 1844, in *JSP-A*, 1:90n231.

CHAPTER 9

1. Joseph Smith, Journal, 29 January 1844, in *JSP-J*, 1:170.
2. The content of Young's discourse on this occasion was recorded in the conference's minutes by Thomas Bullock. Bullock used abbreviations in his minutes. Young's words were spelled out in full in the manuscript history of the church written years later. The text quoted here is from the latter source but verified in the original minutes. See Thomas Bullock, Minutes, 9 April 1844, General Church Minutes, CHL; and Manuscript History of the Church, 1993, CHL.
3. The content of Hyrum Smith's discourse on this occasion was recorded in the conference's minutes by Thomas Bullock. Bullock used abbreviations in his minutes. Hyrum Smith's words were spelled out in full in the manuscript history of the church written years later. The text quoted here is from the latter source but verified in the original minutes. See Thomas Bullock, Minutes, 9 April 1844, General Church Minutes, CHL; Manuscript History of the Church, 1995–1996, CHL.
4. "Special Conference," *Times and Seasons*, 15 April 1844.
5. The precise number of electioneering missionaries who eventually campaigned for Smith is unclear. Margaret C. Robertson estimates a total of 400 missionaries but notes that some of the men who volunteered and were subsequently assigned to a location by church leaders never started their missions while others not included on initial lists did serve electioneering missions. In a comprehensive study of the electioneering missionaries, Derek Sainsbury counts approximately 600 electioneering missionaries. However, Sainsbury includes in his count men who aided the campaign in substantive ways such as writing and publishing but who did not necessarily leave home to campaign for Smith. See Margaret C. Robertson, "The Campaign and the Kingdom: The Activities of the Electioneers in Joseph Smith's Presidential Campaign," *BYU Studies Quarterly* 39, no. 3 (2000): 147–180; and Derek R. Sainsbury, *Storming the Nation: The Unknown Contributions of Joseph Smith's Political Missionaries* (Provo, UT: Religious Studies Center, Brigham Young University, 2020).
6. Council of Fifty, Minutes, 25 April 1844, in *JSP-A*, 1:133.
7. Council of Fifty, Minutes, 25 April 1844, in *JSP-A*, 1:133–134.
8. Stan M. Haynes, *The First American Political Conventions: Transforming Presidential Nominations, 1823–1872* (Jefferson, NC: McFarland and Company, 2012), 5–27; and James W. Davis, *National Conventions in an Age of Party Reform* (Westport, CT: Greenwood Press, 1983), 19–27.
9. Haynes, *The First American Political Conventions*, 27–39.
10. Haynes, *The First American Political Conventions*, 10–18.
11. On the long-held aversion of American politicians and the voting public to candidates directly campaigning to the public, see Gordon S. Wood,

Radicalism of the American Revolution (New York: Knopf, 1991), 287–305; and Mark R. Cheathem, *The Coming of Democracy: Presidential Campaigning in the Age of Jackson* (Baltimore: Johns Hopkins University Press, 2018), 9–11.

12. On the transformation of presidential campaign practices during the 1830s and 1840s, see Cheathem, *The Coming of Democracy*.

13. Sainsbury, *Storming the Nation*, 65–83.

14. "Correspondence," *Northern Islander* [Beaver Island, Michigan], 30 August 1855.

15. Brigham Young and Willard Richards to Reuben Hedlock and the Saints in the British Empire, 3 May 1844, Willard Richards Journals and Papers, CHL.

16. Franklin D. Richards, Journal, 21 May 1844, Franklin D. Richards Journals, Richards Family Collection, CHL. Also see Sainsbury, *Storming the Nation*, 120.

17. Luke 10:14, KJV.

18. Bushman, *RSR*, 152–154; Reid L. Neilson, "Mormon Mission Work," in Terryl L. Givens and Philip L. Barlow, eds., *The Oxford Handbook of Mormonism* (New York: Oxford University Press, 2015), 182–195; John G. Turner, *Brigham Young: Pioneer Prophet* (Cambridge: Harvard University Press, 2012), 20–28; and "History of Willard Richards," *Deseret News* 23 June 1858.

19. Henry G. Boyle, Reminiscences and Diary, typescript, 5–6, CHL.

20. Daniel Durham Hunt, Journal, 1–6, CHL.

21. Nancy Naomi Alexander Tracy, Reminiscences and Diary, typescript, 28, CHL.

22. Jacob Hamblin, "Record of the Life of Jacob Hamblin as Recorded by Himself," 103, CHL. Also see Sainsbury, *Storming the Nation*, 63.

23. Dwight Harding to Ralph Harding, 22 August 1844, Ralph Harding Correspondence, 1844–1846, CHL.

24. Sally Randall to "Dear Friends," 21 April 1844, Sally Randall Letters, 1843–1852, CHL.

25. Daniel H. Wells to Joseph Combs, 31 March 1844, Wells Family Correspondence, circa 1832–1852, CHL.

26. Samuel Hollister Rogers, Journal, 20 June 1844, photocopy, CHL.

27. Henry G. Boyle, "Autobiography and Diary of Henry G. Boyle," typescript, 5–6, CHL.

28. Amasa Lyman, Journal, 25 June 1844, Amasa Lyman Collection, CHL.

29. *Times and Seasons*, 1 August 1844.

30. Wilford Woodruff, Journal, 1 July 1844, CHL; "Communications," *The Prophet*, 13 July 1844. Also see Sainsbury, *Storming the Nation*, 136–137.

31. William Lampard Watkins, "A Brief History of the Life of William Lampard Watkins," typescript, 1, CHL. Also see Sainsbury, *Storming the Nation*, 133.

32. William Lampard Watkins, "A Brief History of the Life of William Lampard Watkins," typescript, 2, CHL.
33. Abraham Smoot, Journal, 29 May and 4 June 1844, CHL.
34. Abraham Smoot, Journal, 25 May 1844, CHL.
35. Sainsbury, *Storming the Nation*, 124–126.
36. William Lampard Watkins, "A Brief History of the Life of William Lampard Watkins," typescript, 3, CHL.
37. On the debate over and nature of slavery in antebellum Kentucky, see Marion Brunson Lucas, *A History of Blacks in Kentucky: Slavery to Segregation, 1760–1891* (Lexington: University Press of Kentucky, 2003), 42, 86, 140; J. Winston Coleman Jr., *Slavery Times in Kentucky* (1940; repr. New York: Johnson Reprint, 1970), vii; William Frehling, *Road to Disunion: Secessionists Triumphant, 1854–1861* (New York: Oxford University Press, 1990), 18, 35, 74; Klotter, *Henry Clay*, 192–193; and Aaron Astor, *Rebels on the Border: Civil War, Emancipation, and the Reconstruction of Kentucky and Missouri* (Baton Rouge: Louisiana State University, 2012).
38. "A Friend to the Mormons," *Times and Seasons*, 15 March 1844.
39. "For President, Gen. Joseph Smith," *Times and Seasons*, 1 March 1844; For President, Joseph Smith, *Nauvoo* Neighbor, 28 February 1844.
40. "Illinois. The Mormons," and "A New Candidate in the Field," *Niles' National Register*, 2 March 1844.
41. "Mormon Movements," *New York Herald*, 23 May 1844.
42. "New Candidate," *People's Organ*, 6 March 1844.
43. *Boston Investigator*, 15 May 1844.
44. *Working Man's Advocate*, 18 May 1844.
45. John Windt et al., to Joseph Smith, 20 April 1844, in "State Convention," *Nauvoo Neighbor*, 22 May 1844; Joseph Smith to John Windt et al., 16 May 1844, in "State Convention," *Nauvoo Neighbor*, 22 May 1844. On the history of the National Reform Association, see Jonathan H. Earle, *Jacksonian Antislavery and the Politics of Free Soil, 1824–1854* (Chapel Hill: University of North Carolina Press, 2005), 58–61.
46. "Life in Nauvoo," *New-York Tribune*, 28 May 1844.
47. *Belleville Advocate*, 18 April 1844.
48. Anti-Mormon newspapers were expectedly critical of Smith's candidacy. Invoking Smith's January 1844 letter to John C. Calhoun, the *Warsaw Signal* pressed Smith on his plan to obtain redress for the Mormons' persecution in Missouri, arguing that Smith's tone suggested retribution for Missouri as unjust as that which the Mormons had experienced in that state. See "To Jo Smith," *Warsaw Signal*, 21 February 1844.
49. The second party system in the United States was characterized in many ways by a large section of the country's electorate voting based on issues more than out of party loyalty. See Graham A. Peck, "Was There a Second

Party System?: Illinois as a Case Study in Antebellum Politics," in Daniel Peart and Adam Smith, eds., *Practicing Democracy: Popular Politics in the United States from the Constitution to the Civil War* (Charlottesville: University of Virginia Press, 2015), 145–172.

50. Council of Fifty, Minutes, 25 April 1844, in *JSP-A*, 1:135.

51. *The Prophet*, 25 May 1844; Peter Crawley, *A Descriptive Bibliography of the Mormon Church* (Provo, UT: BYU Religious Studies Center, 1997), 2 vols., 1:255.

52. Crawley, *A Descriptive Bibliography of the Mormon Church*, 255.

53. "Prospectus of a Weekly Newspaper to be Entitled The Prophet," *The Prophet*, 18 May 1844.

54. Crawley, *A Descriptive Bibliography of the Mormon Church*, 255.

55. Will Bagley, ed., *Scoundrel's Tale: The Samuel Brannan Papers* (Spokane, WA: Arthur H. Clark Company, 1999), 255–279.

56. "Samuel Brannan," *The Saints' Herald*, 25 May 1889; "Samuel Brannan," in Frank Soulé et al., eds., *The Annals of San Francisco* (New York: D. Appleton and Company, 1855), 748–749.

57. "Samuel Brannan," *The Saints' Herald*, 25 May 1889; and "Samuel Brannan," in Soulé et al., eds., *The Annals of San Francisco*, 748–749.

58. "An Appeal to the Freeman of the State of Vermont, 'The Brave Green Mountain Boys,' and Honest Men," *The Prophet*, 18 May 1844.

59. For examples, see "The Globe," *The Prophet*, 18 May 1844; "Nauvoo Mansion," *The Prophet*, 18 May 1844; and "All Is Peace at Nauvoo among the Saints," *The Prophet*, 25 May 1844

60. For examples, see "Public Meeting," *The Prophet*, 1 June 1844; "Jeffersonians Attend," *The Prophet*, 8 June 1844; and "Jeffersonian Convention," *The Prophet*, 8 June 1844.

61. *The Prophet*, 8 June 1844.

62. Jeffrey L. Pasley, *"The Tyranny of Printers": Newspaper Politics in the Early American Republic* (Charlottesville: University of Virginia Press, 2001), 8–9, 173–174, 401–405.

63. Church leaders in Nauvoo had originally scheduled the convention for 2 May 1844 but soon thereafter postponed it for two weeks to 17 May 1844. See "Public Meeting," *Nauvoo Neighbor*, 24 April 1844; Council of Fifty, Minutes, 6 May 1844, in *JSP-A*, 1:157.

CHAPTER 10

1. Joseph Smith, Journal, 4 March 1844, in *JSP-J*, 3:189; Wilford Woodruff, Journal, 3 March 1844, CHL.

2. Joseph Smith, Journal, 4 March 1844, in *JSP-J*, 3:189.

3. Francis B. Heitman, *Historical Register and Dictionary of the United States Army, from Its Organization, September 29, 1789, to March 2, 1903* (Washington, DC: Government Printing Office, 1903), 211; Teunis G. Bergen, *The Bergen Family: Or the Descendants of Hans Hansen Bergen* (Albany, NY: Joel Munsell, 1876), 335; James Bennet, *The American System of Practical Book-Keeping* (New York: Collins and Hannay, 1824). Also see Lyndon W. Cook, "James Arlington Bennet and the Mormons," *Brigham Young University Studies* 19, no. 2 (1979): 247–249.

4. "Military Appointment," *The Wasp* [Nauvoo, IL], 30 April 1842.

5. Smith and Bennet first corresponded directly in 1842. The first letter was from Smith, introducing Willard Richards to Bennet in June. Their regular correspondence commenced in September. See Letter to James Arlington Bennet, 30 June 1842, in *JSP-D*, 10:205–209; Letter from James Arlington Bennet, 16 August 1842, in *JSP-D*, 10:426–430; Letter from James Arlington Bennet, 1 September 1842, in *JSP-D*, 11:11–17; and Letter to James Arlington Bennet, 8 September 1842, in *JSP-D*, 11:74–83.

6. James Arlington Bennet to Joseph Smith, 24 October 1843, Joseph Smith Collection, CHL.

7. James Arlington Bennet to Joseph Smith, 24 October 1843, Joseph Smith Collection, CHL. Also see Joseph Smith, Journal, 9 November 1843, in *JSP-J*, 3:127, 127n568.

8. Willard Richards to James Arlington Bennet, 4 March 1844, Willard Richards Journals and Papers, 1821–1854, CHL.

9. Willard Richards to James Arlington Bennet, 24 October 1842, Willard Richards Journals and Papers, 1821–1854, CHL.

10. Willard Richards to James Arlington Bennet, 4 March 1844, Willard Richards Journals and Papers, 1821–1854, CHL.

11. James Arlington Bennet to Willard Richards, 14 April 1844, Willard Richards Journals and Papers, 1821–1854, CHL.

12. Willard Richards to James Arlington Bennet, 20 June 1844, Willard Richards Journals and Papers, 1821–1854, CHL.

13. Several scholars who have examined Smith's campaign have offered their respective opinions on how serious Smith was about his presidential ambitions. Fawn Brodie wrote that Smith "suffered from no illusions about his chances of winning the supreme political post in the nation. He entered the ring not only to win publicity for himself and his church, but most of all to shock the other candidates into some measure of respect." See Fawn Brodie, *No Man Knows My History: The Life of Joseph Smith*, 2nd edition (New York: Knopf, 1971), 362. Richard Bushman portrays Smith's campaign largely as a gesture designed to attract publicity to the church and its petitioning efforts but acknowledges that "with a large field of candidates and no clear favorite," Smith "may have

thought he could gain votes through convert baptisms and steal the victory in a split vote." See Bushman, *RSR*, 515. In setting forth their conspiracy theory that Smith was assassinated in order to elect Henry Clay president, Robert S. Wicks and Fred R. Foister portray Smith as a serious candidate with a real chance to win. See Robert S. Wicks and Fred R. Foister, *Junius and Joseph: Presidential Politics and the Assassination of the First Mormon Prophet* (Logan: Utah State University Press, 2005). John Bicknell asserts that Smith "understood fully that he would not be elected president" but that "the campaign afforded him a chance to spread the word about Mormonism and put its case before the people and their leaders." Bicknell, *America 1844*, 48–49. Also see Newell G. Bringhurst, "Reflections on a Roundtable Colloquium Dealing with Joseph Smith's 1844 Campaign for U.S. President," *John Whitmer Historical Society Journal* 22 (2002): 153–158; Daniel N. Gullotta, "A Prophet for President: A Study of the Political Thought of Joseph Smith, His Campaign for the United States Presidency in the 1844 Election, and the Imagination of Jacksonian America" (master's thesis, Yale University Divinity School, 2016); and Park, *Kingdom of Nauvoo*, 185–190, 208–210.

14. Robert G. Dixon, "Electoral College Procedure," *The Western Political Quarterly* 3, no. 2 (June 1950): 215.

15. Willard Richards to James Arlington Bennet, 20 June 1844, Willard Richards Journals and Papers, 1821–1854, CHL.

16. Betty Fladeland, *James Gillespie Birney: Slaveholder to Abolitionist* (Ithaca: Cornell University Press, 1955), 1–28.

17. Fladeland, *James Gillespie Birney*, 31–50.

18. Fladeland, *James Gillespie Birney*, 39–50. For a history of the American Colonization Society, see Eric Burin, *Slavery and the Peculiar Solution: A History of the American Colonization Society* (Gainesville: University of Florida Press, 2005).

19. Fladeland, *James Gillespie Birney*, 51–89.

20. Fladeland, *James Gillespie Birney*, 133–160.

21. Reinhard O. Johnson, *The Liberty Party, 1840–1848: Antislavery Third-Party Politics in the United States* (Baton Rouge: Louisiana State University Press, 2009), 6–11; and James G. Birney, *A Letter on the Political Obligations of Abolitionists* (Boston: Dow and Jackson, 1839).

22. One Liberty Party newspaper in Indiana admonished voters: "Vote as you pray. You must do it, or be recreant to your country, recreant to your religion, recreant to your God." See *Free Labor Advocate* [New Garden, Indiana], quoted in John R. McKivigan, *The War against Proslavery Religion: Abolitionism and the Northern Churches, 1830–1860* (Ithaca: Cornell University Press, 1984), 146.

23. Johnson, *The Liberty Party*, 11–21.

24. Johnson, *The Liberty Party*, 11–21; and Fladeland, *James Gillespie Birney*, 188–189.

25. Johnson, *The Liberty Party*, 23–49, quote at 49. Also see Klotter, *Henry Clay*, 308–310.

26. James G. Birney to Joshua Leavitt et al., 10 January 1842, in Dwight Lowell Dumond, ed., *Letters of James Gillespie Birney, 1831–1857* (New York: D. Appleton-Century Company, 1938), 2 vols., 2:645–657; and Grimstead, *American Mobbing*, 69.

27. *New York Emancipator and Free American*, 17 November 1842. Also see Klotter, *Henry Clay*, 308–310.

28. "A New Advocate for a National Bank," *The Daily Globe*, March 14, 1844.

29. "A New Advocate for a National Bank," *The Daily Globe*, March 14, 1844. Poindexter served as a Democratic senator from Mississippi from 1830 to 1835, but his political career ended after he fell out with Andrew Jackson and Martin Van Buren on several issues, including the Second Bank of the United States. See Edwin A. Miles, "Andrew Jackson and Senator George Poindexter," *The Journal of Southern History* 24, no. 1 (February 1958): 51–66.

30. "The Globe," *Times and Seasons*, 15 April 1844.

31. "The Globe," *Times and Seasons*, 15 April 1844.

32. "The Globe," *Times and Seasons*, 15 April 1844.

33. "The Globe," *Times and Seasons*, 15 April 1844.

34. The original letter Smith wrote to Hardin on 19 April 1844 is not extant. However, Hardin copied the letter's text into his correspondence with Blair. See John J. Hardin to Francis Blair, 7 May 1844, Stephen A. Douglas Collection, Special Collections Research Center, University of Chicago. The letter to *The Globe* was also published by the *New York Herald* and the *Nauvoo Neighbor*. See "The Next Presidency—Joe Smith, the Mormon Prophet, Defining His Position," *New York Herald*, 17 May 1844; and "The Globe," *Nauvoo Neighbor*, 17 April 1844.

35. James Arlington Bennet to Willard Richards, 14 April 1844, Willard Richards Journals and Papers, 1821–1854, CHL; Council of Fifty, Minutes, 21 March 1844, in *JSP-A*, 1:57. Bennet's name appeared in one issue of the *Nauvoo Neighbor* as Smith's running mate. However, in the next issue the editors announced that Bennet would not be on the ticket, after all. See *Nauvoo Neighbor*, 6 March 1844; *Nauvoo Neighbor*, 13 March 1844.

36. Robert M. McBride and Dan M. Robison, *Biographical Dictionary of the Tennessee General Assembly, Volume I, 1796–1861* (Nashville: Tennessee State Library and Archives and the Tennessee Historical Commission, 1975), 166–167; Wilford Woodruff, Journal, 19 April 1836 and 19 July 1836, CHL; and Council of Fifty, Minutes, 21 March 1844, in *JSP-A*, 1:57.

37. In the 1830s records of the Academy branch of the church, both Lewis Copeland and Robert Copeland are listed as "Coloured." See Wilford

Woodruff, Membership Record Book, 1835, Wilford Woodruff Collection, CHL.

38. Wilford Woodruff to Solomon Copeland, 19 March 1844, copy, Joseph Smith Office Papers, CHL.

39. Wilford Woodruff to Solomon Copeland, 19 March 1844, copy, Joseph Smith Office Papers, CHL.

40. Council of Fifty, Minutes, 6 May 1844, in *JSP-A*, 1:158.

41. On the rocky relationship between Smith and Rigdon, see Historical Introduction to Letter to George W. Robinson, 6 November 1842, in *JSP-D*, 11:196–199; "Elder Rigdon, &C.," *Times and Seasons*, 15 September 1842; and Joseph Smith, Journal, 11 February 1843, in *JSP-J*, 2:260.

42. Council of Fifty, Minutes, 6 May 1844, in *JSP-A*, 1:158–159.

43. *Nauvoo Neighbor*, 22 May 1844.

CHAPTER 11

1. Haynes, *The First American Political Conventions*, 71–77.

2. For example, see *Jonesborough Whig* [Jonesborough, TN], 5 January 1842.

3. Bicknell, *America 1844*, 71; *New York Tribune*, 3 May 1844.

4. Bicknell, *America 1844*, 71; *New York Tribune*, 3 May 1844.

5. See 1844 Whig Party platform in "The Presidential Question—Singular Prospects," *New York Herald*, 6 May 1844; Michael Holt, *The Rise and Fall of the American Whig Party: Jacksonian Politics and the Onset of the Civil War* (New York: Oxford University Press, 1999), 165–168.

6. "To the Editors," *Washington Daily National Intelligencer*, April 27, 1844. Also see Klotter, *Henry Clay*, 296–299.

7. *New York Tribune*, 3 May 1844; and Holt, *The Rise and Fall of the American Whig Party*, 189.

8. Klotter, *Henry Clay*, 300, 313–315.

9. "Theodore Frelinghuysen," *Centinel of Freedom* [Newark, NJ], 7 May 1844.

10. Bicknell, *America 1844*, 74. Also see Klotter, *Henry Clay*, 313–315.

11. Donald B. Cole, *Martin Van Buren and the American Political System* (Princeton: Princeton University Press, 1984), 269.

12. John Locke, *Epistola de Tolerentia/A Letter on Toleration*, Raymond Klibansky and J.W. Gough, eds. (Oxford: Clarendon Press, 1968), 133.

13. "For the Neighbor," *Nauvoo Neighbor*, 15 May 1844.

14. *Nauvoo Neighbor*, 22 May 1844.

15. Cheathem, *The Coming of Democracy*, 11–12.

16. Henry Clay to Joseph Smith, 15 November 1843, Joseph Smith Collection, CHL.

17. John F. Cowan to Joseph Smith, 23 January 1844, Joseph Smith Collection, CHL.
18. Joseph Smith to Henry Clay, 13 May 1844, in *Nauvoo Neighbor*, 29 May 1844.
19. Joseph Smith to Henry Clay, 13 May 1844, in *Nauvoo Neighbor*, 29 May 1844.
20. Joseph Smith to Henry Clay, 13 May 1844, in *Nauvoo Neighbor*, 29 May 1844.
21. Joseph Smith to Henry Clay, 13 May 1844, in *Nauvoo Neighbor*, 29 May 1844.
22. "For the Neighbor," *Nauvoo Neighbor*, 15 May 1844.
23. "For the Neighbor," *Nauvoo Neighbor*, 15 May 1844.

CHAPTER 12

1. Richard Brookhiser, *America's First Dynasty: The Adamses, 1735–1918* (New York: The Free Press, 2002), 113–121. On Adams's and Quincy's 1844 visit to Nauvoo, Illinois, see Jed L. Woodworth, "Josiah Quincy's 1844 Visit with Joseph Smith," *BYU Studies Quarterly* 39, no. 4 (2000): 71–87.
2. Robert A. McCaughey, *Josiah Quincy, 1772–1864: The Last Federalist* (Cambridge: Harvard University Press, 1974); and James R. Cameron, *The Public Service of Josiah Quincy, Jr., 1802–1882* (Quincy, MA: Quincy Co-operative Bank, 1964).
3. Josiah Quincy, *Figures of the Past from the Leaves of Old Journals* (Boston: Roberts Brothers, 1883), 378–379.
4. Quincy, *Figures of the Past*, 379.
5. Charles Francis Adams, Journal, 14 May 1844, in Henry Adams, "Charles Francis Adams Visits the Mormons in 1844," *Proceedings of the Massachusetts Historical Society*, Third Series, 68 (October 1944–May 1947): 284.
6. Quincy, *Figures of the Past*, 379.
7. Quincy, *Figures of the Past*, 379–380.
8. Quincy, *Figures of the Past*, 380.
9. Quincy, *Figures of the Past*, 380–381.
10. Quincy, *Figures of the Past*, 382.
11. Quincy, *Figures of the Past*, 382–384. On the religious views of Adams, see Sara Georgini, *Household Gods: The Religious Lives of the Adams Family* (New York: Oxford University Press, 2019), 82–118. (Quincy came from a family of devoted Unitarians); Robert A. McCaughey, *Josiah Quincy, 1772–1864: The Last Federalist* (Cambridge: Harvard University Press, 1974), 165.
12. Quincy, *Figures of the Past*, 384–385.

13. Quincy, *Figures of the Past*, 387; Charles Francis Adams, Journal, 14 May 1844, in *Adams*, "Charles Francis Adams Visits the Mormons in 1844," 285.
14. Quincy, *Figures of the Past*, 388.
15. Quincy, *Figures of the Past*, 388–389.
16. Quincy, *Figures of the Past*, 391–392.
17. Quincy, *Figures of the Past*, 397–398.
18. Quincy, *Figures of the Past*, 396–397.
19. Quincy, *Figures of the Past*, 398–399.
20. Quincy, *Figures of the Past*, 399.
21. Josiah Quincy to Mary Quincy, 16 May 1844, Quincy-Howe Family Papers, Massachusetts Historical Society.
22. Charles Francis Adams, Journal, 14 May 1844, in in *Adams*, "Charles Francis Adams Visits the Mormons in 1844," 286.
23. Quincy, *Figures of the Past*, 376–377.
24. Quincy, *Figures of the Past*, 381–382.
25. Quincy, *Figures of the Past*, 394.
26. Hatch, *The Democratization of American Christianity*, 9.
27. Quincy, *Figures of the Past*, 400.

CHAPTER 13

1. "State Convention," *Nauvoo Neighbor*, 22 May 1844; "Minutes of a Convention," *Nauvoo Neighbor*, 22 May 1844; and Joseph Smith, Journal, 17 May 1844, in *JSP-J*, 3:253.
2. "State Convention," *Nauvoo Neighbor*, 22 May 1844; and "Minutes of a Convention," *Nauvoo Neighbor*, 22 May 1844.
3. "Minutes of a Convention," *Nauvoo Neighbor*, 22 May 1844; Joseph Smith, Journal, 15 May 1844, in *JSP-J*, 3:251. The *Nauvoo Neighbor* first published Smith's reply to Clay in its May 29, 1844, issue. See "Gen. Smith's Rejoinder," *Nauvoo Neighbor*, 29 May 1844.
4. "Minutes of a Convention," *Nauvoo Neighbor*, 22 May 1844. The *Nauvoo Neighbor* only published cursory summaries of Smith's and Rigdon's speeches. It stated that Smith "spoke with much talent, and ability, and displayed a great knowledge of the political history of this nation, of the cause of evils under which our nation groans, and also the remedy." Rigdon addressed "the political dishonesty of both Henry Clay and Martin Van Buren," and stated "his views, nd the present condition of this country." See "Minutes of a Convention," *Nauvoo Neighbor*, 22 May 1844.
5. "Minutes of a Convention," *Nauvoo Neighbor*, 22 May 1844.
6. "Minutes of a Convention," *Nauvoo Neighbor*, 22 May 1844; and Joseph Smith, Journal, 17 May 1844, in *JSP-J*, 3:253.

7. "State Convention," *Nauvoo Neighbor*, 22 May 1844.
8. "The Tyler Convention," *New York Herald*, 29 May 1844.
9. Stan M. Haynes, *The First American Political Conventions: Transforming Presidential Nominations, 1832–1872* (Jefferson, NC: McFarland and Company, 2012), 80–81.
10. Cave Johnson to James K. Polk, 27 May 1844, in Herbert Weaver et al., eds., *Correspondence of James K. Polk* (Nashville: Vanderbilt University Press, 1989), 14 vols., 7:157.
11. Church leaders assigned Orson Hyde, Orson Pratt, John E. Page, and David S. Hollister to the Baltimore conventions. See *JSP-A*, 1:133n404.
12. David S. Hollister to Joseph Smith, 9 May 1844, Joseph Smith Collection, CHL.
13. David S. Hollister to Joseph Smith, 9 May 1844, Joseph Smith Collection, CHL.
14. David S. Hollister to Joseph Smith, 9 May 1844, Joseph Smith Collection, CHL.
15. Charles Sellers, *James K. Polk* (Princeton: Princeton University Press, 1957–1966), 2 vols., 2:76–89; and John Bicknell, *America 1844: Religious Fervor, Westward Expansion, and the Presidential Election That Transformed the Nation* (Chicago: Chicago Review Press, 2015), 84–88.
16. Sellers, *James K. Polk*, 2:76–89; and Bicknell, *America 1844*, 86.
17. Sellers, *James K. Polk*, 2:78–89; and Bicknell, *America 1844*, 87–88.
18. Sellers, *James K. Polk*, 2:88; and Bicknell, *America 1844*, 87–88.
19. "First Great Movement for the Presidency—Mr. Webster in the Field," *New York Herald*, 26 May 1844; and Peterson, *The Great Triumvirate*, 354–357, 361.
20. Bartlett, *John C. Calhoun*, 299–304; and Joseph G. Rayback, "The Presidential Ambitions of John C. Calhoun, 1844–1848," *The Journal of Southern History* 14, no. 3 (August 1948): 331–332.
21. "First Great Movement for the Presidency—Mr. Webster in the Field," *New York Herald*, 26 May 1844; and Peterson, *The Great Triumvirate*, 354–357.
22. *The North American and Daily Advertiser* [Philadelphia], 29 May 1844; "National Tyler Convention," *Daily National Intelligencer* [Washington, DC], 29 May 1844. Also see Bicknell, *America 1844*, 86–87.
23. "Two Baltimore Conventions," *The Atlas* [Boston], 30 May 1844; "The Tyler Convention," *New York Daily Herald*, 29 May 1844. Also see Bicknell, *America 1844*, 88.
24. Sellers, *James K. Polk*, 2:89; and Bicknell, *America 1844*, 88.
25. Sellers, *James K. Polk*, 2:89–91; and Bicknell, *America 1844*, 88.
26. Sellers, *James K. Polk*, 2:91–92; and Bicknell, *America 1844*, 88–90.

27. Bicknell, *America 1844*, 91; and Haynes, *The First American Political Conventions*, 83–84.
28. Bicknell, *America 1844*, 91; and Haynes, *The First American Political Conventions*, 84–86.
29. Sellers, *James K. Polk*, 32, 67–76.
30. *Nashville Union*, 14 May 1844 and 18 May 1844.
31. Lee Scott Theisen, "James K. Polk: Not So Dark a Horse," *Tennessee Historical Quarterly* 30, no. 4 (Winter 1971): 383–401; Sellers, *James K. Polk*, 2:70–73.
32. Theisen, "James K. Polk;" and Walter R. Borneman, *Polk: The Man Who Transformed the Presidency and America* (New York: Random House, 2008), 109–110.
33. For a comprehensive examination of Polk's political career prior to 1840, see Sellers, *James K. Polk*, vol. 1; Borneman, *Polk*, 64–66. On the nickname "Young Hickory," see Greenberg, *A Wicked War*, 25.
34. Sellers, *James K. Polk*, 1:421–469, 469–488; Greenberg, *A Wicked War*, 32–33; Borneman, *Polk*, 64–66.
35. *New York Tribune*, 1 June 1844.
36. *Nashville Republican Banner*, 7 June 1844.
37. Bicknell, *America 1844*, 92.
38. "Van Buren's Prospects on the Wane—Tyler's Movements—Gen. Smith, &c.," *Nauvoo Neighbor*, 5 June 1844.

CHAPTER 14

1. "All Is Peace at Nauvoo among the Saints," *Nauvoo Neighbor*, 1 May 1844.
2. Joseph Smith, Journal, 24 March 1844, in *JSP-J*, 3:207.
3. Charles Foster is the man who drew a pistol and aimed it at Smith. See Joseph Smith, Journal, 26 April 1844, in *JSP-J*, 3:236.
4. In January 1844, Smith had accused Law of adultery. Although Law denied the charge, Smith subsequently refused to perform the sealing ritual for him and his wife, Jane. Both Laws were excommunicated from the church on 18 April 1844 "for unchristianlike conduct." See Joseph Smith, Journal, 18 April 1844, in *JSP-J*, 3:231–232.
5. "Nauvoo Legion Officers," *JSP-J*, 3:474. Wilson Law was excommunicated from the church on 18 April 1844 for "for unchristianlike conduct." See Joseph Smith, Journal, 18 April 1844, in *JSP-J*, 3:231–232.
6. Historical Introduction to Letter of Introduction from Sidney Rigdon, 9 November 1839, in *JSP-D*, 7:57–58. Robert D. Foster was excommunicated from the church on 18 April 1844 "for unchristianlike conduct." See Joseph Smith, Journal, 18 April 1844, in *JSP-J*, 3:231–232.

7. Letter from Elias Higbee, 20 February 1840–A, in *JSP*-D, 7:180. Chauncey Higbee had been excommunicated from the church in 1842. See Nauvoo High Council Minutes, 20–24 May 1842, CHL. Francis Higbee was excommunicated from the church on 18 May 1844. See Nauvoo High Council Minutes, 18 May 1844, CHL.

8. Bushman, *RSR*, 526–531. Smith most notably taught about the potential of men and women to become like God in a May 1844 funeral sermon. See Joseph Smith, Journal, 7 April 1844, in *JSP-J*, 3:217–222. As historian Richard Bushman explains this controversial development in Smith's theological teachings, "Critics are wrong when they say Joseph Smith created a heaven of multiple gods like the pagan pantheons of Zeus and Thor. The gods in Joseph Smith's heaven are not distinct, willful personalities pursuing their own purposes. The Christian trinity was Joseph's model; the gods are one as Christ and the Father are one, distinct personalities unified in purpose and will." See Bushman, *RSR*, 535.

9. Joseph Smith, Petition for Writ of Habeas Corpus, 6 May 1844, Nauvoo, IL, Records, CHL; Joseph Smith, Journal, 6 May 1844, in *JSP-J*, 3:244–245; and Bushman, *RSR*, 529–530.

10. State of Illinois v. Joseph Smith for Adultery [Hancock County Circuit Court 1844], Hancock County, IL; Joseph Smith, Journal, 25 May 1844, in *JSP-J*, 3:260–261.

11. Joseph Smith, Journal, 27 May 1844, in *JSP-J*, 3:264.

12. Joseph Smith, Journal, 27 May 1844, in *JSP-J*, 3:264–265; and Bushman, *RSR*, 538–539.

13. Bushman, *RSR*, 539–540; Dallin H. Oaks, "The Suppression of the Nauvoo Expositor," *Utah Law Review* 9, no. 4 (Winter 1965): 868.

14. *Nauvoo Expositor*, 7 June 1844. Also see Bushman, *RSR*, 539–540.

15. *Nauvoo Expositor*, 7 June 1844.

16. Joseph Smith, Journal, 8 June 1844, in *JSP-J*, 1:274–276.

17. Joseph Smith, Journal, 10 June 1844, in *JSP-J*, 3:276–277.

18. Oaks, "The Suppression of the Nauvoo Expositor," 876–877. Also see Joseph Smith, Journal, 10 June 1844, in *JSP-J*, 3:277.

19. Testimony of John R. Wakefield, in "For the Neighbor," *Nauvoo Neighbor*, extra, 21 June 1844.

20. "The Time Is Come," *Warsaw Signal*, extra, 11 June 1844.

21. These remarks by William Law were recorded in an interview years later that was published in the *Salt Lake Tribune*. See *Salt Lake Tribune*, 31 July 1887. Also see Alex Beam, *American Crucifixion: The Murder of Joseph Smith and the Fate of the Mormon Church* (New York: Public Affairs, 2014), 122.

22. Joseph Smith, Journal, 10 June 1844, in *JSP-J*, 3:277.

23. For example, see "The Mormon Disturbances," *New York Tribune*, 6 July 1844.

24. Joseph Smith, Journal, 11 July 1844, in *JSP-J*, 3:279.

25. *Warsaw Signal*, 12 June 1844.

26. "To the Public," *Nauvoo Neighbor*, 12 June 1844; William Blackstone, *Commentaries on the Laws of England* (Oxford: Clarendon Press, 1765). The passage in Blackstone's *Commentaries* that Smith and company referred to states: "A fourth species of remedy by the mere act of the party injured, is the abatement, or removal of nuisances . . . whatsoever unlawfully annoys or doth damage to another is a nuisance; and such nuisance may be abated, that is, taken away or removed, by the party aggrieved thereby, so as he commits no riot in the doing of it." Quoted in Oaks, "The Suppression of the Nauvoo Expositor," 889.

27. "To the Public," *Nauvoo Neighbor*, 12 June 1844.

28. Joseph Smith, Petition for Writ of Habeas Corpus, 12 June 1844, State of Illinois v. Joseph Smith et al. on *Habeas Corpus* [Nauvoo Municipal Court 1844], Nauvoo, IL, Records, CHL; Writ of Habeas Corpus, 12 June 1844, State of Illinois v. Joseph Smith et al. on *Habeas Corpus* [Nauvoo Municipal Court 1844], Nauvoo, IL, Records, CHL; Hyrum Smith et al., Petition for Writ of Habeas Corpus, 13 June 1844, State of Illinois v. Joseph Smith et al. on *Habeas Corpus* [Nauvoo Municipal Court 1844], Nauvoo, IL, Records, CHL; and Writ of Habeas Corpus, 13 June 1844, State of Illinois v. Joseph Smith et al. on *Habeas Corpus* [Nauvoo Municipal Court 1844], Nauvoo, IL, Records, CHL. Also see Joseph Smith, Journal, 12–13 June 1844, in *JSP-J*, 3:279–280 and 280n1278.

29. *Warsaw Signal*, extra, 19 June 1844.

30. Joseph Smith, Journal, 17 June 1844, in *JSP-J*, 3:287–288.

31. Joseph Smith, Journal, 18 June 1844, in *JSP-J*, 3:290–291.

32. Joseph Smith, Proclamation, 18 June 1844, Joseph Smith Collection, CHL.

33. Brent M. Rogers, "'In the Style of an Independent Sovereign': Mid-Nineteenth-Century Mormon Martial Law Proclamations in American Political Culture," in McBride, Rogers, and Erekson, eds., *Contingent Citizens*, 110–127.

34. John C. Calhoun Jr. to [James Edward Calhoun, Pendleton], 19 July 1844, in Clyde N. Wilson et al., eds., *The Papers of John C. Calhoun* (University of South Carolina Press, 1959–2003), 28 vols., 19:397–399. Also see Brian Q. Cannon, "John C. Calhoun, Jr., Meets the Prophet Joseph Smith Shortly before the Departure for Carthage," *Brigham Young University Studies* 33, no. 4 (1993): 773–780.

35. John C. Calhoun Jr. to [James Edward Calhoun, Pendleton], 19 July 1844, in Wilson et al., eds., *The Papers of John C. Calhoun*, 19:398.

36. John C. Calhoun, Jr. to [James Edward Calhoun, Pendleton], 19 July 1844, in Wilson, et al., eds., *The Papers of John C. Calhoun*, 19:398.

37. *Warsaw Signal*, extra, 19 June 1844.

38. Joseph Smith to John Tyler, 20 June 1844, copy, Karpeles Manuscript Library, Santa Barbara, CA. Also see Brent M. Rogers, "'Armed Men Are Coming from the State of Missouri': Federalism, Interstate Affairs, and Joseph Smith's Final Attempt to Secure Federal Intervention in Nauvoo," *Journal of the Illinois State Historical Society* 109, no. 2 (Summer 2016): 148–149.

39. Joseph Smith to John Tyler, 20 June 1844, copy, Karpeles Manuscript Library, Santa Barbara, CA; and Rogers, "'Armed Men Are Coming from the State of Missouri,'" 148–149.

40. Joseph Smith to Thomas Ford, 16 June 1844, Joseph Smith Collection, CHL; and Joseph Smith to Thomas Ford, 21 June 1844, Joseph Smith Collection, CHL.

41. Thomas Ford to Joseph Smith, 22 June 1844, Joseph Smith Collection, CHL. According to legal scholarship by Dallin H. Oaks, Smith was justified under the law in suppressing the *Nauvoo Expositor* but had broken the law in ordering the destruction of the press and type. See Oaks, "The Suppression of the Nauvoo Expositor," 885.

42. *JSP-J*, 3:301. On the record-high water level of the Mississippi River, see John C. Calhoun Jr. to [James Edward Calhoun, Pendleton], 19 July 1844, in Wilson et al., eds., *The Papers of John C. Calhoun*, 19:397.

43. Joseph Smith to Emma Smith, 23 June 1844, copy, Joseph Smith Collection, CHL.

44. Willard Richards, Journal, 24 June 1844, in Willard Richards Papers, CHL.

45. John Taylor recorded this statement in a reminiscent account he wrote later that year. See "The Martyrdom of Joseph Smith and His Brother Hyrum," in *The Doctrine and Covenants of the Church of Jesus Christ of Latter Day Saints*, second edition (Nauvoo, IL: John Taylor), 1844, 444–445.

46. For examples, see Fred R. Foister and Robert S. Wicks, *Junius and Joseph: Presidential Politics and the Assassination of the First Mormon Prophet* (Logan: Utah State University Press, 2005), 157–180; Beam, *American Crucifixion*, 154–187; and Joseph L. Lyon and David W. Lyon, "Physical Evidence at Carthage Jail and What It Reveals about the Assassination of Joseph and Hyrum Smith," *Brigham Young University Studies* 47, no. 4 (2008): 4–50. Also see Brodie, *No Man Knows My History*, 380–395; and Bushman, *RSR*, 546.

47. Rogers, "'In the Style of an Independent Sovereign,'" 110–127.

48. Willard Richards, Journal, 23–27 June 1844, Willard Richards Papers, CHL.

49. Ford, *History of Illinois*, 340–345.

50. Willard Richards, Journal, 27 June 1844, Willard Richards Papers, CHL.

51. Joseph Smith to Emma Smith, 27 June 1844, Joseph Smith Collection, CHL.

52. Willard Richards, Journal, 27 June 1844, Willard Richards Papers, CHL; and Stephen Markham to Wilford Woodruff, 20 June 1856, Historian's Office, Joseph Smith History Documents, circa 1839–1860, CHL.

53. Willard Richards to Governor Ford, General Dunham, Colonel Markham, and Emma Smith, 27 June 1844, Willard Richards Papers, CHL.

54. Almira Mack Covey to Harriet Mack Whittemore, 18 July 1844, photocopy, Harriet Mack Whittemore Correspondence, CHL.

55. Willard Richards, Journal, 27 June 1844, Willard Richards Papers, CHL.

56. LaJean Carruth and Mark Lyman Staker, eds., "John Taylor's June 27, 1854, Account of the Martyrdom," *Brigham Young University Studies* 50, no. 2 (2001): 28n6.

57. Willard Richards to Thomas Ford, Jonathan Dunham, Stephen Markham, and Emma Smith, 27 June 1844, Willard Richards Journals and Papers, 1821–1854, CHL.

58. This argument counters that of Fred R. Foister and Robert S. Wicks. See Foister and Wicks, *Junius and Joseph*. Regarding the attempted assassination of presidential candidates, Frederick M. Kaiser compiled a list of all assassination attempts made on American presidents, presidential candidates, and presidents-elect in a special report for the United States Congress, but he omitted Joseph Smith. See Frederick M. Kaiser, *Direct Assaults against Presidents, Presidents-Elect, and Candidates*, Congressional Research Service Report RS20821 (Washington, DC: Office of Congressional Information and Publishing, 2008). Also see Frederick M. Kaiser, "Presidential Assassinations and Assaults: Characteristics and Impact on Protective Procedures," *Presidential Studies Quarterly* 11, no. 4 (Fall 1981): 545–558.

59. "Fourth of July," *Sangamo Journal* [Springfield, IL], 11 July 1844.

60. "The Mormon Difficulties," *Sangamo Journal*, 4 July 1844.

61. For a detailed history of the "Bible Riots" in Philadelphia, see Michael Feldberg, *The Philadelphia Riots of 1844: A Study of Ethnic Conflict* (Westport, CT: Greenwood Press, 1975); and Amanda Beyer-Purvis, "The Philadelphia Bible Riots of 1844: Contest over the Rights of Citizens," *Pennsylvania History* 83 (summer 2016): 366–393. On the public denouncement of such anti-Catholic violence in Springfield, Illinois, see "The Philadelphia Riots—Resolutions of a Whig Meeting," *Sangamo Journal*, 20 June 1844.

62. Vilate Kimball to Heber C. Kimball, 30 June 1844, photocopy, CHL.

63. Almira Mack Covey to Harriet Mack Whittemore, 18 July 1844, photocopy, Harriet Mack Whittemore Correspondence, CHL.

64. Sarah M. Kimball letter to Sarepta Heywood, circa 1844, Joseph L. Heywood Letters, CHL. For a summary of many of the written reactions to the deaths of Joseph and Hyrum Smith, see Jeffrey David Mahas, "Remembering the Martyrdom," in *Revelations in Context* (Salt Lake City: The Church of Jesus Christ of Latter-Day Saints, 2016), 299–306.

65. Smith's family and friends worried that anti-Mormons would attempt to steal and desecrate Joseph and Hyrum Smith's bodies. Accordingly, they buried coffins filled with bags of sand in the public cemetery while quietly interring the bodies in the basement of the unfinished Nauvoo House. Several months later, the bodies were quietly moved to an unmarked grave near the banks of the Mississippi River. See Bushman, *RSR*, 553.

66. Willard Richards to Brigham Young, 30 June 1844, Willard Richards Journals and Papers, 1821–1854, CHL.

CHAPTER 15

1. "Mormon Meetings," *Cleveland Herald*, 8 July 1844.

2. Wilford Woodruff, Journal, 15–17 July 1844, CHL. Woodruff stopped in New York City before departing for Nauvoo. See Wilford Woodruff, Journal, 24 July 1844. The reactions of many of the electioneering missionaries are described in Sainsbury, *Storming the Nation*, 153–164.

3. "The Mormon National (Presidential) Convention," *Niles National Register*, 29 July 1844.

4. In his diary, electioneering missionary Joseph A. Stratton wrote simply of what business was attended to at the Baltimore convention when he wrote, "nothing done." See Joseph A. Stratton, Journal, 12 July 1844, CHL.

5. For examples, see Matthew J. Grow, *"Liberty to the Downtrodden": Thomas L. Kane, Romantic Reformer* (New Haven: Yale University Press, 2009), 71–73.

6. "Death of J. Smith, The Mormon Imposter," *The Millennial Harbinger*, September 1844.

7. On American Protestants' view of the Mormons and other religious minorities as too "fanatical" to deserve religious freedom, see Fluhman, *"A Peculiar People."*

8. Boyle, "Autobiography and Diary of Henry G. Boyle, 1832–1855," 8.

9. Wilford Woodruff, Journal, 6 August 1844, CHL.

10. Minutes, 8 August 1844, Historian's Office General Church Minutes, 1839–1877, CHL. The minutes of the August 8, 1844, meeting were recorded in shorthand and later transcribed in long form. A recent transcription of the minutes varies from the earlier longform transcription. See Robin Scott Jensen and LaJean P. Caruth, eds. "Sidney Rigdon's Plea to the Saints: Transcription of Thomas Bullock's Shorthand Notes from August 8, 1844, Morning Meeting," *Brigham Young University Studies* 53, no. 2 (2014): 121–139.

11. Richard S. Van Wagoner, *Sidney Rigdon: A Portrait of Religious Excess* (Salt Lake City, UT: Signature Books, 1994), 352–360. Also see Turner, *Brigham Young*, 111–114; Ronald K. Esplin, "Joseph, Brigham and the Twelve: A

Succession of Continuity," *Brigham Young University Studies* 21, no. 3 (1981): 1–40; Ronald W. Walker, "Six Days in August: Brigham Young and the Succession Crisis of 1844," in David J. Whittaker and Arnold K. Garr, eds., *A Firm Foundation: Church Organization and Administration* (Provo, UT: Religious Studies Center, Brigham Young University), 161–196; and *JSP-A*, 1:208.

12. "An Epistle of the Twelve," *Times and Seasons*, 15 August 1844.

13. Voter turnout in Nauvoo was low, with only 720 casting votes. See *The Warsaw Signal*, 13 November 1844. Just days before the election, the *Nauvoo Neighbor* published an editorial in which it described its disappointment with both the Whig and Democratic parties in the wake of Smith's assassination. Alas, the editors determined that there were more redeeming characteristics among the Democrats than there were among the Whigs and thereby implied that the Mormons should vote for Polk. See "The Election," *Nauvoo Neighbor*, 6 November 1844. In New York, *The Prophet* officially endorsed Polk on October 19. See "The Consequence of One Vote," *The Prophet*, 19 October 1844.

14. Theodore Frelinghuysen to Henry Clay, 9 November 1844, in James Hopkins et al., eds., *The Papers of Henry Clay* (Lexington: University Press of Kentucky, 1959–1992), 10 vols. and supplement, 10:143.

15. Klotter, *Henry Clay*, 322–327.

16. Henry Clay to William Henry Seward, 9 November 1844, in James Hopkins et al., eds., *The Papers of Henry Clay* (Lexington: University Press of Kentucky, 1959--1992), 10 vols. and supplement, 10:143.

17. *Charleston Southern Patriot*, 25 November 1844. Also see Klotter, *Henry Clay*, 327.

18. Klotter, *Henry Clay*, 328–353.

19. Klotter, *Henry Clay*, 354–372.

20. Fladeland, *James Gillespie Birney*, 255–294.

21. Oaks and Hill, *Carthage Conspiracy*, 48–63.

22. Oaks and Hill, *Carthage Conspiracy*, 52–53.

23. Oaks and Hill, *Carthage Conspiracy*, 97–98, 186.

24. Council of Fifty, Minutes, 4 March 1845, in *JSP-A*, 1:292–295.

25. Council of Fifty, Minutes, 9 September 1845, in *JSP-A*, 1:465–477.

26. Hosea Stout, Journal, 26 September 1845, in Juanita Brooks, ed., *On the Mormon Frontier: The Diary of Hosea Stout, 1844–1889* (Salt Lake City: University of Utah Press, 1964), 2 vols., 1:73.

27. Leonard, *Nauvoo*, 525–550.

28. Leonard, *Nauvoo*, 551–562.

29. Leonard, *Nauvoo*, 574.

30. Turner, *Brigham Young*, 116–118; and Robin Scott Jensen, "Mormons Seeking Mormonism: Strangite Success and the Conceptualization of

Mormon Ideology, 1844–50," in Newell G. Bringhurst and John C. Hamer, eds., *Scattering of the Saints: Schism within Mormonism* (Independence, MO: John Whitmer Books, 2007).

31. Michael Scott Van Wagenen, *The Texas Republic and the Mormon Kingdom of God* (College Station: Texas A&M University Press, 2002), 52–63.
32. Bringhurst and Hamer, eds., *Scattering of the Saints*.

CONCLUSION

1. For instance, Mark A. Noll described his expansive work on religion in the early United States as an examination of "how religion influenced the early United States," but he mentions the rapidly expanding Mormon movement in only three sentences scattered throughout the book. See Mark A. Noll, *America's God: From Jonathan Edwards to Abraham Lincoln* (New York: Oxford University Press, 2002), 115, 183, 184. Gordon S. Wood describes the utility of using the history of the Mormons as a microcosm of many of the major trends and developments in nineteenth-century American history. See Gordon S. Wood, "Evangelical America and Early Mormonism," *New York History* 61, no. 4 (October 1980): 359–386. The significance of the Mormon past to the broader history of the United States is similarly demonstrated in Howe, *What Hath God Wrought*, 312–310, 723–731. Also see Nathan O. Hatch, *The Democratization of American Christianity* (New Haven: Yale University Press, 1989), 134–141. A recent exception to this trend is Benjamin E. Park, *Kingdom of Nauvoo*.
2. David Sehat, *The Myth of American Religious Freedom*, 4.
3. On perception among some segments of the nineteenth-century American public that Mormons and other religious minority groups were too fanatical and superstitious to deserve full religious liberty, see J. Spencer Fluhman, *"A Peculiar People": Anti-Mormonism and the Making of Religion in Nineteenth-Century America* (Chapel Hill: University of North Carolina Press, 2012).
4. For example, see Sotrios A. Barber, *The Fallacies of States' Rights* (Cambridge: Harvard University Press, 2013). Also see Spencer W. McBride, "When Joseph Smith Met Martin Van Buren," 150–158.
5. McBride, "When Joseph Smith Met Martin Van Buren," 150–158.
6. Joseph Smith to John C. Calhoun, 2 January 1844, Joseph Smith Collection, CHL.
7. Joseph Smith, Journal, 9 July 1843, in *JSP-J*, 3:55.
8. Joseph Smith to John C. Calhoun, 2 January 1844, Joseph Smith Collection, CHL.
9. T.J. Stiles, *Jesse James: Last Rebel of the Civil War* (New York: Knopf, 2002), 37–55.

10. David Rice Atchison to Jefferson Davis, 24 September 1854, David Rice Atchison Papers, Western Historical Manuscripts Collection, State Historical Society of Missouri, Kansas City, Missouri.

11. Brent M. Rogers, *Unpopular Sovereignty*.

12. Rogers, *Unpopular Sovereignty*, 288–291; Paul W. Reeve, *Religion of a Different Color: Race and the Mormon Struggle for Whiteness* (New York: Oxford University Press, 2015), 44–45.

13. Sehat, *The Myth of American Religious Freedom*.

ABBREVIATIONS

. . . .

CHL   Church History Library, Salt Lake City, Utah.

JSP-A   Ronald K. Esplin, Matthew J. Grow, and Matthew C. Godfrey, eds., *The Joseph Smith Papers*, Adsministrative Series, 1 vol. (Salt Lake City: Church Historian's Press, 2016)

JSP-D   Dean C. Jessee, Ronald K. Esplin, et al., eds., *The Joseph Smith Papers*, Documents Series, 7 vols. to date (Salt Lake City: Church Historian's Press, 2013–).

JSP-II   Dean C. Jessee, Ronald K. Esplin, et al., eds., *The Joseph Smith Papers*, Histories Series, 2 vols. (Salt Lake City: Church Historian's Press, 2008–2012).

JSP-J   Dean C. Jessee, Ronald K. Esplin, et al., eds., *The Joseph Smith Papers*, Journals Series, 3 vols. (Salt Lake City: Church Historian's Press, 2008–2015).

JSP-R   Dean C. Jessee, Ronald K. Esplin, et al., eds., *The Joseph Smith Papers*, Revelations and Translations Series, 3 vols. to date (Salt Lake City: Church Historian's Press, 2011–).

LC   Library of Congress, Washington, DC.

NARA   National Archives and Records Administration, Washington, DC.

Bushman, *RSR*   Richard Lyman Bushman, *Joseph Smith, Rough Stone Rolling: A Cultural Biography of Mormonism's Founder* (New York: Knopf, 2005).

INDEX

. . . .

For the benefit of digital users, indexed terms that span two pages (e.g., 52–53) may, on occasion, appear on only one of those pages.